TWO VIEWS OF MIND
Abhidharma and Brain Science

TWO VIEWS OF MIND
Abhidharma and Brain Science

R. Christopher deCharms

with translation by
Gareth Sparham, Sherab Gyatso, and Tsepak Rigzin

Snow Lion Publications
Ithaca, New York

Snow Lion Publications
P.O. Box 6483
Ithaca, New York 14851 USA
607-273-8519

Copyright © 1998 R. Christopher deCharms

First edition USA 1997

All rights reserved. No portion of this work may be reproduced by
any means without prior written permission from the publisher.

ISBN 1-55939-081-6

Library of Congress Cataloging-in-Publication Data

deCharms, R. Christopher, 1966-
   Two views of mind : Abhidharma and brain science / R. Christopher deCharms:
with translation by Gareth Sparham, Sherab Gyatso, and Tsepak Rigzin.
-- 1st ed.
       p.   cm.
   ISBN 1-55939-081-6
   1. Abhidharma. 2. Buddhism--Psychology. 3. Perception.
4. Neuroscience. I. Sparham, Gareth. II. Sherab, Gyatso
BQ4200.D43 1997
128' .2' 0882943--dc21   97-41162
                                                                                            CIP

 PRINTED IN CANADA

Table of Contents

SECTION I
THE PURPOSE OF THIS BOOK

For many minds, something in the body changes, and from this, mind comes. There is also, you see, another kind of mind which controls the *body*. So how to prove this? I think that there is still a lot of work to be done. More discussion, more experiments.

—H. H. the Dalai Lama

One thing I would say might be common between us—no matter that the approach may be different, science or Buddhism—is that when we study, contemplate, and even meditate, we see our investigating nature. Even in meditation we are investigating. We analyze and try to understand things in their proper perspective. I believe that scientists are also analyzing things, examining things, observing things; they are doing research. That is what I value very much. So, in fact, they come to a common ground. I feel that in this way we complement each other. So our sacred books, spoken by an enlightened being, meet with your ideas....

—Lati Rinpoche

Introduction

TIBETAN PHILOSOPHY AND NEUROSCIENCE?

There are many books available making the point that parts of Asian thought are similar to parts of Western thought, and this will not be another one. The claim has been made many times now that mystical traditions including Buddhism are ultimately scientific in nature and that the modern physical sciences are becoming more and more aligned with ancient mystical teachings. This book takes a quite different perspective, asking what we can learn by comparing these two systems, rather than whether they support one another's convictions. The primary emphasis of this book is not whether the two systems justify each other's conclusions by their agreement, because neither system needs justification. Each is already soundly established within its own purview. The emphasis is on what we can learn about the mind by viewing it from two differing perspectives. In this book I try to share in a simple way some ideas of mind from the two endeavors of human culture which have probably had the most to say on this subject in human history: ancient Buddhism and contemporary empirical science.

Why read about a tradition of thought different than your own? People often have either extreme skepticism or enthusiasm for approaches to the questions of mind that come from perspectives outside of their own tradition. My own view is that variety breeds creativity; learning a very foreign approach to familiar puzzles has helped me to frame questions in new ways.

On the other hand, unrealistic expectations are often disappointed. To the Western reader unfamiliar with Asian thought, Tibetan philosophy of mind will probably be found to be just that, another system of philosophy of mind. Like traditionally taught Western philosophy, it has its own views and conundrums, methods and results, and can add new insights in approaching the fundamental question of what it is to have experience and a mental life. Similarly, the reader unfamiliar with the findings of contemporary science will probably find the current accumulations of facts about the brain to give tantalizing and previously unknown insights into the nature of the mind and its relationship to the body, but will certainly find more questions raised than answered. I find both traditions to be more interesting and helpful in providing new means of thinking about the mind than in providing decisive and definitive new answers.

My feeling from spending time with the texts and the teachers of the Tibetan Buddhist presentation of mind, and in the labs of neuroscience, is that each one gets undue respect by outsiders as being hard to understand. In my own experience, I have found that in each case a great deal of the difficulty comes not from the ideas themselves, but from trying to get through a foreign system of presentation. The basic aim of this book is to see whether the Tibetan Buddhist understanding of consciousness, when presented in simple terms, can be helpful to the general student of mind, and similarly, how the Western scientific view can complement it. This book is also my contribution to a dialog which is just beginning to take place between Western scientists of mind and Buddhist scholars, a dialog which I hope has thus far only seen its very beginning.[1] In the past, this dialog has mainly considered the links between Buddhism and Western physics, a field that does not take as its purpose the central purpose of Buddhism, understanding the mind. Fortunately, in recent years the cognitive sciences have become involved in this discourse as well. In my opinion the area of Western thought which is most closely allied with Buddhist thought as a corpus is cognitive neuroscience—the discipline which is presented here.

HOW THIS MATERIAL IS PRESENTED

The Tibetan presentation of mind is a living tradition. The tradition is preserved in detailed texts, but lives in a system of education that involves extensive study of these texts together with discussions, debate, and presentations from teachers. To try to convey the flavor of this enterprise and the wisdom of the Tibetan masters that have conveyed this system to me, I am including parts of the discussions that I have had with a number of lamas concerning the Tibetan Buddhist presentation of mind and the views arising from cognitive neuroscience. I hope that my struggles, the problems of conversing in translation, and the (often difficult) insights of these remarkable teachers, will give a feeling for what the living transmission of Tibetan Buddhism into Western scientific culture might consist of.

In addition, I am presenting highly condensed and simplified presentations of similar topics taken from works on Tibetan Buddhism already found in English translation, and from Western scientific papers (which I will also try to translate into comprehensible English). This book should of course not be taken as a definitive source on either Tibetan Buddhism or cognitive neuroscience, just as a simple introduction.[2]

Finally, I am presenting many ideas arising from the interface of these two traditions that have emerged from discussions like the ones presented here, and from allowing these diverse ideas to settle together for a while. If someone is interested in just a single topic that is covered here, the extensive outlining will make it possible to go directly to that area. Also, for people who want to read the teachings of a particular teacher, these are presented separately from the remainder of the text.

The book addresses four principal topics: the compatibility between Buddhism and a scientifically based Western view of mind; how we perceive reality; how we think about it; and how we remember our thoughts and experiences. Each of these topics is presented in a fairly self-contained way, usually including material from Tibetan texts, an introduction to this topic from the perspective of Western neuroscience, and discussions of these points with Tibetan teachers.

SOURCES OF THIS MATERIAL

In order to narrow the scope of this enormous topic at least somewhat, the Tibetan views presented in these articles are restricted for the most part to a single source, the Gelugpa monastic order's presentation of the views from the historical Sautrantika school of Buddhism. This is a presentation of one from a number of different philosophical schools of Buddhism, each with its own set of teachings on the mind. The Sautrantika school's teachings that I present here are thought by Tibetan teachers to be an important starting point, particularly regarding the issue of concept formation. Within traditional Tibetan education this set of teachings is taught as the second of four schools of Indian Buddhism in terms of the subtlety of its presentation, and students study the "higher" schools later in their training.

Tibetan Buddhist teachers are grouped into four lineages, or monastic orders, each of which presents the teachings of the four schools of Indian Buddhism from a somewhat different perspective. The material in this book is from the perspective of the Gelugpa order, an order founded by the master Tsong-kha-pa in the fourteenth century, and which is now led by the Dalai Lama, spiritual and temporal leader of the Tibetans. In a few cases I present views from alternative perspectives for comparison, and these are duly noted.

Most of this material is drawn from a series of teachings and discussions between myself and a number of Tibetan lamas which took place in Dharamsala, India throughout 1992.[3] These discussions were often based upon traditional topics of debate from Tibetan monastic texts, and also upon topics commonly debated within contemporary neuroscience. Again, the points presented here, particularly regarding Buddhist philosophy, are distilled from secondary written sources and translated oral teachings, and for this reason they should be considered to be comparative introductions to these points rather than authoritative or comprehensive statements.

The scientific understanding presented here has been restricted to contemporary cognitive neuroscience, the Western field of physical science which deals most intimately with issues of the physical basis of mind, and which is my principle discipline of research.

1 The Usefulness of an Exchange: A Discussion with His Holiness the Dalai Lama

The fourteenth Dalai Lama, known with great respect and affection by the title "His Holiness" within the Tibetan community, is the spiritual and temporal leader of the Tibetan people, a Nobel laureate, and probably the most influential advocate and well known personal example of Buddhist ideals alive today. For many years His Holiness has shown an interest in learning about Western science in general and about neuroscience in particular, and he has repeatedly advocated its importance for Tibetan Buddhism. He is without doubt the most well informed Tibetan lama regarding the issue of Western neuroscience.

We spoke mainly in English but were assisted by the excellent translation of the Ven. Lobsang Jordan. In transcribing the text from tape, care was taken to remain very close to the exact words used, particularly by His Holiness, although small grammatical changes were necessary to make the text more readable. My additions and comments have been included in brackets, which will be the convention throughout the book.

USEFULNESS OF AN EXCHANGE FOR PRACTITIONERS AND FOR ACADEMIC STUDY

CdC: I have been here since Losar [Tibetan New Year] studying the correspondence and relationship between the understanding of the mind in Western neuroscience and the philosophical understanding

His Holiness the Dalai Lama with the author

in Tibetan Buddhism. I have been concentrating on the Sautrantika system of tenets in particular. I am hoping to compare the understanding of the mind from Buddhist philosophy with the understanding from Western neuroscience. As you know, there are a number of interesting relationships between the two, and these are what I have been exploring.

I know that in the past you have made comments on the importance of the interchange between these two disciplines. I wondered if you have anything to say now about the benefit to Tibetan Buddhism, Tibetan practitioners, and Tibetan philosophy that could come from an understanding of the brain drawn from neuroscience.

His Holiness: For practitioners, I don't know. My interest is for academic study about the mind and about the explanation of the relation between mind and this body. There are some rough explanations, or vague explanations on how this works. The detailed explanations are not yet available.

For example, sometimes it is obvious: due to emotion, immediately there is a change in the body elements. When, for example, someone gets angry, immediately the body will change. If somebody should have desire, attachment, so the body elements will change. In *sutrayana* there is very little explanation of this. In *tantrayana* there is more.[4]

However, the scientific explanation of this relation is much more detailed. I think [that within the scientific view] the relation is mainly that something happens to some body elements...something happens, so that these emotions develop. Scientists accept a type of brain that is [composed of parts of the material] body. So, you see, first some kind of movement happens in the body, then they accept the reaction, the so-called mind or emotions that come out. In any case, there is a more detailed explanation. There is some change in the body and due to that this happens and this happens [His Holiness makes gestures of thoughts and emotions]. This is very interesting. So that is the main reason for my interest. For us, in that field regarding the brain, it is very useful to learn the scientific findings.

For the practitioner, without knowing any of these things, they practice, so it doesn't matter [laughing deeply]. Their main concern is change, they are not concerned in how change takes place, but *how to change*. That is their business.

A SCIENTIFIC PERSPECTIVE ON ANCIENT DEBATES OF TIBETAN BUDDHISM

CdC: So do you think that certain points in Gelugpa philosophy, such things as how a conceptual consciousness is formed, or how an "aspect" which reflects the properties of a perceived object is taken up by the consciousness during perception of the object, some of these debated points, might have answers from the understanding coming from neuroscience? Do you think that this is likely to have a new impact on the understandings of some of these ancient debated issues?

His Holiness: The findings of neuroscience can indeed solve some of these debated points. I do think so.

For example, in the different levels of tenets[5] there are two classes of models where seeing an object is explained. One is called "with the aspect of an object." You see an object first by getting an aspect of that object in your mind.[6] Another version suggests that you do not have to depend on getting an aspect, that you can directly see the object. The explanation with aspect, with a kind of reflection, is closer to the scientific explanation. When we both see one table, we are both seeing one table, we can touch it simultaneously, but in a real sense there is some kind of reflection, some kind of aspect of that table on our mind, and the mind sees that aspect, not this [he places his hand on the physical table]. Therefore, some may see this table darker, some lighter, things like that. So therefore, the five senses of human beings have five perceptions of different appearances. So this is the scientific explanation. In the Buddhist explanation according to the Sautrantika school and the higher schools, this is also the way. So this is very useful for comparison.

So now suppose today, if there is someone who believes the Vaibashika school of thought [the lowest of the four schools of tenets, which holds that perception does not depend on an aspect], not only can we use logic, but also we can use the arguments of science to demonstrate the superior understanding of the higher schools of thought.

[In the following chapters I will consider in greater detail the mechanisms by which perception takes place. The aspect of a perceived object, which the higher schools posit is formed in the mind during perception, will be directly compared with physically manifest spatial patterns of neuronal activity which are found in the brain.]

SECTION II
A GLIMPSE OF THE TIBETAN VIEW
OF MIND

The body is like a wall, the consciousness or mind is like a painting.

—H. H. the Dalai Lama

2 Approaching the Tibetan View of Mind

Before departing into more detailed descriptions of mind, I would like to start off by presenting a "glimpse." This glimpse is designed to give the reader a feeling for how different the Tibetan view of mind can often be from our own, both in terms of its conception, and in terms of its typical forms of presentation. My hope in this section is to lead the reader away from the idea that Tibetan Buddhism will necessarily seem intuitive from a Western cultural viewpoint. I suspect that many Western readers, particularly those greeting Tibetan thought for the first time, will find elements of the Tibetan position mystifying or alien at first. Perhaps even inconceivable, as was often my own experience.

From personal experience, I would like to suggest that the reader needs neither to accept nor to understand the entirety of the Tibetan philosophical program in order to gain substantial insights from its individual parts. If particular segments seem elusive, impossible, or wrong-headed at first, they are perhaps better seen as the results of cultural context rather than as grave philosophical errors. Often, what seem like gaping differences between viewpoints, in fact come down to very different use of language and the difficulty of translating culturally bound conceptions.

It is also difficult to appreciate at first the extent to which one is ignorant of the cultural and philosophical basics of Tibetan thought. This has the tendency to provoke premature judgments of the Tibetan position which seem self-evident from a Western perspective, but are based on misunderstanding. What follows is an example that I hope will encourage the reader to proceed with the caution of a beginner, however experienced.

A LITTLE PHILOSOPHICAL GAME, FROM TWO CULTURAL PERSPECTIVES

1) A phenomenon exists (has individual existence).

2) The phenomenon does not exist.

For many Westerners these two sentences would seem to cover all of the relevant possibilities, with one or the other (but not both) being necessarily correct. From the Tibetan viewpoint, there are two additional possible (and philosophically important) viewpoints:

3) The phenomenon both exists and does not exist.

4) The phenomenon neither exists nor does not exist.

Which of these are correct for a given phenomenon, such as a simple physical object? On first sight, statement 1 is the obvious answer. What about a unicorn, or the tooth fairy, or some other made-up object? Here statement 2 is true, but perhaps statement 3 as well (in that these things do exist within our ideas). What about our experience of "self"? Even from a Western perspective this question can quickly become tricky. What is the Tibetan answer? The accepted (and even philosophically "proven") answer to this question from a Tibetan viewpoint, even for a simple physical object, is that this list does not contain all of the possibilities, and that the correct understanding is that each of these four viewpoints is in error.

How does this make sense? The answer within Tibetan formal logic is that an error in trying to understand the nature of experience arises from holding and defending any one of these views at all, regardless of which one. The error is essentially in maintaining the position that experienced phenomena are the kinds of things that are explained by one of these four perspectives. This is not a suggestion of nihilism, but a suggestion that experienced phenomena must be comprehended in a different way. My aim at this point is not to fully explain this, nor to try to present the alternative, but just to point out that even the basic and obvious elements of Western logic and reasoning cannot always be wisely applied to Tibetan thinking. Our reasoning itself arises within a particular cultural context, so trying to apply it within a different formal logical system, we can often widely miss the mark through misunderstanding.

MEETING THE TIBETAN LAMAS

In order to begin to set the cultural stage for the Tibetan presentation of mind, I would like to present some context regarding the role of the teachers with whom I spoke as well as my own experience of the discussions we had. In traditional Tibetan culture, lamas have very broad duties because they represent the major source of cultural authority and power on matters of religion, politics, scholarship, and even medicine, law, and divination. In a given day, a lama may take on a monastic administrative role and several teaching responsibilities—from instructing individual students at many levels to leading formal organized educational debates; he may need to settle civic disputes among members of the community, prescribe remedies for the sick, give blessings and or names for newborns, and even chart the likely course of the future. Of course, since the lamas are leading figures of Tibetan culture, sought after by many, it can be extremely difficult to arrange to meet with them.

Many of the more highly placed lamas spend a significant portion of their time entertaining brief visits by guests in their quarters and answering questions, and this was the context in which our meetings took place. The places of our meetings were all in the village of Dharamsala, an exile community on a mountainside in northern India that now houses the Tibetan government-in-exile, the Library of Tibetan Works and Archives, the traditional medical school, and several large monasteries. The rooms that we met in were often decorated with many types of Tibetan art, from traditional paintings to elaborate sculptures of religious figures or offerings that had been brought to the lama by past visitors.

As an example, my interviews with Lati Rinpoche took place in his private rooms at Namgyal Monastery, one of the several monasteries rebuilt in Dharamsala. Our meetings often took place over Tibetan butter tea served by Rinpoche's assistants. Rinpoche typically presented himself to us in a disarmingly simple way, wearing only the plainest and most meager coverings of a monk. During our discussions Rinpoche sat on a platform at one end of the room where he received visitors for many hours a day, and the translator and I sat in front of him. We sat beneath a number of Tibetan *thankas* (traditional paintings of Buddhist images) and figures of deities which were arranged on the opposite wall. The Dhauladar range of the Himalayas towered to six thousand meters in the distance outside of the window, and the adjoining monastic courtyard was often loud with the noise of hundreds of young monks yelling and clapping their hands in heated formal debate. Some of the lamas live in long-term seclusion, often for months or even years at a time, either in small stone cells hidden up in the mountains, or in retreat caves which can be found throughout the Himalayan region.

Often during the course of our discussions Tibetans would come in to consult Rinpoche for advice, to ask for a divination, or to ask for a blessing for themselves or a loved one. Typically, their brief meetings would begin by the visitor bowing at the feet of the lama and making several offerings, including a ceremonial scarf called a *khata*. For Tibetans, as well as visitors from outside of the Tibetan community, the opportunity to meet with one of the lamas is a rare and very important occasion in many respects. The visitors would often ask for advice on some topic, or ask to have some form of blessing made, which the lama would perform in elaborate ceremonial fashion. I was particularly fascinated to watch the performance of divinations, for names of newborns or for good fortune.

Many aspects of the Tibetan teachings on mind were historically considered "secret," and were made available to advanced monks only. This arose for many reasons, not the least of which is that these teachings can easily be severely misunderstood without proper training in basic Buddhist thought. In recent years, particularly due to the views of the current Dalai Lama, much of this secretiveness is being lessened. Nonetheless, I attempted to respect the Tibetan culture, to the extent that I could control my curiosity, by not pressing those points which were considered secret teachings.

I hope that this brief bit of flavor has given a small hint of the cultural context within which these ancient Tibetan teachings have been preserved to the present day. Through a combination of oral and written transmission these teachings have been maintained largely unchanged for many hundreds of years in Tibet.

In the next two sections I present two perspectives on the Tibetan view of mind which I hope will give some sense of the unique character and the mystery that can often be associated with the Tibetan system of understanding. These first two views may seem the most foreign to some Western readers coming from scientific or materialist traditions, but I would encourage them to read on. I believe that the material in the sections that follow will seem more easily accessible, less mysterious, and will begin a more formal and systematic presentation of the Tibetan position.

3 A Very Different Metaphor of Mind—
His Holiness the Dalai Lama

In this short section taken from a longer discussion, His Holiness gives a clear view of the uniqueness of the Tibetan view of mind compared with traditional Western perspectives. I find it a wonderful place to start an exploration of the relationship of mind and physical form from the Tibetan Buddhist and scientific perspectives.

THE TIBETAN APPROACH TO MIND—A PAINTING WITH NO WALL

His Holiness: In this essential way our explanation of the mind is different from yours. Your explanation is that the body is like a wall, the consciousness or mind is like a painting. If the wall is there then the painting can exist; as soon as the wall disappears, then there is no more painting.

Here is our response, the Buddhist response: We say, yes, the grosser level mind is just like that. The more subtle level mind is not that way. Even without a wall, it is still there. Otherwise, what is the cause of taking birth? What is the cause of evolution? We accept evolution, Darwin's theories, no problem. From empty space eventually the energy and different elements developed, and finally, this human body exists. Why did it happen? This is the question. We believe that there is no creator of this being who utilizes the universe. It is their *karma*, mainly their desire, that leads eventually to evolution of sentient beings.

From that viewpoint, we believe that there is a very subtle consciousness, a subtler kind of consciousness which can be identified independently from this body. There is a more subtle body that is the subtle energy. How to prove that? Very difficult. How to explain that? Very difficult. Unless there is some individual who through practice, through meditation, the grosser level of mind....I never met someone completely dissolved. But some kind of change takes place for practitioners through deep meditation for long periods. In them some different kind of light has been getting strong. Their mental state is almost like...faint. There are, for them, some different experiences, so that means that through meditation one can mentally move the energy somehow.

The energy goes everywhere, no control. Once you put this energy under your control, into one place, eventually there is some kind of immersion. This shows or demonstrates that the energy, or mental consciousness, through meditation, is controlled. Control your mind, and you automatically control your energy, so the body element is eventually controlled. *Now* the indication is that the mind is the supreme controller of this body. So, *not* body changes, mind comes. Not that way. For many minds, something in the body changes, and from this the mind comes. There is also, you see, *another* kind of mind which controls the *body*. So how to prove this? I think that there is still a lot of work to be done; more discussion, more experiments. I think that next century we may produce some new ideas.

4   A Discussion with the Venerable
Lobsang Gyatso: Mind and Mental Factors

*I intend this chapter to be another form of introduction, which I hope will
give a feel for the overall approach to mind which is found in Tibetan Buddhist thought. As the reader may sense from this interview, I left feeling that
I had been presented with a great deal of understanding, but unable to pin-
point exactly where it was. This is probably the most elusive of the interviews
that I present. This exposition is drawn from the Sautrantika view, which is
the basis of this book, but also from the teachings of the more complex
Prasangika school, and from tantric teachings. Lobsang Gyatso, with whom
I spoke, died in February, 1997. He was the principal of the Institute of Buddhist Dialectics in Dharamsala, India. He was an authority on the Tibetan
teachings of the mind in general, and on the topic of "mind and mental factors" in particular.*

THE PRESENTATION OF MIND AND MENTAL
FACTORS IN TIBETAN BUDDHISM

Lobsang Gyatso: I will start off with those things in reality which do
and do not have awareness. We are going to make that division. Something which has awareness does so dependent upon five elements.
[Within Buddhist thought there are many different divisions of mind
and matter into constituent parts of varying subtlety and number. This
is one of the very simplest. It is a metaphorical division designed primarily just to clarify the nature of different objects; here it clarifies the
difference between objects being perceived, and aware subjects that
do the perceiving.]

Ven. Lobsang Gyatso (Photo: Sidney Piburn)

We start with these five elements or *dhatus*, the most ancient and traditional ones: earth, air, fire, water, and space. Then you add on top of that a further element which you define as awareness, and you then can describe the things in the universe with six elements which are defined as those with awareness.

What about non-awareness? If you talk about everything in the universe forever, if you are absolutely inclusive, what about the things which do not have awareness? You must have this fifth element or *dhatu* of space. The fifth element allows the non-aware in the sense that anything which *is* needs a place to *be*—needs a space and a locality—and the space which provides its locality is what is meant by the fifth element, which is necessary even for the non-conscious things to be.

Then you add to that complex of necessary elements awareness, and you get a different sort of thing in the universe, a thing which is called sentient. It is the presence of this sixth element which allows that specific sort of thing in the universe to have experiences, along the lines of "this hurts," "this is nice," and so forth. If you say, "Well, fine, what about a beginning to it, what about the fundamental origin of these six fundamental elements?" There is no such beginning possible. It really makes no difference in terms of measurement of the things in the universe.

Let me speak in terms of beginnings and ends or beginninglessness and endlessness of things. Where you have secondary, or built up realities, or objects, or things in the universe, these things can be talked of in terms of beginnings and ends. In other words, things that come into being and go out of being. When we get down to a much smaller level, then the concept of beginning and ending is no longer applicable to things in the universe. Just as when you take these five elements, when you are talking in terms of a rougher level of complexity, the whole level of presentation of things with beginnings and ends, creation and dissolution, is applicable and functions well. When you move to a lower, more subtle level, when you break them down into smaller things, that whole language is no longer applicable to things in the universe. Similarly, with the sixth element of mind or awareness, to the extent that you are talking about rough levels of awareness, it is correct to say that they come into being and go out of being. When you are talking about very small, subtle levels, then the language of beginning and ending of awareness is no longer applicable.

When you get down to a subtle analytic level, the level of the very subtle awareness, at this level the language of beginnings and endings does not apply. It is just like when you are putting two planes of glass together, there is no beginning or end. At the level of the elements, at that very subtle level, the functions of the very subtle awareness and other elements have a clear aspect to them like two planes of glass put together. If you have two absolutely clean panes of glass and you put them together, it is very hard to see where one ends and the other begins. Similarly, the very subtle sixth element, awareness, and the very subtle other five elements which make up matter, form, and so on—they are together when you are talking about a living creature. At that point, both are clear, and it is difficult to see where one begins and the other ends. At the subtle level, it as if there really is no ending of one and beginning of the other. It is like if you have six incredibly clear panes of glass and you look straight through them, it would be very hard to see where one was ending and the other beginning. What is the reason? It is that they have clarity as their nature. It makes no difference the size of the panes of glass.

Similarly, this explains why this extremely subtle union of six elements together, this extremely subtle mind with its basis, cannot be seen. Wherever they go, we cannot see them. It is not something that we can see—no matter how big or small they might be. The clarity of them is such that you cannot see where they are beginning or ending.

When they are in association with rougher things in the universe, when the six elements looked at in their most subtle form are in connection with something rough, then we can begin to see them. Then *that* can be seen. It is like if you had an incredibly clear mirror, you would not know that there was a mirror there. You would just walk straight into it. If there is a little bit of dust on it, then you would immediately be able to see that there is something there and to know that it is a mirror.

Thus it is said that the nature of awareness is clear and knowing (*rig pa*).When you talk about clear and knowing, whatever is meant by the word clear, which is a translation of other words coming from other languages, the mirror fulfills that part of the definition, but it does not fulfill the knowing part. What you put in *with* the clear part is *rig pa*, some knowing part, and then you get the sixth element.

Just as, for example, when we fall asleep there is awareness, but we ourselves do not have awareness of that awareness. That parallels or exemplifies that when this clarity and knowing is associated with rougher levels, then we can know it; but when it becomes more and more and more subtle, then we cannot know it. When it becomes more and more subtle, it gives rise to the idea that it is not there at all, but it *is* there.

For example, our perceptual awareness is generated out of our eyes, ears, nose, tongue, and so forth. Coarse states of perceptual awareness are generated out of the connection of extremely subtle elements of awareness with rougher physical elements. Thereby they give rise to these rougher states of awareness.

It can be imagined sort of like one electron, where an electron here is understood as one very basic part which would give rise to an electrical current. When you have enough of the electrons all together you are going to have a current, and then you are going be able to see if it is burning something or lighting something up or whatever, but in its very smallest element you cannot see it. When they are all together, and when it gets together with these rougher things, then you can see it. For example, in this rough level, in it you see the whole room lit up. Similarly, when there are extremely subtle elements, and the subtle elements get associated with rough elements, at that point you get situations like being able to be *aware* of the whole room, you get awareness on this kind of level. What I am saying, in other words, is that you have a movement between two sorts of levels, a level of grosser, extended, surface realities, and a level of subtle, smaller, *underlying* realities (realities necessitating analysis to be perceived). There is a movement between these two going on continually. Thus we have the differentiated awareness.

In terms of the cycle of existence, that whole presentation is not applicable to the very, very subtle mind (*rlung*) which remains in its fundamental underlying reality. Only the rougher states of awareness elements go through the process of cyclic existence. The extremely subtle mind of every living creature is the same. As you move into a more coarse mode, you have difference. The whole talk of karma in Buddhism leads back to this. Were there no karma and *samsara*, there would be no purpose in the attempt to achieve liberation or the state of enlightenment. To the extent that there *is* a continuum, to *that* extent it is possible to continually improve, and there is a meaning in attempting to achieve an improvement which is not lost.

It is also said that this awareness, this knowing aspect of mind, has infinite capacity for increase. The expansion in it is infinite, and that is the fundamental position behind the Buddhist position that enlightenment is possible.

CONSCIOUSNESS AS CLEAR AND KNOWING

If awareness is defined as clear and knowing, then we need to begin to present the lengthy explanation of this. Just what is this clarity? When you are talking about the non-aware things, the clarity in them is to do with light or luminosity. Another word used is *dawa*, which means nothing sticking to it, nothing obstructing it in the way that something which is sticking obstructs a mirror. Its being luminous is its *selwa* and its not having anything stuck to it is its *dawa*, and thus you have its clarity.

When you are talking about awareness, what you actually mean is the appearing of the object, which is described in terms translated as "light" or "clarity." It is the appearance of the object to awareness which is the light or luminosity. Then there is something grabbing it. That grabbing it is what is known as *rig pa* or knowing. So thus you have clear and knowing as the description of mind.

If you didn't have it shining, then you couldn't get hold of it, you couldn't have knowing (where knowing here means getting hold of it). Just the shining. If it wasn't shining out, you couldn't have knowing, this sense of *rigpa*. You couldn't have the getting hold of it unless you have something shining out which is going to be gotten hold of.

CdC: So the clarity isn't a clarity that is inside the mind itself, the clarity is partly a clarity of the object such that the awareness includes the clarity. The clarity is an aspect or feature of the combination and relationship of the mind and the object which together are the awareness. It is not part of the mind by itself. Similarly, the knowing is a feature of the relationship between the knower and the object. Is this correct?

Lobsang Gyatso: Yes, this is the point. Thus, you have the defining characteristic of consciousness as clear and knowing.

CONSCIOUSNESS AS AUTHORITATIVE REGARDING APPEARANCE

Such consciousness, thus defined, is authoritative about the appearance of an object. There is no conceptuality about that consciousness whatsoever, it is a bare authoritativeness about appearance, where appearance is the same as light coming up to it. Awareness is self-validating in this sense, that one simply knows. It is authoritative about that fact, that there was knowledge.

If you look at your experience of a dream, when you are sleeping, if you think back about what your experience or awareness was, you will notice that there was a continuum. Although there are many instants—one after another—together, what you experience is a continuum. That observation is itself the formal demonstration that awareness is authoritative regarding the mere fact that awareness existed. In terms of human experience, a dream is experienced as a connected experiential sequence. The fact that the continuum of awareness is experienced even deep in a dream as a connected experiential sequence is itself a demonstration: it "self-demonstrates" that each moment of awareness must be authoritative that something appeared to it. Later you can think, "I saw something in that dream, I remembered something back then." Because of that fact, we say that awareness is authoritative regarding appearance. This is why you can begin to have that kind of memory of your dream.

How can you have such a remembrance? Because the awareness was itself authoritative to the fact that something was appearing to it. It is *pramana*, it validly cognizes the fact that something appears. Were this not to be so, if a moment were not an event which does indeed know that something appeared to it, then it would be impossible for it to be consciousness. It simply couldn't be.

INTENSITY OF CLARITY

Then there is the intensity of clarity. There are strengths of appearances. Some have stronger or lesser light, as you might say. Where you have stronger light things leave more of an imprint. For example, you might be able to say of something "it was ten years ago when I dreamt that" and be absolutely positive because of the intensity of the light to the awareness. Consider if an awareness brings back to mind something which was seen before, that is, a remembrance. Let's say that there are one hundred things in a list that you are going to repeat. You are going to have an authoritative awareness to each one in turn; if you do not have an authoritative awareness to the appearance of one, then you are going to miss out that one.

The awareness is authoritative to its appearance. In other words, the mind is authoritative to its appearance. Say you are thinking about something, you recall that which you are thinking about to mind. If you have a clarity to your awareness, to that extent you can begin to talk about the fact that you are remembering. You must have that clarity to awareness. At that point you can say "I'm remembering, I'm remembering." Just thinking about these examples, you can see what is meant in talking about awareness as clear and knowing.

If you notice, sense generated perceptions are separate. This whole line of analysis does not apply directly to them. They are just out there and clear. This analysis of awareness that I have been explaining can only be done when you think about what is going on "inside," as you might say, when you think about thoughts, or recollections. This itself is a demonstration that we are not talking about awareness being something physical.

AWARENESS IS NON-PHYSICAL

Awareness is not physical. You can only have a concept of it when you are looking inside. "Out there" you will never find it, it has to be inside. Thus it is not physical.

It is not part of the physical universe because it is inside. You can't point to the place where it is. You look and you see it there, but it is not like something in the physical universe where you can point and say, "Oh yes, there it is. It's over here, and it's over there." In that sense it is a non-dimensional, non-physical thing. You can think about it, but it is not locatable. Say, for example, that one is getting irritated. If you say, "Okay, where is it?" It is unlocatable. If it were something physical you would be able to stop and point and say, "It is there." Similarly, you look out and you have a clear awareness of something out there, generated through the eyes, and if you say, "Where is the awareness?" It is unfindable. There is an awareness, but it is unfindable.

Similarly with neurologists themselves, there is no possibility that their investigations into the physical world are ever going to locate an awareness in that sense, because it is not a part of the physical world. It is non-physical. Say you are looking in the distance, you are having a "looking in the distance" awareness. Clearly the awareness is not inside the eye, nor outside the eye, nor in the distance, nor anywhere else. It is non-locatable in the physical universe in that sense. It is not to be pointed to anywhere.

CdC: I just wanted to comment that I think it is interesting that although we neuroscientists can find the hardware parts, and even find the activity which corresponds to the function of an awareness, I think that it is very true that having done that we have not found the awareness itself, although we may have found a counterpart.

[I would like to elaborate on this to avoid a potentially serious confusion regarding the argument that awareness is non-physical. I personally believe beyond any doubt that the functions of awareness can be localized within the brain, and I believe that the brain is the physical "seat" of awareness. In my interpretation the argument presented above is in no way necessarily at odds with this understanding and does not necessarily suggest that there is something "extra," beyond the brain, which mediates awareness somehow. The argument suggests to me that the awareness from the subjective viewpoint itself will not be found in the brain (or anywhere else), not that its substrate cannot be found. In a somewhat parallel example, water is clearly the substrate of wetness, but the wetness itself cannot be "pointed to," only the water. Subjective awareness as spoken of above is in a different category of description than localizable objects, it is known from a different perspective, and this is why it cannot be found as a localizable object. This suggests that to imagine looking for subjective awareness itself in the brain as an external entity is logically incorrect. However, this does not imply, in my opinion, that awareness does not have a physical substrate in the brain which functionally corresponds to it exactly. That would be a different argument. A similar point is made below by Lati Rinpoche, who suggests that the brain has the potential for creating illumination, but is not the illumination itself. I see the puzzle of how the substrate and the subjective awareness are explicitly related, in concept and in detail, to be one of the greatest challenges facing neuroscience. This is also a challenge that has been addressed by Abhidharma in many ways.]

Lobsang Gyatso: You will never find it in the brain! It is a matter of experiencing it. There is no possibility beyond experiencing awareness to ever find it in the physical universe.

AWARENESS AND PHYSICAL BEING

If you start to intensely contemplate something, focusing your mind upon it, and if your contemplation seems to follow a successful sequence of individual moments, then as you move through that sequence of contemplating you will find that the mind inside you, your awareness, seems to start to glow. It will come up with a tremendous vibrancy or clarity. You will find yourself sitting with great vibrant clarity of awareness. You will feel this awareness within yourself. During that kind of moment one feels very comfortable and very nice, but when that awareness starts to go away the pleasant physical feelings may recede as well, you might even begin to notice the whole body beginning to hurt a great deal. So, what you find through experience, if you are looking in this way, is that awareness itself has an expanding and shrinking quality to it. As awareness narrows one can find all sorts of difficulties, both mental and physical.

The intellect itself is similar. When the intellect really gets into a sharp mode, and is just roaring as you might say, when you are thinking about something which is absolutely captivating and the intellect is earnestly and eagerly grappling with it, and the intellect is going on and on with wondering and thinking and trying to understand, when you are caught up in that sort of clarity of the intellect, you can find that any sort of physical ailment just does not impinge upon the experiential world. Time also seems to be a nonentity. When you start to look you find that hours have gone by since you started to involve yourself in the intellectual process. Then, as your ability to investigate or analyze or wonder looses it sharpness, if you do keep trying to go on, you may feel quite uncomfortable. Not only that, but the clarity may have completely gone away. When you get that really clear feeling of awareness, that feeling almost of what awareness is, there is a stability. There is a concentratedness, a concentration, that can come. That concentratedness can stay buoyant for quite some time.

It seems to me, therefore, that where you have awareness or mind in a very forceful and clear state, and very strong, it begins to take over the physical being, it begins to dominate what the physical body does. Where it looses its strength, the physical begins to dominate.

AWARENESS CAN INCREASE AND DECREASE WITHOUT LIMIT

Think of an increase in awareness in a metaphorical sense, like having something grow up or jump up. If you think of the increase in a physical sense, what is the highest that a person could possibly learn to jump? There is no way that this physical increase can increase in the way that an awareness increases within. Awareness can go from almost a blank mind, almost no awareness whatsoever, to an infinite feeling, an infinite awareness. It can increase without any limit whatsoever. This increase is related to the clarity of the appearance to awareness. To the extent that there is a growing clarity in the appearance to an awareness, the awareness increases in accord with that clarity.

It is like this light, the light from this little lamp. This is a really strong light, relative to the things that it right now casts its light upon in the room. Similarly, you talk of a strong light of awareness relative to the amount of things that are known. But this physical light has a certain limit to it, it can only beam out with strength to a certain limit. The mind is different from that. There is a "one on the other" relationship acting between the awareness and the light. You get a clearness in awareness, a light thrown in awareness, which is itself intimately related with the amount of light coming in from the object.

There is a relationship like that, a "one on the other" relationship, which allows a tremendous throw of light, metaphorically speaking, when you come to awareness. How vast the things it throws its lights upon. To the extent that there is a penetration into, an investigation into more and more detail of a particular thing being looked at, that causes a corresponding increase in the throw of the light of awareness onto that thing.

Its increase, the increase in the scope of the awareness, is related to the habituations of the mind as well. In other words, the habituation of the mind is what causes the greater and greater clarity, the greater and greater throw of the light of awareness. When you are bringing up awareness again and again and again, that is what is meant by habituating to an awareness. Making that continuum of awareness go on and repeat functions with the objects that those repeated awarenesses are aware of, they work in relation to one another. This causes more and more awareness, more light. For example, as you meditate, applying the mind again and again and again, the clarity of awareness increases more and more and more. This entails that the object which awareness is focused upon and is being clear *about* is becoming clearer and clearer. As that object becomes clearer, the mind becomes clearer.

Imagine someone out there that you can't stand, and imagine that you keep bringing the person to mind in terms of your thought of them. You keep bringing that thought to mind again and again and again. You are habituating that mind (or meditating that mind). It is getting bigger and bigger and bigger, clearer and clearer, and more and more intense. It can turn into a situation where just to hear the person's name causes rage. You can work in the opposite direction, thinking, I have got to stop thinking again and again and again that way. You think about the thoughts, and when those thoughts come you put them out of your mind. By putting them out of your mind, it won't be long before they stop coming. Eventually it will be that even if you see the person you will not feel so bad.

Awareness is seen as something which is capable of great increase and decrease, and thus is not part of the physical world. What do I mean by this increase of awareness? If one thinks about a young child, about the breadth of their knowledge, how small it is relative to the highly educated person! The increase of awareness from one to the other is really quite huge. With an educated person the depth can be really quite staggering. Conversely, as the person moves into the process of death, as the senses close down, that whole huge, highly expanded awareness begins to shrink so small that it becomes an incredibly small size once again. To the extent that it gets smaller, to that extent the relationship of the awareness with that which makes up the physical part of a human being or living creature becomes more and more tenuous. For example, say you are deep in sleep and dreaming, even if someone touches you, you have no awareness. It is like that. Where the consciousness is very small, there is less relationship with the physical organism.

In the process of death the consciousness's size decreases and decreases and decreases, the feelings and so forth of the physical being begin to disappear. Finally it disappears to such a point that it looses all connection with the physical, with the body, and is simply no longer related to it; the person is dead then.

I would like to bring up another example. Have you ever had the experience that you are asleep and you are dreaming, but you do not have enough bedclothes on you and it is quite cold in the room. What you end up getting in the dream is that you are in a thunderstorm or something. There is an impact coming in, but the strength, the size, the impact of the awareness has gone down. With its going down, the feeling which is associated with it must necessarily also go down. So what you find is that the feeling of cold cannot penetrate enough because the mind has gone down, so the feeling cannot really get through. So it is not really able to grip. What I am pointing to is how feeling also can go up and down. There becomes less connection with this rough body. Finally, awareness is associated only with the very subtle body and goes away. That is not to say that the continuum is broken. The continuum of awareness remains.

SECTION III
BUDDHISM AND SCIENCE

I have a great interest in the close relationship between Eastern philosophy, particularly Buddhism, and Western science. My basic aim
as a human being is to speak always for the importance of compas-
sion and kindness...but in order to develop these it is very important
to know more about the nature of mind or consciousness.

It is important for Western science and material development, and
Eastern mental development, to work together. Sometimes people have
the impression that these two things are very different, even incom-
patible. However, in recent years this has changed.

—H. H. the Dalai Lama, *Gentle Bridges*

Looking at the amount of authoritative statements which have been
generated out of direct perception, empirical knowledge, the amount
which scientists have been able to learn, it is absolutely staggering.
Similarly, the amount of statements that can be generated out of this
second authority, out of reasoning or logic, is again vast.

—Kamtrul Rinpoche

5   Is Buddhism Scientific? No

Having given a preliminary bit of the flavor of the Buddhist presentation of mind, I think that its differences from the scientific approach are manifest. There is a growing popular literature from the last few decades, both in English and in Asian languages, suggesting that metaphysical traditions, including Buddhism, are in some sense scientific in nature, or that the modern physical sciences are becoming more aligned with ancient mystical teachings.[7]

While a general case has sometimes been made for this kind of viewpoint, this book takes a different perspective. The issue of whether the two traditions seem similar or justify each other's convictions through similarity is largely bypassed. My interest here is not to compare traditions to find similarities, but to find what the two systems can learn from one another. From this perspective, differences between the two systems are in many respects more interesting and useful than similarities. The purpose of this section of the book is to explore some of the overall conceptual differences between the two systems, based on material taken both from their formal presentations and from discussions with lamas.

The clear distinctions between Buddhism and science seem patently obvious in many respects, but there has been a trend towards discounting the differences in search of finding similarity. This recent trend notwithstanding, the conceptual differences between the two systems are very substantial, and they have important implications when trying to understand how the two traditions bear upon one another. The attempt to find lines of communication between Eastern and Western thought has often led to a stress on the superficial, and this has often gone to the point of being simply misleading and untrue to the systems being considered.

It is certainly possible to describe science and Buddhism generally enough that they become mutually inclusive, emphasizing that they are both observational in some sense, that they both have a presentation of matter based on particles and causal laws and so forth. This pursuit has done a great deal to start an "intereducation" process, but these sorts of description can often misrepresent fact and miss the real beauty of each system by not conveying its true detail. More important, they often fail to point to comparisons between systems of thought which will lead to further learning. Overarching descriptions of similarity between systems of thought are often attempts to justify one in terms of the other, or attempts to justify one's understanding of one in terms of the other, rather than attempts to pursue new insights by exploring what each one has to offer in its own right. It appears manifest that however much Buddhism and science may have in common, they are certainly not the same, and it may be the differences that provide the real opportunities for exploration. The following sections point out some major differences between the two systems of understanding, and what some consequences might imply about each approach to mind in general.

A DIFFERENCE IN AUTHORITY: MEDITATIVE OBSERVATION VS. EMPIRICAL VERIFICATION

It has often been said that Buddhism is based on careful observations, so it is "objective" in the same sense that science is held to be objective. But this presentation of similarity obscures a real beauty of the Buddhist system from the vantage point of Western science. The observational methods of Buddhism are what the present science of mind largely *lacks* in systematic form, and could almost certainly learn from. Their main value to Western thinking may be that they are both subjective and systematic to a level of detail that current Western systems of observation have not yet reached. They are subjective in the sense of being "internal" observations, observations made of one's own experience. To call them objective exactly negates their main potential value to science—which is to provide a basis for carefully observing the mind from the "inside."[8]

The fundamental authority in Buddhist understanding is what the clearly perceiving mind can see from within, an authority that holds almost no weight whatsoever in current scientific thinking and has therefore gone almost completely unexplored. This authority is then expanded, using a detailed system of internally coherent logic, (which is discussed in the interview with Kamtrul Rinpoche presented in the next chapter). The importance of Buddhism to scientific learning can be seen most clearly if this difference in authoritative base is held in sight, rather than obscured.

If scientific observation is going to explain the mind, not just the brain, then producing a systematic approach to measuring and describing mental processes cannot be avoided. Only to the extent that the mind can be carefully described in its own right can its functions be explained in terms of neural substrates. No amount of neural data alone can completely explain the functioning of the mind, for mental states are not experienced as neural impulses nor are they describable in those terms alone. Recording from every neuron in a human brain simultaneously for a month, measuring every molecule's concentration, and observing every pattern in the complex network, will not in itself explain the mind. It can only serve as a substrate upon which a theory of mind can rest, as a physical basis in terms of which mental states can be explained.

At a minimum, for even a rudimentary understanding of the mind, a system of description at the experiential level must accompany the neural level of explanation. More profitably, the two descriptive systems must ultimately be directly related to one another through precise definitions and identities. Obviously, no matter how precisely either the nervous system or the mind is understood, this will only aid in an understanding of their relationship to the extent that the phenomena of one can be clearly explained in terms of the other. The need for more powerful and more systematic empirical methods for describing mental phenomena is a great problem for understanding the mind both at the psychological and neurological levels. At present, Western science cannot produce anything close to a consensus of how to define the key terms regarding the mind, or how best to make empirical measurements regarding most mental states beyond simple perceptions.

Moving in the opposite direction of inquiry, to suggest that basic scientific observations share the same status with those of Buddhism neglects their own cardinal virtue—consensus based on simple verifiability. Science has become so successful and powerful, and has come to be held as the final authority in so many areas of knowledge, because it is held that in principle everyone can agree on its observations. In practice agreement is much less uniform, but on the major points it is sufficient to allow standards to be set and technological achievements to be made.

The fundamental authority of science is consensus based on verification. This consensus arises because of the demand for verifiability in the scientific method, the demand that the claims of science be relatively easily and quickly testable by anyone with modest technical expertise and access to proper technical equipment who cares to question them. In fact, a scientific law is considered certain only to the extent that it has been tested and reproduced and a consensus has been reached. The point here is not that science is always right, nor that its views do not change, but that science's value comes directly from its verifiability, which leads to common usage. People trust science and technology by believing that if they follow its instructions they will get the same results every time, the same results seen by others.

This broad consensus through testing and verification, particularly regarding details, is exactly what is missing from the many mystical presentations of the mind. Although many argue that eventually each person can verify all of the statements of the historical Buddha through observation, as teachings profess, in the meantime there is no strong *consensus* on many of the points of esoteric knowledge, and many contradictions between different schools of thought. By using the methods of science, methods based on commonly verifiable observations, it might be possible to start to find a similar kind of consensus regarding debated points within Buddhism, or even debated points between traditions, as will be discussed in detail below. Again, this striking difference in method points to an opportunity for new exploration.

A DIFFERENT DUALISM: THE MIND-BODY
PROBLEM AND THE SUBJECT-OBJECT PROBLEM

The question of whether perceived reality is unified or can be broken into parts is central both within the tradition of science and in Buddhist thought, but it is discussed from very different angles. Although this question is sufficiently broad to encompass many volumes on its own within each field, and sufficiently subtle that it does not fair well in brief presentations, it seems important to at least acknowledge the major differences in approach between the two systems, since these greatly color the resultant presentations of the mind.

Within the tradition of Western philosophical thought, at least since the ideas of Descartes[9] and perhaps since Plato, a division has been made between dualistic views in which the mind and body are treated as different kinds of entities, and monistic views in which all of reality is considered to be a single entity which includes both matter and mind. The current bias within the scientific community is towards a type of materialist monism in which the mind is held to be merely a function which springs forth or emerges from the properties of the brain. It is thereby posited that the problem of mind will be finally solvable by means of scientific observations and laws. This is a view of the mind as a mechanism in action: mind is the functioning of a mindless machine. In this vein there have been numerous arguments regarding whether it would be possible to build an artificial consciousness machine, and even whether consciousness is necessary at all in order to behave and survive as an organism. In this view, then, the problem is solved by dismissal. The universe is considered as one physical reality, a mind is considered to be a fancy type of object but nothing more, and the existence of the problem is denied.

In the Buddhist tradition the problem of duality is posited quite differently, and this leads to a substantially different view of what a mind is. Here the paradox is between unified experience, and a split dividing subject and object, rather than a split dividing mind and body. Buddhist dualism separates the experienced self from the experienced other, whereas cognitive dualism[10] separates the mental from the material. From the Buddhist standpoint there is nothing more or less material about subjects in comparison with objects, they share equal status in this regard. Buddhist thought posits that reality shares both sides of a nature, which seems paradoxical from a simple Western perspective. The Tibetan tradition suggests that it is neither correct to suggest that reality is completely unified, nor that it is divided, and it can only be truly understood from this perspective.[11] In this tradition there are two alternate views which correspond to the two sides of this paradox, and which seem contradictory, but are both held to be "truths."

Within "conventional understanding" there is an apparent experience of division between observing subject—the conventionally understood "I"—and observed object. In conventional language a subjective, conscious mind is described as separate from that which it takes as its object. This form of description or explanation is held to be largely a matter of linguistic convenience, a tool. The other viewpoint, translated as the "ultimate understanding," is that reality is not separated into subjects and objects at all, and hence there is no essential "identity" or "self," nor "non-identity" or "other" in anything. This is an aspect of the Buddhist terms translated as "selflessness" and "emptiness."[12] In this case the problem of duality is solved by inclusion— both the divided *and* the unified perspectives on mind are considered to be valid in different ways and for different purposes.

A DIFFERENCE IN METHOD: DESCRIPTION VS. MECHANISTIC ANALYSIS

In addition to being different in their philosophical approaches to mind, these two systems are different in the methods that they employ, and these differences can be very instructive. The Tibetan approach to mind is largely *descriptive*, explaining by illustration and metaphor, whereas Western science is predominantly *mechanistic*, explaining in terms of simple material forces acting on small constituent parts. The next chapter presents a discussion of these two methods of description that I had with Kamtrul Rinpoche. In this section, I use parallel explanations taken from the presentation of mind in Tibetan thought, and from contemporary neuroscience, to illustrate the contrast between these two approaches.

The Buddhist perspective on the mind—descriptions of consciousness

The Tibetan descriptive method is well illustrated by the descriptions of vision in the tantric medical texts, called the *Gyu-zhi*. This example is chosen because these texts provide the closest thing to a mechanistic description of mind found within Tibetan thought. The mind in general is described as being supported by the flow of a bodily humor, called *lung (rlung)*, through bodily channels "in the same way that a swift horse supports its rider."[13] Vision is explained in a similarly metaphorical, descriptive, and practical fashion. The Tibetan medical explanation of vision is not concerned with exactly which functions are taking place on what substances at the instant that one sees, as is the case in a scientific description, but with what bodily constituents support the faculty of sight overall. For this reason, looking to the Tibetan presentation of vision for physical, mechanistic details to compare with those found in Western science produces limited results.

The general elements that are said to be the most involved in vision are called the "life sustaining wind," which is associated with the visual awareness, the "sight bile," which is associated with the eye itself, and the "satisfying phlegm," which combines with the others to maintain the ability to see. For vision to occur these humors must all be present in their correct balance in the eyes, the brain, and a series of channels which emanate from both. Any imbalance will impair vision, and most impairments of vision can be diagnosed and treated by rebalancing these humors through medical intervention in one form or another. The pattern here is this: practical, metaphorical descriptions are given of what happens and what should be done to make things happen differently. Mechanistic details are not involved and are even avoided as extraneous.[14]

Tibetan philosophers and meditators explain consciousness in general using a similar method to that of the medical texts. The descriptions of vision used in meditation, for example, present a series of bodily channels which the meditator seeks to visualize and purify internally.[15] There are differences between the channels described in the medical texts and those visualized in meditation, but the purpose is the same: to alleviate suffering by purification and balance, and thereby to transcend ignorance and suffering. Mechanistic details of how the channels function are not needed to describe their purification and are considered extraneous. As H.H. the Dalai Lama put it, "For the practitioner...their main concern is change, they are not concerned with how change takes place, but *how to change*. That is their business."[16]

Tibetan philosophical presentations explain consciousness, including vision, using a similar method. Rather than presenting causes and machinations, it presents catalogs and descriptions. Taking the example of vision, one is said to see "directly," with a complete, nonconceptual ascertainment of an object, or "indirectly," using a general, conceptual mental image of the object, which is inherently limited (as will be described in detail in the following chapters). In the many volumes on how these two processes of seeing work, virtually no mention is made of what physical mechanism allows them to function. The philosophical treatment seeks to demonstrate how to strive towards the kinds of seeing which will lead one to see absolute truth, and how to get away from the kinds of seeing that are mistaken or limited. These categories describe *what* the different types of consciousness do, not *how* they do it—this is not considered relevant and is often even considered counterproductive.

The neuroscience perspective on the brain—mechanisms of behavior

The scientific descriptions of the brain could hardly be considered more different in method. They seek to describe how processes work in terms of minute causes and physical matter, and almost entirely neglect the nature of the objects of mind themselves. In the case of vision, there are volumes on *how* we see, and very little on classifying the types of sight that we have based on their objects. In order to allow comparison, a preliminary outline of the scientific ideas of the mechanism of vision is presented, and this example will be explained in greater detail in the discussion of perception.

Scientists have discovered individual cells in the eye that receive light and form an image of the world, a function perhaps conceptually similar to that provided by "clear internal form" described in the Abhidharma presentation of visual perception. These cells are each individually connected to cells in the brain through a nerve which carries all of their millions of fibers. Once in the brain this information is processed through many individual "maps" of the visual world, with each map containing an image of the entire current visual scene in the activity of its many cells, much as a world map contains a representation of the entire earth's surface. The individual maps are arranged in a hierarchy, with the visual information flowing from the eye to the first map and then on to the higher maps which abstract particular aspects of the visual scene. One of these maps is particularly involved in representing the colors that we see, another in representing motion, and another in representing the angles and orientations of visual forms, just as different maps of the same world might represent political borders, climatic regions, and mineral deposits. As we progress upwards through the hierarchy more and more complex features are represented until, at the top of the hierarchy, the maps are used in representing things as complex as familiar faces or how we are spatially situated relative to our environment. These most complex representations are thought to be built up from the combination of simple features at lower levels. In this way visual images are recognized without the need for any "internal observer" to recognize them; the recognition is simply a product of the functioning nervous system.

A chief difference between these scientific descriptions and those in Tibetan texts is that at each level neuroscience attempts to be thoroughly mechanistic and reductionist in its viewpoint. It seeks to explain each complex part as resulting from a series of material forces acting on smaller constituent parts. Each of the visual maps have been physically observed inside the brain by recording the activity of nerve cells. For example, the image of the world inside the eye is explained as the electrical activities of an array of individual receptor cells. This electrical activity is in turn reduced to mechanisms at the next simpler level: it is explained as resulting from the flow of electrical current into the cells when they are struck by light. The operations of these currents are further explained in terms of a whole cascade of chemical reactions which are triggered by light and ultimately lead single molecule channels in the cells to open and close and allow current to pass. This current is even further dissected into the flow of individual types of atoms through these micro-channels. If one desires, one can continue this progression down through the physics of the atoms and even further.

This is mechanistic analysis. The point is certainly not that the entire process from atom to brain has been explained, it is that this type of mechanistic, reductionist approach is the stated method of science and that it has proven to be an extremely powerful means of explanation. Its weakness is that at present it has not been able to reach far enough upwards to grasp conscious awareness. In any case, it is certainly very different from the descriptive emphasis found in Tibetan Buddhist thought.

DIFFERENT VIEWS OF CAUSATION

Buddhist philosophy and Western science both have principles of causation and attempt to analyze reality into minute causes and conditions. The descriptions in the two systems often sound surprisingly similar, which has encouraged some to imagine that the two are really very nearly the same. The Buddhist presentation of causal relations that govern mind and matter based upon the principle of dependent arising are set out in the Abhidharma Pitaka, which the Buddha himself is said to have called the highest understanding of reality. The causal relations of Western science are to be found embodied in any of its physical laws, from those of Newton's physics to modern molecular biology. Since many of the details of the two sets of causal laws sound quite similar, it is worth investigating the extent to which the two systems of causal explanation are truly related overall.

The texts of the Abhidharma contain detailed causal descriptions of mind and an analysis of consciousness and matter into discrete conditions and elements, much like a periodic table. The Buddhist theory of individual "atoms" flashing into and out of existence has very often been compared to the understanding of modern physics.[17] In translation, the Abhidharma can sound very similar to scientific reductionism. For instance, describing vision, the *Treasury of Knowledge* (*Abhidharmakosha*) of Vasubandhu asks:

> What is the use of this quarrel about 'who sees' and 'who is conscious'? It is like chewing on empty space! A visual perception is a fact, conditioned by two other facts, an organ of vision and some color.... There is nothing but elementary facts appearing as cause and effect.[18]

A similar perspective echoes throughout neuroscience. It is embodied in the first words of many students' first neuroscience textbook:

> The key philosophical theme of modern neural science is that all behavior is a reflection of brain function. According to this view...the mind represents [only] a range of functions carried out by the brain.[19]

Although many of the causes and elements described in Abhidharma sound strikingly similar to those found in science, which certainly may be no coincidence, these causes and constituents are of a very different *kind*. It is possible that Abhidharma and science have come, through different means, to very similar conclusions, but the basis and purpose of Abhidharma is entirely distinct from that of science. Abhidharma is metaphysical, science is mechanistic. This means that even if the laws within the two systems are similar, they operate over very different domains of experience and should not be taken to be describing the same aspects of reality.

The elements and karmic causes described in the Abhidharma are fully realized only by the Buddha himself—they are a very different stuff from the simple, materially observable objects and physical forces seen by any scientist. This means that an ordinary individual cannot expect to observe the laws of Abhidharma in motion or to make definite predictions from them in the same simple ways that he or she can observe gravity acting or predict simple effects from scientific laws. The purpose of Abhidharma is not to provide a useful mechanistic explanation of mundane physical events and how to control them, which it does not do, but to lead one to liberation from the ignorance of conditioned existence. The karmic causal relations described by the

Buddha are on a different plane of understanding from the material causes of the scientist and the two should not be confused; they draw on different realms of experience because they are born of separate perspectives.

THE IMPORTANCE OF THE DIFFERENCES BETWEEN THE TWO SYSTEMS

Although the understanding of Tibetan Buddhism may in many ways be similar to that of Western science, to suggest that the Abhidharma is itself scientific only invites the scientist to confuse the mystic with the concrete, and then to subject Buddhist esoterica to a mechanistic analysis which it simply could not withstand. If scientists look to Abhidharma to find explanations of physics, biology, or chemistry they will not find scientifically verifiable empirical answers because this is not what Buddhism provides. Similarly, if Buddhists look to science to find answers to mystical questions they will be either disappointed or confused, for this is not the realm of scientific explanation. Considering Buddhism and science to be equivalent pays credit to the wisdom of neither tradition because it ignores the real value of what each contains. The greatest value of comparison can be found by acknowledging the differences between the two systems and finding the virtues of each.

Another reason that the distinctions which have been outlined above must be born in mind is that otherwise unrealistic expectations will form which will likely end in condemnations. There is no reason to allow science to do battle with Buddhism for overstating its bounds and claiming authority over all of reality, as science has done battle with Western religions already. Similarly, in Tibetan culture where mystical tradition holds the dominant influence, there is no reason to suggest that science produces a valid basis of mystical understanding. The value obviously lies in finding the merits of each system where they actually lie, in its own realm of inquiry.

Photo of Kamtrul Rinpoche (Photo: Jeanne Stone)

6   A Discussion with Kamtrul Rinpoche—
A Different Authoritative Base

The following is a discussion of one of the key differences between the science of mind and the Tibetan Buddhist presentation, a difference in the source of authoritative statements about reality. In this interview I discussed with Kamtrul Rinpoche some of the methods and findings of Western neuroscience regarding the brain, and he presented to me some of the very different methods and conclusions arising from his own tradition. If there is any simple message which I took from this discussion, it is probably that each tradition offers an interesting contrast to the other's methods, often on similar topics.

Kamtrul Rinpoche is a highly respected teacher of the Nyingma lineage. He is designated as "Rinpoche," a term of respect which means "precious one," to reflect this fact. The Nyingmapa is another of the four orders of Tibetan Buddhism, in addition to the Gelugpa order, which is the primary focus of this book. This addition seemed appropriate both to add a taste of variety and because Rinpoche presented such a clear, elucidating view of the mind, often from the perspective of the Dzog Chen or Absolute Completion teachings. These discussions were graciously translated by Gareth Sparham (see discussions with Lati Rinpoche as well). Rinpoche was very interested in the value of the unique perspective that the scientific method gives in addressing questions of the mind, and he made presentations of Tibetan teachings that were directly related to central issues in contemporary science, often in the guise of fanciful stories.

This discussion began with my giving a presentation of some of the views of science regarding the formation of perceptions and the storage of memory.

Much of this material is presented later in this volume. The principal topic I wish to emphasize from this interview is Rinpoche's comments on the differences in methods between science and Buddhism, and their mutual value.

THE POWER OF TWO TYPES OF AUTHORITY: OBSERVATION AND REASON

Rinpoche: I liked the presentation of the scientific view of the brain very much. It strikes me that the presentation that you have given is one which is based upon empirical evidence. In other words, you have *seen* those sorts of things that you speak about; people have *seen* those sorts of things, and they have generated out of this a model of what is actually there in the mind. There is no quibbling with that. Each of these things which you describe strike me as a thing which *is* there in the mind.

There are things said in the Buddhist texts which are quite beyond the ability of the human faculties to directly see. For example, it is said in one of the texts that on one small atom there are as many Buddhas as there are atoms in the universe. Something like that our faculties are not capable of seeing, so we must just listen to those who can see that as being the way that things are.

This being the case, our Tibetan presentation is one which is generated out of an internally coherent logic. Inferential recognition is the main thing which is used to generate our understandings. The first sort of authority is thus the authority which is given to statements or models by the faculties of those who set them forth by experiencing them directly, using developed observational faculties which ordinary people like myself do not have. A second source of authority is the authority of inference drawn from another person's statements through logic. That authority is not just one Tibetan's authority. It is still an authority which is handed down, this second level of inferential or logical authority. It is essentially those things that one thinks of as being reasonable. It is an authority which comes down from the historical Buddha himself, who originally put forth many of the points of Buddhist logic which have been pondered ever since. Looking at the number of authoritative statements that have been generated out of direct perception through science and empirical knowledge, the amount which scientists have been able to learn, it is absolutely staggering. Similarly, the amount of statements that can be generated out of this second authority, out of reasoning or logic, is again vast.

If you take, for example, your presentation of the ever smaller pathways [found by anatomists within the brain], finally leading down to the smallest pathway, the neuron, with each of these ever smaller pathways being grouped together into larger pathways, this would be, I think, just about impossible to arrive at through this second level of authority, through reasoning and meditative experience. To come at these findings through reasoning would be incredibly difficult. One would have to take it in and get at it through what one sees. It would be very hard to come at it through this second level. It is the case, is it not, that up until the ability of science to utilize this authority of seeing and to make these authoritative statements about the brain, it has never been possible to do so before.

Therefore, up until the time of science being able to do this, what has happened is that there has been this other level of authority, perhaps best called logic based on observation, trying to understand what is out there. In the earlier presentation of the Buddhists there are channels, energy moving through channels, and drops or winds, which were arrived at fundamentally from a logical approach to what *has* to be, based on meditative experience. It is really wonderful that this is now being given investigation by this other level of authority. This would not have been available before, because we did not have the power to make these types of observations.

SECTION IV
PERCEIVING THE REAL

Our perceptual awareness is generated out of our eyes, ears, nose, tongue, and so forth. Coarse states of perceptual awareness are generated out of the connection of extremely subtle elements of awareness with rougher physical elements.

—Lobsang Gyatso

7   Perception in Tibetan Abhidharma and Western Neuroscience

Having considered the presentations of mind from the Tibetan and neuroscientific traditions in their broadest sense, we will now go on to address some central issues in greater detail and in more precise language. This section will address the presentations of the nature of perception and how it is that we understand our experience. The first part of the chapter will describe the kinds of perception that the Sautrantika school asserts, the importance of perception to Buddhist thought, and the mode of functioning of perceptual awareness. Next, I will present some points from the scientific understanding of the brain, as it relates to the perceptual process. The conclusion will make comparisons between the two systems, particularly noting how some persistent philosophical problems and debates within Tibetan Buddhism might be addressed by the findings of science. Although these two systems of thought are very different in many ways, their presentations of perception are surprisingly complementary, which leads to a wealth of possible points of comparison and areas where each system can gain new insights from the other.

THE SAUTRANTIKA VIEW OF DIRECT PERCEIVERS

Definition of a direct perceiver

The Tibetan Buddhist view of perception is founded on an understanding of the directly perceiving consciousness, which can access the ground of reality. As stated in Geshe Jam-bel-sam-pel's *Presentation of Awareness and Knowledge,*

> The definition of a direct perceiver is a non-mistaken knower that
> is free from conceptuality.[20]

In this definition a perceiver should not be taken to be a person who occasionally has perceptions, as in Western thought. Here, a direct perceiver is *a moment of awareness itself*, not a person who "has" such a moment. This reflects a basic underlying difference between these two systems for viewing the mind. In this presentation a perceiver is not understood as a type of thing (like a person) which is from the "mental" division of reality and is thereby in some way capable of being aware, and so capable of perceiving objects from the physical world. Here, a perceiver is a moment of awareness itself, a subject, which is neither understood as solely mental, nor as solely physical. A subject in this sense is defined in terms of the type of object that it takes, the types of conditions that bring it about, whether it apprehends its object directly, indirectly, or not at all, and in general, the detailed nature of its relationship to the object that appears to it and is apprehended by it. These relationships will be described for different types of subjects and objects in this and the subsequent chapters.

The separation between direct perception and conceptual thought which this definition puts forth forms a basic division of types of knowledge within the Sautrantika system. In brief, objects of awareness are divided into two categories whose names are translated as "conventional truths," which are known by thought, and "ultimate truths," which are known by simple and direct perception. The purpose of direct perception within Sautrantika Buddhism is clear and fundamental—it is to gain access to the truth from one's direct experience of perceivable reality, which is what leads to overcoming ignorance. For this reason, the Sautrantika system is at pains to emphasize that perception does indeed have direct access to the bare ground of experience, and a considerable part of this chapter addresses how this can be the case.

This "ultimate truth" is *not* a complete or ideal conceptual understanding of the world. The term used in translation unfortunately connotes that an "ultimate truth" might be something conceptually sophisticated coming from an approved body of reason or dogma superior to all others. In fact, it is intended to convey largely the opposite impression. In the Sautrantika context, an ultimate truth is something that one directly perceives from experience, in both its fundamental simplicity and its richness of detail. It is considered to include objects which are external to the subject in that their defining characteristic is that specific features exist "from the object's own side."[21] These perceived objects are directly contrasted with objects that are constructed entirely internally by thought: our concepts, mental images, and so on.[22]

Perception is described as direct and non-mistaken because it is said to faithfully reflect the aspect of its object like a mirror reflects a precise image of what is in front of it. That is not to say that direct perception has access to reality in the sense of directly entering into its realm, nor that all objects are necessarily correctly ascertained, but that the aspect of the object which is cast to the perceiving mind is complete, so the mind has the *possibility* of full ascertainment of what is experienced. Perceptions can be mistaken, but there is nothing inherently missing from perception in general to prevent the perceiving mind from fully ascertaining its objects. This delicate balance is struck to give the mind direct access to reality, but not necessarily ascertainment, and this interplay will be a major theme of this chapter, as it is in the Sautrantika position. The presentations of the different kinds of direct perception and its general mode of functioning all reflect its basic purpose for Tibetan Buddhism, which is to gain direct, ultimate access to the "real" ground of experience, which can liberate one from ignorance.[23] The next section describes how this process is said to function.

The mode of functioning of direct perception in Tibetan Buddhism

DIVISIONS AND TYPES OF DIRECT PERCEIVERS

In Abhidharma all existent phenomena are defined as being knowable, so descriptions of the types of objects of perception are closely related to descriptions of the kinds of matter. The types of matter are typically described and divided into categories according to the perspective that they are experienced by the directly perceiving mind. For direct perception there are six "doors" or avenues for the entry of awareness into the consciousness, which correspond to the five traditional Western senses plus one. In the authoritative text called the *Treasury of Knowledge*, the historical master Vasubandhu categorizes phenomena into eighteen *dhatus*, or constituents, which correspond to the six types of objects of direct perception, the sense faculties that they use, and the types of consciousness that result, as follows:[24]

External Objects	Sensory Faculties	Consciousnesses
1. Form, Color and Shape	7. Sense of Vision	13. Visual Consciousness
2. Sound	8. Sense of Audition	14. Auditory Consciousness
3. Odor	9. Sense of Smell	15. Olfactory Consciousness
4. Taste	10. Sense of Taste	16. Gustatory Consciousness
5. Tangibles	11. Sense of Touch	17. Tactile Consciousness
6. Mental Objects	12. Mind Sense	18. Non-Sensory Consciousness

This categorization sets out two important points which will be described more fully later: the division of the experience of perception into an object, a sense power, and a consciousness, and the presentation of a nonconceptual type of perceived object which can be the object of a perceiving mind, but not of thought.

Direct perceptions can also be divided into four categories by the types of objects that they take: [25]

1. Sense direct perceivers.
2. Mental direct perceivers.
3. Self-knowing direct perceivers.
4. Yogic direct perceivers.

In this classification the different types of perceivers are divided according to the complexity (or "subtlety") of their appearing objects. A sense direct perceiver is defined as

> a non-mistaken, nonconceptual knower that is produced from its own uncommon empowering condition, a physical sense power.[26]

These take the five types of sensory phenomena which are traditional from the Western viewpoint as their appearing objects. Direct perceivers are defined to exclude incorrect perceptions of experience and conceptualizations, which will fall into different categories of mind described below. The uncommon empowering condition of a direct perceiver is one of the necessary conditions which together bring it into being, and it corresponds to the related sensory faculty.

Following after a sense direct perception, "one smallest moment" of mental direct perception arises from the uncommon empowering condition of a "mental sense power." This means that a moment of direct perception (a directly perceiving mind) is generated in the aspect of the immediately preceding moment of perceptual awareness. This previous moment can have been one of the five types of sense direct perceiver, or it too can have been a mental power (with a common example being the mental power that is produced by meditative stabilization).

Self-knowing direct perceivers allow for self-awareness. They take as their appearing object another moment of awareness, with this moment of awareness taking its own appearing object.[27]

Finally, yogic direct perceivers are described as those which are produced in the mind of a "'superior' (*arya*)...from a meditative stabilization which is a union of calm abiding and special insight." This is the type of direct perceiver that is cultivated in Tibetan Buddhist meditation to allow realization of the impermanence of experience and (in the Madhyamika school) of selflessness.[28]

THE TWO TRUTHS IN BRIEF

The mode of functioning of direct perception is explained in comparison with conceptualization in terms of a division into two distinct types of objects, translated as the two types of "truths." In this context, the translation "truth" is not meant to apply to an entire corpus of correct wisdom, but to an individual object of experiential awareness. This distinction between two types of objects is used to make clear what is experienced through direct perception and what is not.

Conceptual truths: the objects of thought

This type of truth is defined as being a mental convention only; its object is a mental semblance, a "meaning generality" which is imputed by thought, and is conventionally used in language and day to day activities. These translations of technical terms lead one to understand that a concept of an object, although it can clearly relate to the object itself, is nonetheless a creation of the mind, and it resembles the object only in a general and relative way, although it can nonetheless be useful. The mental semblance does not have all of the real object's own features, nor the real object's full richness of detail. For this reason a conceptual mind is said to be mistaken (or deceptive). It does not distinguish between the incomplete mental image of an object, which is formed largely from preconceptions, and the actual object itself in all of its detail.

More technical characterizations of conceptual objects of thought from the Sautrantika perspective include: (a) they are "permanent" or "static" in the sense that while a mental image exists it does not have as an inherent characteristic that it disintegrates from moment to moment in the way that real matter does, nor that it can "organically grow" with time; (b) semblances cannot be mentally or physically divided and maintain their same sense;[29] (c) they can be perceived whether their appearing object is physically present or not;[30] (d) they abide "mixed in place, time, and nature," meaning that they generalize or share features between different actual objects which are similar;[31] (e) they are unable to produce physical functions;[32] and (f) they are not "products" (this is the translation of a technical term and means that they are not created from causes and conditions in the way that perceived physical objects are).[33]

In short, although conceptual objects of mind are held to be real phenomena which can be usefully employed in day to day life, in sophisticated reasoning, as well as in the Buddhist path, they are only posited to exist in our "mistaken" thoughts and never to be ultimately concordant with reality, in that something is always missing.

Nonconceptual truths—the objects of direct perception
The type of truth experienced by perception is considered to be an ultimate truth by Sautrantika psychology; it is the direct apprehension of experienced reality. The objects which we directly perceive exist "from their own side" instead of being merely imputed by thought. They are typically the substantially existing physical objects that we find in the world, with all of their wealth of detail. The use of the term "ultimate truth" as a translation should not be thought to imply "vague realms of misty truth," but something much simpler, and directly experienced in perception.[34] These "ultimate truths" are not "correct" conceptual understandings of reality, they are direct experiences of it. Technically, these "truths" are also defined as: (a) impermanent, or non-static in the sense that their constituents disintegrate with every moment in the way that ordinary matter does in the Buddhist view;[35] (b) they can be broken into component parts and maintain their (divided) existence;[36] (c) they can only be perceived when they are physically present;[37] (d) they abide "unmixed in place, time and nature," meaning that they are specific rather than general; (e) they are able to produce functions, as physical objects typically can;[38] (f) they are unsuitable to be mixed with conceptual thoughts and cannot be fully expressed in words because of their infinite detail; and (g) they are products (produced from causes).[39] Direct perception allows access to the richness of the experienced world.

This presentation of two types of reality often seems quite counterintuitive from a Western perspective. It posits that ultimate truths, the objects of experience, are impermanent and thereby exist for only a single moment before they cease, whereas conventional truths, our concepts, are permanent and unchanging. An example to illustrate this counterintuitive definition is that the object of direct experience of a mind aware of a tree is impermanent and an ultimate truth, whereas the idea of impermanence is permanent and only a conventionally existent truth.

DIRECT PERCEIVERS KNOW THEIR OBJECTS COMPLETELY AND WITH BARE AWARENESS

Direct perception is described as being a "complete engager," which means that it has complete access to all of the specific characteristics of its objects. This is not, of course, meant to suggest that one can consciously perceive all of the tiny details within objects all at once, but it does mean that all of the features of an object can be accessed by direct perception, including an object's tiny constituent elements and its more subtle features, such as its impermanence.[40] It is posited that we directly perceive these characteristics of objects—they are cast to the mind which faithfully reflects their various aspects—but we may not become aware of them because of our lack of ascertainment.[41] The Sautrantika presentation suggests that although our mind "directly perceives those features [which we do not become aware of]...it is unable to induce ascertainment of some factors. This is due to thick predispositions [and other factors]." Why would one posit that perception is taking place in the absence of awareness? The reason for this presentation by the Sautrantikas appears to be to maintain the status of direct perception as being a complete engager of specifically characterized phenomena—of objects characterized by all of their specific details—and thereby of "the real."[42] If only some of the object's characteristics were reflected by direct perception, this would contradict the notion that it is intimately linked with the ultimate reality of what is experienced.

Direct perception is a "bare" awareness of an object in its entirety, without anything added. The idea that perception apprehends the world in this crystal clear way is traceable to the historical master Dignaga's statement:

> The object of the sense (*indriya-gocara*) is the form (*rupa*) which is to be cognized [simply] as it is (*svasamvedya*) and which is inexpressible (*anirdeshya*). [43]

This statement strongly supports the division of awarenesses into the two kinds explained above, direct perception of inexpressible, ultimate truths of experience, and conceptual understanding of conventional objects.

> For direct perception, but *not* for conceptuality, an object's mode
> of appearance to the eye consciousness [for example] accords with
> its final nature. That is to say, all its uncommon specific
> characteristics...vividly appear to the visual sense.[44]

This description of the characteristics of bare awareness found in direct perception is intended to convey that the direct perceiver is in intimate contact with the ultimate reality of existent phenomena. This is another key element to the mode of functioning of this type of awareness. I shall now turn from the mode of functioning of perception to the issue of how perception unfolds.

Mechanisms of direct perception

THE CONDITIONS OF DIRECT PERCEPTION

One description of the unfolding of direct perception is based upon the causal elements which lead to it. Direct perception is said to be brought about by three conditions:[45]

1. The observed object.
2. The uncommon empowering condition.
3. The immediately preceding moment of consciousness.

These three conditions are taken from each of the three groups of *dhatus* described earlier.[46] When these three conditions together are met, then direct perception can take place. The observed object is a physically existent experienced object. In technical terms, it is a specifically characterized, impermanent phenomenon in the category of an ultimate truth.

The uncommon empowering condition is one of the traditional five sense powers or the mental faculty. The sense powers are all described as matter which is "clear internal form." The texts describe each individual sense power in a highly metaphorical way, based on the introspective sensation of the sense rather than an empirical dissection of its effector. The visual sense power is described as being in the shape of a flower, the auditory power as being in the shape of a bundle of wheat, the olfactory power as two copper needles, the gustatory power as a cut half-moon, and the tactile power as smooth skin.[47]

The final of the three conditions is the immediately preceding condition of the mind, which includes such elements as one's interest in an object, concentration, mental stabilization, attention, and so on. It is described as a "knower" (moment of awareness) which leads to engagement in the object. It is technically defined as "a knower which

principally and directly produces a sense direct perceiver apprehending a form only as an experiencer which is a clear knower."[48]

ASPECTED DIRECT PERCEPTION

The next point regarding how direct perception unfolds is the important issue of how the object comes to interact with the mind through
casting its aspect. In order to solve the philosophical problem of how
three independent, impermanent, and completely disjointed conditions are able to meet and lead to the direct perception of an object, the
Sautrantika school posits the notion of an aspect of the object, which
is "cast towards" a consciousness. Since the object cannot physically
enter the consciousness, and the consciousness cannot become the
object but it must still be technically considered to be "one entity"
with the object,[49] the idea is presented that the consciousness exactly
reflects its object in the way that a mirror reflects an exact image:[50]

> Just as a glass placed over a blue cloth takes on the color blue
> without itself becoming blue and without blue actually entering
> into the glass, the eye consciousness perceiving a table takes on a
> likeness of table without actually becoming a table and without a
> table actually entering into it.[51]

It is interesting to note that by using the analogies of a mirror and a
plate of glass the Sautrantikas give consciousness a relatively passive
role in taking on the aspect of its object. The following section will
describe a strikingly similar presentation from modern brain science,
which suggests that the brain contains neural images of external objects, but also suggests, in contrast to the metaphor of a mirror, that
when the brain takes on the image of a perceived object it actively
participates and changes dynamically as a part of this process.

The reason for the presentation of aspected direct perception is clear:
the Sautrantika school is trying to maintain the individuality and sepa-
rateness of objects while at the same time positing that direct perception is able to fully apprehend reality.[52] In order to preserve this separation the Sautrantikas assert that "direct perception does not know
actual phenomena nakedly but knows them through certain types of
sense data." This is asserted explicitly to address the criticism that if
there were no intermediary aspect between the consciousness and the
object then the two would have to be considered to be one substantial
entity;[53] in other words, they would not be separate objects at all.[54] As
Jang-gya Rol-bay Dor-jay writes in his *Presentation of Tenets:*

> If the object itself were known clearly without [any] aspect, that object would be an entity of illumination [a conscious entity] and in that case would be apprehended even without reliance on a [separate] consciousness.[55]

What exactly is an aspect, and how is it involved in the unfolding of the process of perception? In general, an aspect is described as something which an object casts towards a consciousness, into the form of which the consciousness is generated, and which is similar to the object which casts it. The fact that the aspect which an object casts is similar to the object is given as an explanation of why direct perception is incontrovertible with respect to the object which appears to it, at least for Sautrantika, if not for the later schools.[56]

The role of the aspect in the unfolding of perception is also explained in terms of two types of aspects, one of which is involved in each of two successive stages in direct perception. The distinction between the types of aspects is considered in greater detail in the discussion with Gen Damcho below. For now, during the unfolding of an individual perception, the objective apprehension object is succeeded by the apprehension aspect (or consciousness aspect), and serves as a temporal intermediary in this process.[57]

The complex topic of the aspect which an object casts and how this is involved in the mechanism of perception is not uniquely resolved within the Gelugpa presentation of Sautrantika. There are a number of different debates within the tradition regarding the specific nature, number, location, and implications of the two kinds of aspect just described. Later, we will consider the different notions of the aspect of perception in greater detail and in light of the findings of contemporary neuroscience, in an attempt to answer some of the remaining (and long debated) points about the mode of functioning of perception from within this new context.

THE UNITS OF DIRECT PERCEPTION

The last issue in this section regarding the functioning of direct perception concerns the nature of the individual objects taken by perception and whether they can be divided into parts or are inherently unified, and this is again a debated topic. Although different understandings of the Sautrantika view agree that direct perception incontrovertibly cognizes ultimate truths, there is a general division of interpretation regarding what type of objects this definition includes, specifically regarding whether perception is made up only of tiny, indivisible units, or can include whole, unified objects. The contrast and debate between these two positions will be presented in brief form here, and considered in greater detail later in the context of a view from contemporary neuroscience.

The debate over the unity of perceived objects within the Gelugpa tradition is discussed thoroughly by Anne Klein, who notes that there is a great deal of controversy regarding the exact nature of the objects of direct perception, which stems from different interpretations of classical texts.[58] The Tibetan term for the object of direct perception is typically translated as "the real," and there is general agreement concerning the points that these real objects, or units of direct perception, are (in technical terms) impermanent, specifically characterized phenomena which can perform functions. However, there is a great deal of controversy regarding further details. As Klein mentions, there is evidence that as early as the time of the historical figure Dignaga, there existed the beginnings of a conflict between the notion that the aggregated objects of our experience, tables and so on, are specifically characterized and impermanent phenomena, and Vasubandhu's statement from the *Treasury of Knowledge* that the ultimate objects of direct perception are tiny particles which are indivisible in space and time.[59]

Klein argues that while the common view is that objects of direct perception are indeed "partless particles," the Gelugpas take the position that whole objects are equally "real." She cites Stcherbatsky's definition of an object of direct perception as a typical example of a prevalent interpretation of the Buddhist view:

> [It has] no extension in space and no duration in time.... [It is] the point instant of reality.... We can cognize only the imagined superstructure of reality, but not reality itself.[60]

This interpretation clearly puts the aggregated objects of our everyday experience into the realm of conceptual, conventional truths, not the objects of direct perception. On the other hand, the Gelugpas interpret the historical master Dharmakirti's statement from the *Pramanavartika* that "Whatever exists ultimately is able to perform a function," to mean that composite objects, which they hold to perform functions, are themselves ultimate truths. For example, a table is a composite object, made up of many particles, but as an aggregate it can perform the function of holding a plate, and can thereby be argued to "exist ultimately" in the sense of being an object of direct perception.

Klein suggests that the Gelugpas solved the apparent discrepancy between unified and divided objects of perception by teaching two separate divisions of the historical Sautrantika school, one holding to each belief. The Sautrantikas Following Scripture, the lower of the two schools in the Gelugpa presentation, are held to support the notion that specifically characterized phenomena are partless particles and individual moments of consciousness. The Sautrantikas Following Reasoning, the higher school, are presented as teaching that all objects of direct perception, including aggregated wholes as well as their parts, are ultimate existents. This second position maintains that all impermanent objects, regardless of their size or whether they are aggregates, are specifically characterized objects of direct perception which perform ultimate functions.[61] The emphasis of the Sautrantikas Following Reasoning is shifted from the characteristics of the physical object of perception to the characteristics of the mind which apprehends the object:

> The chief distinction between specifically and generally charac-
> terized phenomena is not, as in other interpretations, their size,
> or their designation as whole or a part, but whether or not they
> are imputed by thought.[62]

This once again stresses the division of awarenesses into two types, conceptual and perceptual, based upon the kind of object which they take. From this perspective the essential remaining question is whether aggregated phenomena are imputed by thought or exist "from their own side." Although the Gelugpa scholars attempt to solve this riddle through textual analysis, Klein suggests that there are statements which adequately support both sides, and that there are simply no clear statements from the authority of Dignaga, Dharmakirti, or Vasubandhu which decisively resolve this question. As was alluded to already, there are a number of insights into this issue which can be gained from the scientific understanding of what kinds of perceptual objects are possible based on our knowledge of the perceptual mechanism, and this will be taken up later.

In summary, the Gelugpa position on perception is that the directly perceiving mind is incontrovertible with respect to its appearing object, meaning that perception does in principle have direct access to reality. Perception is contrasted with conceptual understandings in that each takes its own form of object, with perception taking objects that "exist from their own side" and contain the full richness of experiential detail, rather than being imputed by thought. The types of direct perception are enumerated in several ways, along with the conditions which bring them about, and the directly perceiving consciousness is explained to gain access to experience by reflecting the aspect of its object, which is at once described as a unified whole, and also as an indivisible entity. These points are all made from the perspective of experience itself; the direct perceiver is not a person who sometimes perceives, but an experienced moment of awareness. With this as our basis of comparison, we will now turn to a perspective taken from the contemporary Western science of the brain.

THE UNDERSTANDING OF PERCEPTION FROM CONTEMPORARY NEUROSCIENCE

Definition of perception

Within science, the motivation for considering the issue of perception is completely different than it is within Buddhism, and for this reason the term "perception" itself refers to quite different things within these two traditions. In Buddhism perception is understood as a means of gaining access to the truth about experienced reality, whereas in science it is understood as a physical, biologically necessary process which is studied empirically. The resulting definitions are extremely different. Francis Bacon's early scientific definition of perception presents an historical example of this separation:

> [Perception is] the being affected by an object without contact, though *consciousness is absent.*

A more contemporary definition, taken from a standard text on neurobiology, presents a view equally disparate from that of Sautrantika:

> Our *perceptions are not direct records of the world* around us but are *constructed internally,* at least in part, according to innate rules and constraints imposed by the capabilities of the nervous system. [Italics added for emphasis.][63]

Although limited, perhaps a generally representative definition of perception within science is one cited in a contemporary introductory psychology text by Mark McGee and David Wilson:

> Perception is the term we use to describe the brain's interpretation of sensory information.[64]

Within the neuroscience community perception is commonly treated as the cognitive aspect of sensation, which discovers important information about the environment in order to ensure beneficial behavior. In marked contrast to the Buddhist emphasis on the urge for knowledge and liberation from ignorance,[65] the general biological and evolutionary view is that our fundamental urge is one for survival. Accordingly, while Buddhism defines perception and awareness in terms of their ability to know objects fully and apprehend the truth, science defines them in terms of their ability to apprehend features of the environment that will help an organism to survive, and the issue of whether or not they are "true" in any more abstract sense is largely ignored.

The issue of consciousness receives very sparse treatment in biological descriptions of perception because it is considered in some ways a separate matter, as the first quotation above makes clear. While the assumption of Buddhism is that consciousness of reality is the very purpose of perception, a prevalent assumption in biology is that perception exists only to allow effective behavior. In the extreme, there have even been theories put forth regarding why consciousness exists at all, given that a hypothetical organism would be able to survive without it. In making comparisons of the understanding of perception within Buddhism and that within science, this striking difference regarding what perception is must be born clearly in mind. Particularly given these ideological differences of approach, and the inherent differences between a theory born of introspection and one born of external measurement, it is in some ways very surprising how compatible these two views of perception in fact are.

The functions of perception

Within neuroscience, sensory perception is no longer divided into the five traditional senses, as it once was, but into a larger number. The human body has many organs for sensation which are as important as those of the five traditional senses but are not routinely considered in the Buddhist presentation. For example, the ear contains not only the apparatus which allows us to hear, but also three round canals of fluid which allow us to perceive our movements, and additional organs which allow us to detect the orientation of our body in space. Without these additional senses, normal bodily posture and movement would be completely impossible. The body also contains, among many other examples, an array of stretch, pressure, and chemical sensors that lead us to the feelings of body position, hunger, or the need to breath.

Another difference in the presentation of perception is that within neurobiology, "non-sensory mental objects" are usually considered within the context of conceptual thought, rather than perception, although the division between percept and concept is not drawn nearly so decisively as in the Sautrantika tradition.

The objects of the traditional senses are also divided differently within neuroscience than within Buddhism. For example, in Buddhism the objects of hearing are categorized by whether or not they are articulate, pleasant, or derived from a conscious source.[66] In neuroscience sound is studied in terms of its physical properties (such as pitch or frequency) and its ability to allow an organism to localize an object, judge its distance, extract cognitive information about the sound source and, in the case of humans at least, recognize language. Each of these examples illustrates the biological view of perception as a means of acquiring information about the environment.

Perhaps the most significant difference is that neuroscience fully acknowledges that the perceptual mechanism itself is flawed and can be fooled by its objects, even when it is in perfect working order. The best examples of this come from the visual and auditory illusions, which demonstrate our misapprehension of external forms. A typical and universally recognized example is that after walking along a path for some time looking down, upon looking up, the clouds and sky will appear to recede. A number of studies have been conducted to try to find the biological substrates for perceptual illusions and it has been possible to demonstrate in some cases that the perceptual apparatus perceives illusions in the way that it does simply because of the way that it is built.[67] Philosophically, this suggests that there are "errors" built into the design of our sensory system, and that any knowledge which we obtain from it must be viewed with a skeptical eye. Interestingly, this same point is important to the later Gelugpa presentation of the Prasangika school's refutation of Sautrantika thought.[68]

The measurement of perception

Within the scientific tradition of this century, there has been a strong tradition of measuring the details of the accuracy and characteristics of perception objectively. To this end, the field of psychophysics has performed thousands of experiments that probe subject's abilities to experience different types of stimuli. Here, the word subject is used in the traditional scientific sense—as a person who can be repeatedly tested using a variety of sense objects—not as a moment of mind. The two simplest examples of this type of experiment are detection and discrimination threshold measurements. The ability of a subject to perceive a sensory object at all (be it a tone, a light, a light touch to the skin, etc.) can be measured by presenting sensory objects that are just more intense than the subject can detect, and sensory objects that are just less intense than can be detected, in order to define the exact intensity which is the subject's threshold for detection. Similarly, the subject can be asked to differentiate very similar stimuli in order to find the threshold for detecting the differences between stimuli. Interestingly, near the sensory detection threshold, subjects typically have the experience that they are guessing blindly about what they perceive, but they can nonetheless quite accurately report the correct answer most of the time.

This type of research has defined in great detail the limits of human perception of simple objects, and illustrates one of the scientific system's greatest achievements in the area of measuring the mind. Unfortunately, measuring or explaining the more complex or subjective aspects of experience, such as emotions or thoughts or plans, has proved to be much more difficult and is still comparatively unexplored. I will focus on the areas of mind that the field of neuroscience in particular has made the greatest progress towards understanding, and the greatest example is surely visual perception.

Mechanisms of perception—vision

A brief overview of the biological understanding of the mechanism of vision will serve to illustrate this approach to perception in general, so that comparisons and contrasts can then be examined. Neuroscience suggests that the process of sight begins in the eye, which is known to function somewhat like a sophisticated, automatic camera. The lens in the front of the eye is automatically controlled to focus the image of the world onto the eye's back surface. The size of the hole through which light passes (the pupil) is also automatically adjusted based on the amount of light, in order to ensure optimum "viewing." This analogy quickly breaks down, however, because while a camera merely produces an image for an outside observer, the visual process as it progresses through the brain is itself presumed to *be* the observer.

Once a visual image of the world falls onto the retina on the back surface of the eye, it is translated into a neural code which will become the basis of awareness. The retina is made up of a sheet of several million individual receptor cells, each of which responds to light from a particular part of the visual picture, changing light into the electrical energy of a neural coding signal. This is somewhat analogous to a video camera that turns the amount of light falling on each point in a picture into its own electrical signal which can be projected onto a screen. Just as the camera that one uses limits the kinds of things that one can take a picture of—because of the amount of light that is needed, whether it is black and white or color, and so on, there are also physically defined limits on the possibilities of visual perception that are due to the mechanisms of the eye, a point often overlooked in the Buddhist view of perception.

Two important limits to the eye's capacity, which will be considered in more detail later, are that the biological eye cannot see things that happen too fast nor distinguish details that are too small. If one imagines looking through a television camera which takes images thirty times per second, one would simply not be able to see events that were much shorter than this. Similarly, if one's camera can just distinguish a one centimeter object at ten meters distance, then it will not be able to capture events that are far smaller. The receptors in the eye (and the ones that they are connected to in the brain) operate rather slowly, slowly enough that when we see a movie go by at twenty-three frames per second the eye usually does not perceive the flickering. Also, no matter how much we may train our perception, we will never be able to spatially discriminate two single events of light which, when projected on the retina, fall within the boundary of one receptor cell.[69] Some of the consequences of these limits will be presented below in a comparison to different Buddhist views of the individual units of perception.

THE VISUAL PROCESSING HIERARCHY OF THE BRAIN

The visual images of the world which come from each of the two eyes are combined together in part of the cerebral cortex at the back of the brain. This information is processed through a hierarchy of many individual "maps" or "images" of the visual world as summarized in Figure 1. Each of the many maps (which are collapsed and shown as boxes in this diagram) represents the entire extent of the visual scene coming in through the eyes, just as a world map represents the entire surface of the planet; but each map represents a different group of features, much like political or geologic boundaries are represented by different world maps. It is equally valid to use a common Buddhist analogy and imagine these maps to contain something like mirror reflections of the visual world. The image in each map is created by the

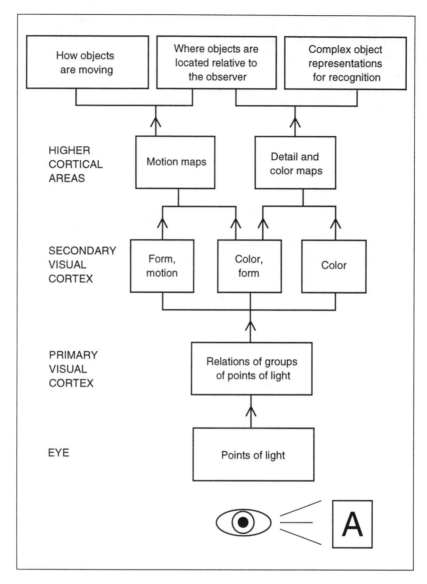

Figure 1. The Visual Processing Hierarchy of the Brain

A simplification of the current notion of how visual perceptual information is processed within the brain. Information flows upwards from the eye through neural signals, with each level of the diagram upward representing a progression further into the brain.

activity of the many nerve cells which make up the map's surface, with salient parts of the visual image represented by areas of energetically active cells. Thus, a number of physically measurable correlates (or images) of visual consciousness do indeed exist in discrete locations in the brain. These maps have been measured using many different methods by hundreds of scientists, and although many crucial details remain unresolved, the basic fact of their existence is beyond any doubt.

The individual maps are arranged in a hierarchy, with the visual information flowing from the eye to the first map and then on to the higher maps, which abstract more complex aspects of the visual scene. In this way the perceptual apparatus builds up representations of whole complex objects, which are found further into the brain and higher up the hierarchy from the simpler individual visual features represented below. One of these maps is more involved in representing the colors that we see, another is more involved in representing motion, and another represents angles of orientation and form, just as different complex maps of the same world might represent political borders, climatic regions, and mineral deposits. Progressing upwards through the hierarchy more and more complex features are represented until, at the top of the hierarchy, the maps represent things as complex as faces or spatial relations within the environment.

An interesting question about this understanding has been asked by both eminent scholars of biology and of Buddhism alike: Where do all of the lines lead?[70] What is at the "top" of this hierarchy which "perceives" these representations? At what point in the hierarchy does awareness take place? Although somewhat difficult to grasp, and certainly not completely clear, the notion of this presentation is that there *is no* observer which exists separately from this system, and no point in the hierarchy where the awareness "sits." Much as in the Buddhist presentation of Abhidharma, the notion is that it is possible to describe perception merely taking place as this process, without the need for any sort of substantially existent being residing alongside of the process and serving as the subject which observes. The activity of this hierarchy is itself thought to be the physical correlate of awareness, with awareness of simple features taking place near the bottom, and more abstract features nearer the top. Within science, perception and awareness can be viewed as simply being a product of the functioning nervous system, without the need for any separate subjective mind or self.

AWARENESS TAKES PLACE OVER TIME AND SPACE

A major difference between this view and traditional Buddhist presentations of perceptual consciousness is that here "a single" perceptual consciousness is explicitly described as taking place over a rather long period of time, being spread over a large area within the brain, and taking place concurrently with other processes. Perception is definitely not thought of as taking place in individual instantaneous moments which come about one at a time in a series and are completely indivisible. Although there is compelling data that many types of information are processed through perception in fairly long "chunks" of time, rather than in a completely continuous fashion (with the chunks being about a tenth to half of a second),[71] a prevailing view is still that consciousness flows from one moment to the next not in discrete and tiny instants but more as an ongoing stream of processing. It takes time for information to progress upwards through the visual processing system from the eyes—nearly a quarter second for the higher maps to become fully active in fact—and this is part of why it takes time to react to something that we see. Also, while this information is percolating through the system, new information is coming in at the bottom, and information may also be coming in from all of the other senses, as well as from conceptual thought. These different types and different objects of consciousness do not seem to take place in a discrete series but concurrently. It also takes time for the information about the same object from different senses to be put together again. These are some of the reasons that the most popular current models of brain functioning rely on the idea of "parallel, distributed processing." Consciousness is not thought of as happening as a series of discrete points, but as a continuous web of signals which are distributed into different parts of the brain and are all evolving at once. Although it is possible that somehow these ongoing processes do break awareness into small pieces, it does not seem at all likely that they are entirely discrete, nor that they occur at rates beyond tens or hundreds per second. These ideas are somewhat at odds with the traditional Buddhist presentation that thousands of discrete moments of awareness fly by in sequence within the blink of an eye.

PERCEPTUAL ILLUSIONS

There have been a number of studies addressing the question of whether it is a subjective or mental element which is fooled in perceptions of illusory phenomena, or whether the nervous system itself can bear the blame. One issue at stake here is whether there is some con-

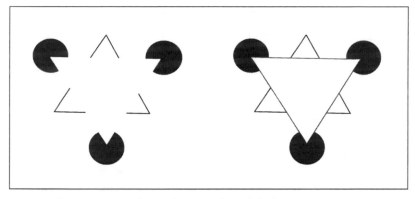

Figure 2. Illusory contours that trick the mind—and the brain

When we observe the figure on the left, we have the natural experience that there is a white triangle which covers the remainder of the figure. Our experience corresponds roughly to that shown in the figure on the right, only with the "top" triangle having no dark edges. In fact, as is plain to see, there are no edges or triangles at all, just line segments, corners and partially occluded circles. Von der Heydt and colleagues have shown that neurons in the visual cortex respond to the figure on the left in a fashion analogous to the way they do to the figure on the right. Roughly speaking, neurons in the visual system respond as if they "see" the edges of the top triangle, even though these edges do not in fact exist. These visual neurons are presumably part of the root of our perception in this simple case.

scious *observer of* the nervous system that is mistaken or whether the mistake can be located in the neural mechanism itself. The clear answer has been that many of the errors that we encounter in our perceptions can be directly attributed to quirks in the perceptual apparatus. For example, von der Heydt and colleagues, and more recently Sheth, *et al.*, have shown that when some types of visual illusions are presented to the eyes, even the early and middle level maps within the perceptual system represent the illusions as we perceive them, that is, incorrectly.[72] Figure 2 shows an example of these types of figures, and the perceptual "mistakes" which they lead to. The demonstrations of mistakes built right into the fabric of the perceptual apparatus have clear implications for the Sautrantika notion that direct perception is a non-mistaken knower which fully cognizes its object. Another example of a mistake of the perceptual nervous system will be discussed in the section on the mistakes of thought and of direct perception.

COMPARING THE TWO SYSTEMS OF THOUGHT

Having presented an overview of some important aspects of the two presentations of perception, this section will compare particular issues from the two systems. The aim of this book is certainly not to show that the two systems of thought have found the same answers. It will probably never be possible to prove the correctness or the errors of particular Buddhist assertions through science, or vice versa, because the two systems come from such different perspectives. However, if one chooses to draw analogies between the two systems of metaphor, mechanistic and allegorical, they turn out in many cases to be surprisingly similar. This becomes most interesting when the language and observations found in one system can be brought to bear on old problems from the other system.

The question of aspected perception

According to the Gelugpa presentation of perception, the aspect which a perceived object casts to the mind is an impermanent phenomenon and, therefore, is, "at least in theory, [a] specifically located and findable [object]." This brings up the obvious question of whether neuroscience has ever found such a thing in the physical structure of the brain, a place where Buddhists have not heretofore had the opportunity to look. As is probably clear from the above discussion of neural maps, the answer seems to be yes. This leads to the possibility of presenting new perspectives on some of the age-old debates of the Gelugpa order, which were formulated long before modern investigations of vision had begun, to see if convincing arguments can be made from new information.

WHERE IS THE ASPECT OF ASPECTED AWARENESS?

From the traditional Gelugpa standpoint, the issue of locating the aspect of awareness is somewhat problematic. Some Gelugpa scholars asserted that the subjective apprehension aspect (the consciousness aspect) exists in the pupil of the eye, and that the objective apprehension aspect exists somewhere between the object and the perceiving consciousness,[73] but there are a number of problems with these ideas which were recognized by the early Gelugpas. Support for this notion was levied from the empirical observations of the day: if the pupil deteriorates then so does vision, and if an object is too close to the eye then it cannot be perceived clearly (as if there is not enough room in between the eye and the object for the generation of the aspect).[74]

One obvious problem with this idea is that if a second observer looks for the objective apprehension aspect where it is supposed to be (between the eye and its object), he will not find it. Also, since the three causes of perception (the observed object condition, the sense power, and the previous moment of consciousness) are causes, they must (by Buddhist formal logic) all have ceased to exist the moment before a perception begins; so it is also unsuitable to posit any of these obvious candidates as the physical manifestation of the consciousness aspect. Another problem is that since the subjective apprehension aspect is not the object, but sounds in this theory like it is appearing to consciousness, one could incorrectly conclude that the perceptual consciousness is mistaken with respect to its appearing object, just as a conceptual mind is. Perhaps the trickiest problem, as described by Klein, is this: "If the subjective apprehension aspect is a consciousness, why would cognition of a table require the presence of [another consciousness], an eye consciousness?"

From a modern standpoint, many of these difficulties seem to stem from the ancient scholars not having had access to information about the actual mechanisms of perception and assuming that consciousnesses are unitary, point-like phenomena. Now that the complex interrelations between sense objects and brain processes are beginning to unfold, it becomes possible to address these questions in new ways.

The modern perspective may be able to resolve some of these problems and provide a clarifying view. One can draw a clear analogy between the maps, or images, found in the brain, and the subjective aspects posited to reflect an object as described by Sautrantika, and from this perspective several questions come to have clear answers. If one chooses to draw this analogy, then the modern biology of the visual system can be viewed in direct parallel with the assertion made by the ancients that consciousness, or at least an underlying physical substrate, is indeed generated in the aspect of its object. The aspect of an appearing object can indeed be thought of as a reflection of the object which exists in the material of consciousness, as a physical image which exists within the brain. These images are *in fact* "specifically located and findable," and one can examine their properties directly. However, positing that the subjective aspect of visual consciousness takes place within the pupil will simply no longer suffice.

If one wishes to maintain the clear division between subjective and objective apprehension aspects, which is the Gelugpa position, then one can argue that the objective aspect, which is not of the nature of consciousness but is similar to the object, is the image formed in the eye, whereas the subjective aspect, which *is* of the nature of consciousness, is the manifestation of this image found in the maps of the visual processing hierarchy. Although this would be a valid parallel to draw, it seems somewhat arbitrary. As will be discussed in the forthcoming presentation of conceptual consciousness, it is simpler to imagine a continuum existing between the objective and subjective sides of perception which spans the perceptual processing system, and this view remains otherwise consonant with the Sautrantika presentation of awareness.

An understanding of aspected awareness which parallels the findings from neuroscience appears to be largely compatible with the ideas of Sautrantika and to give clear solutions to many of the historical problems of this heavily debated issue. Since the objective and subjective apprehension aspects can both be physically located, they can both be very clearly seen to be specifically characterized impermanent phenomena in the Buddhist sense. This view also allows a strong further clarification of the difference between direct perception and conceptualization in terms of the aspect of awareness, since a mind imagining a mental image (a meaning generality) obviously does not have a physical image of this object on its retina, and hence no objective apprehension aspect.

Finally, if consciousness is understood to exist along a physical hierarchical processing system rather than as a unitary point in space, then it is no longer problematic, as it has been held to be in debates, to believe that one consciousness contains both a subjective apprehension aspect and an eye consciousness. They are different parts of the same process of awareness.

IS THE MEDIUM OF THE ASPECT STATIC AND PASSIVE, AS IN A MIRROR REFLECTION?

The metaphors used by Gelugpa scholars to describe the apprehension aspects of consciousness suggest that the aspect itself is only "clear," and plays a completely passive role, whereas the interpretation coming from neuroscience suggests a much more active function. The images in the brain which are thought to dance across neural maps from moment to moment as perception takes place should not be thought of as passive reflections in the looking glass of the mind. Although it is indeed true that the brain of a person perceiving blue does not become blue, as the Gelugpas point out, it nonetheless does change considerably. The image is maintained through the electrical activity of the many nerve cells of the map, not through simple physical reflection. This is a decidedly active function, with the system expending considerable energy and relying on precise internal machinery in order to bring it about. Furthermore, the fact that these images, or aspects, are actively generated in the brain through precise neural mechanisms means that they reflect not only the properties of the object but also the properties of the reflecting medium. They are the result of an active combination of the object and the processing system of the brain and mind.

HOW MANY ASPECTS APPEAR TO CONSCIOUSNESS AT ONCE?

As described above, within the Gelugpa presentation of Sautrantika there are three competing factions regarding the issue of whether an object casts a single, unified aspect to perception or many different aspects, and how consciousness comes to reflect this—a question that neuroscience can perhaps give new insights into. The Non-Pluralists, supported by the founder of the Gelugpa order, Tsong-kha-pa, maintain that an object casts many aspects at once, but that consciousness takes on just one combined aspect. In his *Presentation of Tenets*, Jang-gya Rol-bay Dor-jay presents what is used as the standard example:

> Although many aspects of blue, yellow, and so forth of a mottled object are cast to the sense consciousness apprehending a mottle, the eye consciousness is generated into having not that number [of aspects] but just the aspect of a mottle.[75]

The Half-Eggists, in contrast, maintain that an object casts only one, single, combined aspect, and that its perceiving consciousness likewise takes on just this one. The Proponents of an Equal Number of Subjects and Objects maintain that an object casts many aspects and a separate consciousness takes on each one individually. Within this group there are those who, like Shantarakshita in his *Ornament to the Middle Way*, assert that, "Consciousnesses arise serially with respect to the white and so forth [of a mottle. Because they arise very quickly fools think they are simultaneous.]" There is another group, described by Jang-gya Rol-bay Dor-jay, who posit that "many aspects are cast [toward a consciousness], and the consciousness is simultaneously generated into having that number of aspects." As Anne Klein, who has translated these texts and studied them extensively, states clearly, "Any of these positions can be supported, depending on one's choice of quotations and interpretations."[76]

If one accepts the notion of a neural correlate for aspected perception, then the answer to this riddle coming from brain science becomes clear. The notion from contemporary neuroscience is that the brain contains many maps (or images, or aspects) of a perceived object all at once, and that the different maps represent different types of information about the object. These different "aspects" would not correspond to the white and blue of a mottle, but rather to the color, shape, and motion of a mottled object, and certainly many other features as well. This interpretation strongly suggests that our consciousness is generated in the many different aspects of an object all at once, as the Proponents of an Equal Number of Subjects and Objects would suggest. However, an unsolved riddle of the brain that is now a hotly debated topic is how these different feature representations can somehow be "bound" together to yield a coherent whole percept in some sense.

What is a particular, a unit of perception?

As was alluded to previously, there has been an ongoing debate within Buddhism, even among Tibetan schools, regarding whether the object of direct perception is a composite whole or a partless particle.[77] The Tibetan approach has been to try to resolve this issue from the works of the ancient masters, but we now have another source of authority upon which to draw. The issue will be presented in its typical Tibetan form, and then it will be considered from the perspective of modern scientific understanding.

A strong critic of the Gelugpa interpretation was the fifteenth century Tibetan scholar Dak-tsang, who asserted that ultimate truths are indivisible, as in Vasubandhu's passage:

> A conventional truth is any phenomenon which, when broken or
> mentally subdivided is no longer understood as that object, like
> a pot or like water.[78]

Dak-tsang suggested that composite impermanent objects are not specifically characterized, only their component parts are. In this view, a table, for example, exists only as an imputed notion of what many aggregated particles correspond to. While the particles themselves perform ultimate functions, such as acting as conditions for our perceptions and aggregating together, the table itself is only conventionally imagined to perform functions. The mind observing a table is thus not an ultimate mind nor a direct perceiver because it has imputed the notion of "table" onto a mere collection of particles.[79]

Within the Gelugpa presentation of Sautrantikas Following Reason a different series of textual interpretations is used to support the opposite view: that perceptions cognize whole, aggregated objects. Support for this is drawn from Dignaga's interpretation of the *Abhidharmakosha* which suggests that direct perception is caused by "many objects [in aggregation]." Dignaga also supports the view that an object of direct perception is a specifically characterized imperma- nent phenomenon. The Gelugpas interpret his presentation to sug- gest the converse as well, that whatever is an impermanent phenom- enon must necessarily also be an object of direct perception.

The Gelugpas place wholes and parts on an equal ontological foot- ing by suggesting that an aggregate is no more imputed by thought than are its component parts and that the collected object itself casts an aspect to consciousness.[80] As Klein explains the Gelugpa position:

> Direct perception does not see wholes and parts as separate: they only appear that way to thought. It is one of the errors of conceptuality that in reflecting, for example, on a pitcher...it will appear to thought that the pitcher...is different from all of its parts.[81]

As will be seen shortly, the mechanisms of perception found within the brain seem to support a similar view and a similar status for parts and wholes within perception.

DOES ONE PARTLESS PARTICLE OF PERCEPTION EQUAL ONE PHOTON?

In searching among the findings of modern science for a correlate of a partless particle of perception one is drawn immediately to the pho- ton, the single unit of visual energy, and this correlate has been duly noted informally.[82] In many ways the two concepts do sound very simi- lar indeed. The photon is said to have no spatial dimensions and to exist essentially timelessly or, for a given observer, for only a very brief instant. However, the first problem with this notion is that there is no obvious parallel unit of objective matter which can be found for any of the other senses; there is no known quantum unit of sound, tactile pressure, odor, or taste, not to mention mental objects.[83] It is possible to argue that these "missing" partless particles have just not yet been discovered, but the question remains as to whether the ap- proach itself is particularly useful.

In the Buddhist framework, perceptual objects and existent phe- nomena are held to be equivalent notions, so looking to matter to understand perception is a straightforward approach. Within the context of Western science the unity between the two is less clear, which suggests that a more effective way of understanding perceptual units within this paradigm may be to study the perceptual apparatus, rather than to study physical matter itself. In trying to understand perception, most scientific study has addressed the perceiver, rather than the perceived, so this is where the most can be learned from science.

IS THERE A PARTLESS PARTICLE OF PERCEPTION AT ALL?

Taking visual perception once again as an example, let us investigate whether neuroscience constrains the viable possibilities of what a partless particle of perception might consist of. As has already been mentioned, our biological eyes have distinct limits in their capabilities that arise as a result of the way that they are built, and hence there are clear constraints on what kinds of objects our eyes are able to register, both in terms of time and in terms of size. Although the visual receptor cells in our eyes (called rods and cones) can indeed respond to single photons under ideal circumstances,[84] the visual information coming from groups of these receivers is immediately combined, summed, and passed on to second order cells which respond to the collected response from a small but averaged area of the visual world. This means that even by the very first processing step in our eyes, any information about partless light particles has been irretrievably mixed and lost in a crowd, and can never reach the brain in its pure form.

There is a similar situation with short spaces of time. The receiving cells sum up the numbers of photons which enter them over a short period of time, and the second order cells sum this information over time once again. It is as if these cells are constantly signaling the number of photons that have arrived recently, over a time which is very long compared to the time that a single photon is actually present (which would only be for trillionths of a second). Once again, the brain receives an averaged signal of how many photons have entered the eye recently from a given area, rather than exactly when one arrives. Visual perceptual information is averaged over space and time, so that the information about single photons simply does not leave the eye or get to the brain.

This means that the only way to posit that the unit of perception is a photon, a partless particle of light energy, is to suggest that all of direct perception takes place in the first layer of the retina and that the remainder of the brain is completely unimportant for this process. This would force one to assert that only the eye itself experiences the world directly and that the entirety of visual consciousness takes place within the simplest level of the system, while the brain remains uninvolved and functions only conceptually. That is biologically unsatisfying since the entire perceptual apparatus is found in the brain, not in the eye. It also leads to a seemingly unresolvable logistical problem, that since there would be no way for the eye to communicate this information to the brain, there would be an uncrossable void between perceptual understanding and conceptual understanding, precisely the void that the Gelugpa presentation is at pains to prevent.

In the other sense modalities there is no clear candidate for a physical unit of sensation at all, but the fact of sensory integration of information remains. In short, science seems to agree with the Gelugpa presentation of Sautrantika; the notion that we perceive individual, indivisible units of experience which correspond to physical units of matter does not seem either biologically or philosophically viable. Whether there is some sort of unit of unified perceptual experience that arises later in the brain from the way in which the whole physical system works is an unresolved question.

RECOGNIZING AGGREGATED OBJECTS

If we leave the notion of the photon as partless particle behind, then we find that there is no clear dividing line which can be drawn within the nervous system between parts of objects and whole objects. There seems to be no clear line where an existent object stops and a mental imputation starts. Although it seems that in the physical world there are clearly objects and there are parts, the fact is that all we encounter are patterns of light—all the rest is up to our perceptual system. The world of sensation is divided up into parts in the retina and then put back together again arbitrarily to form the percepts we experience in the brain. Although the parts of objects that we perceive *seem* to aggregate into unique wholes and to separate from one another by their very nature—although it seems as if there is no other way that it could be—this merely reflects the success of the perceptual system in grouping our experiences into usable and recognizable objects. This is easier to realize if one tries to imagine building a machine (like a brain) which can recognize external objects from the patterns of light which fall on it. The process of recognizing objects, first finding the separate parts of an image and then putting them together into wholes and then "recognizing" them, is a very difficult task indeed (which we have not yet succeeded in solving well for machines).

There is simply no inherently existing and general separation between the wholes and the parts within a visual scene that the nervous
system can access directly; the brain itself must create and define the
distinctions of parts, aggregates of parts, and aggregated wholes in
patterns, using methods of combination and separation. This analysis
is intended to suggest that when perception is viewed as a mechanistic process, any division between whole objects and their parts clearly
becomes an arbitrary division based on the mechanism of perception.

This suggests that parts and wholes share the same status in the
perceptual system, but are they to be designated as conventional or
ultimate in the Sautrantika sense? These two choices seem to correspond roughly to the presentations of two schools within the Gelugpa
tradition. If one chooses to consider the process of separating and designating objects from patterns of light as "nonconceptual," then one
has a system roughly compatible with Gelugpa Sautrantika. Here parts
and wholes are both directly perceived objects which have specific
characteristics and exist "from their own side." Both are considered
impermanent phenomena which can perform functions, and both are
to be contrasted with conceptual objects which are imputed by thought.

If one considers this process of recognition to be "imputing" the
distinctions between objects in a conceptual way, then one is left with
an understanding which seems similar to the more subtle teachings of
Prasangika Madhyamika.[85] Here both parts and wholes of perceptual
objects are considered to be imputed conceptual objects which are
subject to the errors of the process. The choice between these two possibilities is one of subtlety of understanding and pragmatic utility. Both
views, however, support the general Gelugpa notion that we perceive
whole aggregated objects, not separate "partless particles."

WHAT CAN NEUROSCIENCE LEARN FROM THE BUDDHIST PRESENTATION OF PERCEPTION?

The question of what the Western neuroscientist can learn from the
Tibetan presentation of the mind is obviously very broad, but a few
very general points will be made here to round out this comparison.
These are principally intended as "teasers" to scientific readers who
might want to look into this issue further. The Buddhist understanding of perception found within Abhidharma presents a detailed cata-
log of the many types of perceptual awareness not found in the West.
The Buddhist understanding also seems to predate the progress of

neuroscience in granting an equal causal status in perception to the previous moment of consciousness, the observed object, and the sense power of perception, a notion of increasing importance to recent scientific research. Perhaps the most profound lesson which Buddhism has to offer in this area is the notion of the centrality of consciousness and the knower for understanding perception and awareness. It is from this perspective, from the perspective of the experience itself, that the Tibetan presentation of perception arises. The issue of addressing the neural substrate of experience itself is arguably the single biggest challenge facing the field of neuroscience today.

8 A Discussion with His Holiness the Dalai Lama: Aspects of Perception

Having concluded a more formal presentation of the issue of perception, I would now like to present some selected discussions of this topic with Tibetan lamas and scholars. In addition to the formal teachings that I discussed in the preceding chapter, the Tibetan tradition also includes detailed descriptions of the individual moments of awareness that make up the ongoing sequence of experience, as perceived by very advanced meditative practitioners, often after years in seclusion. Unfortunately, many of these descriptions can only be found in the esoteric and "secret" teachings of Tantrayana, which are accessible only to advanced practitioners and were therefore difficult or impossible for me to learn about. I hoped that His Holiness might present a first-hand account of some of these matters. In the second section of this interview we discussed the issue of how individual components of awareness might be separated from one another, and thereby distinguished.

CdC: I wanted to ask you about what your personal understanding of the mechanisms of mundane awareness is, especially regarding the issue of perception of objects and forming concepts. In reading the literature and speaking with the lamas that I have met with, "mundane" awareness of everyday objects by people not advanced in meditation is not discussed so much, it is mostly a discussion of the supramundane.

His Holiness: Oh, not necessarily. I think that many of the discussions in *Lo Rig* are on the mundane level. But when we talk about the spiritual levels and the paths, then we discuss the supramundane truth.

CdC: I was wondering, from your personal perspective, if you could give a view of how this process of perception and concept formation takes place. As I understand, it is possible for extremely advanced meditation practitioners to be very aware of the conscious process of perception moment by moment, to be aware of the individual states of consciousness and the individual energies or *lung*, how they are flowing and how this process in detail takes place.[86] I have had a very difficult time trying to find an answer to this. That is where the most detailed comparison to neuroscience might be made. I was wondering if you could suggest your understanding of this and also which parts of the Tibetan understanding of this process might be most important for the understanding in the West.

His Holiness: The subject of energy or inner air, called *lung*, is only explained in Tantrayana. It mentions each set of organs and their energy and how they work. There are some explanations of how they develop from the time of conception [of a newborn]. First week, second week, then first month, second month, there are some things like that. At the beginning the subtle energy develops, then the other energies develop. Again, when you are dying, there is a discussion of the process of the dissolution of the different energies. But daily, [in mundane experience] when you see something, when you hear something, how it works in terms of the inner energies, there is no such explanation.

HOW THE ASPECT OF AN OBJECT IS CAST TO THE PERCEIVING MIND

One of the most "mechanistic" and detailed descriptions of the act of perception that is given in the Tibetan presentation concerns the "aspect" which an object casts to a directly perceiving mind. I discussed with His Holiness a particular part of this somewhat contentious presentation, which was examined in detail in the preceding chapter. In brief, the issue at hand was whether one object casts only one image to the perceiving mind at a time, or whether an object casts a number of aspects simultaneously. This issue is quite central to the understanding of the resulting moments of conscious experience of the object. In this section I present the view that there are many aspects taken by consciousness at one time, based on analogy with brain functions, and His Holiness takes the traditionally favored position that consciousness takes just one combined aspect.

CdC: There are several different views within Sautrantika regarding what kind of aspect an object casts. There are the so-called Non-Pluralists, Half-Eggists, and Proponents of an Equal Number of Subjects and Objects, who have different views regarding whether an object casts only one aspect or many aspects. [These are the names given to different schools of thought on this topic; they are described in the preceding chapter]. I have been trying to see which of these accords most closely with the findings of neuroscience.

His Holiness: What is your opinion? Were you able to make a correlation with your scientific understanding?

CdC: Well, I think that the correspondence is very interesting. As Your Holiness well knows, scientists have found that the brain contains structures that can be thought of as maps of percepts, or images, or perhaps as aspects of perceived objects. These are precise patterns of neural activity in particular brain regions that correspond to features of the object. They are arrayed spatially and they can be thought of as images or reflections of the object. This is a part of what I do in my own lab research in fact. One can find that for a single object, like the table, there are different representations, different aspects or images of the one table that are all there in the brain at the same time. This seems to me to support the view of the Proponents of an Equal Number of Subjects and Objects of the Sautrantika school, who assert that one object casts many aspects simultaneously.

His Holiness: Just the opposite. As I remember the five colored object, [which is a standard example used], the consciousness also has all five. For one object there is just one subject. If there are five objects, the consciousness is just one. You mentioned just the opposite. [His Holiness is supporting the position of the Non-Pluralists, a different sub-school favored by Tsong-kha-pa, the founder of the Gelugpa order, and many other historical Gelugpa authorities.]

CdC: One consciousness perhaps, as you were saying, but taking up the many aspects of the object at the same time, as the Proponents of an Equal Number of Subjects and Objects within the Sautrantika school posit. They suggest that if you see a mottle of colors, then the object is cast as a whole object, just one, but that each of the colors is a part, so that there can be multiple aspects cast by the same object. In the brain you find, for one object, like a table, there are physically distinct images reflected, physically separate representations, that one might think of as different aspects. For a visual percept, it seems that you find the lines, and the colors, and the corners in many different representations or images that the brain reflects all at the same time. So that is why it seems to me that there is a greater similarity there.

His Holiness: Perhaps. I think you are mentioning about nonconceptual, direct perception. Now for seeing, the impermanence of this table is seen, but the conceptual level cannot realize it. Seeing, color is color, impermanence is impermanence, not just one [undifferentiated] concrete thing [with one aspect]. So that is perfect. Just the same.

SEPARATING THE INDIVIDUAL FUNCTIONS OF THE PERCEIVING MIND

His Holiness: One problem for me is still not very clear. According to the Buddhist teachers, the different senses of consciousness, such as the eye consciousness or the ear consciousness, are quite independent. But, according to modern science, the eye organ is [only] something like a door, the retina reflects some kind of image—that is the responsibility of the eye organ, but the factor which is actually seeing that image is in the brain, not in the eye [which is not the same as the historical Buddhist teaching]. So here, you see, according to Buddhist teachers, the eye consciousness is due to the eye organ and also due to the brain. The cognitive power [of seeing an object] develops, but once that cognitive power is developed, it is something like independent of the brain, or consciousness, or mind. It is quite autonomous. Both for the eye and for the ear [and the other senses].

CdC: We would say a somewhat similar thing. Let me show you a figure that I have for illustration, taken from an article that I am writing (see Figure 1. above). This very simplified diagram is for the eye consciousness. You can see that this is the eye at the bottom and this is where the brain starts at the next level up. This is where the neural energy flows, first upwards from the eye and then from the simplest details of the object, like the lines and the colors, and then up to the more complex details till, at the very top, is the representation of the entirety of the table and its spatial relations and other complex things. For the ear there is another one of these sets of pathways of the flow of neural activity and of the representation of an object; that also starts at the ear, then progresses through simple details such as pitch (frequency), and then progresses upwards to the more complex things, such as the recognition of speech. The two pathways only come together at the highest, most complex levels. They are independent through the perceptual process until the very most complex and general levels.

[This is well documented in the anatomy of the brain. The pathways leading from the eyes, ears, and skin (for the sense of touch) do not reach common points of contact until they have moved well into the brain. At this point the information is highly "processed," or altered, or abstracted by the intervening steps. This suggests that the simplest details of sights, sounds, and touches do not interact directly, only through more general or abstract features.][87]

Eventually I can hear your words and see your face and know that they come from the same person. So, the streams are independent for much of the process carried out by the brain for early perceptual processing, and only at the end are they put together. This is born out in the brain by the fact that if I start with the eye and follow the channels of connections, follow the neuro-anatomical projections, and start with the ear and follow the connections also, I have to go a long way into the brain before they meet. They only meet, in the end, at quite abstract, high level parts of the perceptual apparatus of the brain.

His Holiness: Can we experiment? Can it be possible some way, seeing the table, color, shape, everything, but not to have any kind of discrimination that this is a table.

CdC: Yes, there are very good examples of that. In fact, if I can take a similar example that I have talked about in some of my work. In Sautrantika, there is an issue of the fusion or separation between words and concepts, between term generalities and meaning generalities. [These are the translations of technical terms which can be thought of somewhat like a separation between descriptive (word-like) and depictive (picture-like) components for visually based concepts.] In fact, as you suggested, with a surgical operation you can take the two apart in the brain. There are some patients that have had surgery that physically separates their understanding of an object from the word for the object.

[This type of surgery has sometimes been necessary for devastating and intractable epilepsy. In some cases cutting the link between the two halves of the brain has prevented epileptic seizures from spreading from one side to the other and has been the only hope for patients with frequent seizures. In many cases, amazingly, these patients recover from the surgery almost completely unimpaired by this drastic measure. I discussed this same issue further with Lati Rinpoche and have provided some of the text of that discussion below. These patients are the main source of the present understanding of the differences between the functions of the two sides of the brain, which have now become generally known.]

If you present such a patient in just the right circumstances with a pen to one side of the patient's body, then only one side of his brain will receive the information. He will be able to use the pen to write, showing that he understands it visually and by use as an object, but he will not know the name. If you show the same patient the pen to the other side, thereby making it available to the other side of the brain, then he will be able to say "this is a pen," but he will not know what to do with it. He will not understand it as an object, or know its use. This is an example where these two kinds of awareness are physically separated in the brain by an operation.

[This is actually not quite the experiment that I think His Holiness was referring to. He was suggesting the possibility of separating the directly perceiving part of consciousness from the conceptually understanding part. As far as I am aware, such a thing has never been documented.]

His Holiness: So it is like separating the conceptual from the nonconceptual? Not all of the nonconceptual, seeing and realizing is still there. But just the bare eye consciousness, just seeing all of the qualities of the table or the object, but it cannot be aware. Seeing, but not aware. But both are related to the brain? The eye organ cannot function independently itself.

CdC: Yes, you have to have the eye and the part of the brain for the eye in order for even this "bare" vision to take place.

His Holiness: So where is the image, on the retina or on the brain?

CdC: Both. The first image is in the eye, as on the diagram. Later, there are simple images in the back of the brain. These are very simple images, like just the colors and the points of light on an object. Then you come up to higher levels of representation and then there are images of lines and corners and patterns, and then you come up here and there are more complex images, like legs maybe, and then at the top is the most complex image, the table. And the same is also true for the ears.

His Holiness: That is also the way that perception finally comes to the conceptual level?

CdC: That's right. [Or at least that is a common belief among neuroscientists.] So it is possible, as you said, if you have an ear representation and an eye representation, to surgically cut the two apart. A person with that kind of separation might not be able to associate the sound of your voice with the sight or image of your face. They would not understand conceptually that the two go together. As you suggested, you might be able to physically separate them in the brain.

[This has never been done to a patient deliberately for any reason so far as I am aware, but there are many syndromes like this that have arisen following brain injuries, typically in stroke patients.[88] The catastrophic and curious examples that result from brain injury abound. They give human form to the argument that the brain is the physical seat of awareness. There are patients who can only experience one side of the world because they have had one side of their brain damaged; patients who can recognize spatial relations among objects, like directions on a map, but cannot recognize the objects themselves, and so do not know their own house when they reach home; patients who can recognize objects and people perfectly, but not remember ever having seen them even a moment later; the list goes on and on.]

9 A Discussion with Lati Rinpoche: Perception and the Illuminating Nature of Mind

Lati Rinpoche is one of the foremost scholars and debate masters in the Gelugpa tradition. He has received many high honors including being selected to debate against His Holiness the Dalai Lama, and being selected as the Abbot of Ganden Monastery. He has also taught Buddhism in Western countries on a number of occasions and some of his presentations have been published in English.[89] The two outstanding translators who were generous enough to offer their efforts for this project were Gareth Sparham, a monk of many years, graduate of the Buddhist Institute of Dialectics, and translator of a number of Tibetan texts, and Tsepak Rigzin, who has been selected to translate for Lati Rinpoche on trips to the West in the past, and is the author of The Tibetan-English Dictionary, *among other works.*

Lati Rinpoche and I had a series of in-depth discussions about the characteristics of phenomena of the mind, the relationship of mind to body, and the relationship of the Tibetan to the neuroscientific views in general. This particular discussion concerned the Tibetan presentation of direct perception, a cornerstone of the Tibetan presentation of mind in general.

CdC: I am very grateful for your offering of time to give teachings from the Tibetan wisdom concerning the issues of mind and consciousness and how they relate to modern science.

Rinpoche: Certainly anything that I know I will tell you, what I don't know I cannot tell you. [Rinpoche laughs.]

Lati Rinpoche (Photo: Donald Lopez)

DIRECT PERCEPTION: ITS CAUSES AND THE ROLE OF THE PREVIOUS MOMENT OF MIND

CdC: If Rinpoche is interested in hearing about some of the Western understanding of neuroscience, I would be very pleased to discuss this with him or to answer any questions that he might have. I hoped that we might talk about the mechanisms of direct perception of a directly perceiving consciousness. Perhaps an eye consciousness is the best example. As a starting point I will present very briefly something of the Western understanding.

[At this point I presented a description of the present understanding of visual perception found in neuroscience similar to that presented in chapter 7.]

I would now like to ask, what is the detailed chain of events, from the external object to direct perception, as understood from the Tibetan perspective?

Rinpoche: There are four conditions for direct perception to take place. The first is the objective support condition [the external object]. Second, the eye sense faculty is the uncommon empowering condition. The immediately preceding condition would be the mental consciousness. The fourth condition is called a causal condition, and would be a karmic potential or seed or memory which can ripen into the perception of, for example, a table.

[The presentation given in the accompanying text does not include this fourth condition, which is of a different sort from the other three. This karmic condition is treated differently by the different Buddhist philosophical schools and constitutes a topic in itself. The remaining three are direct translations of Tibetan technical terms.]

With the meeting of these conditions you have the coming about of the present experience of reality. If you take any of them away you won't get it, if you put them all there then you will. Indeed, you have to rely upon the sense faculty in order to have the arising of an eye consciousness.

The arising of different discursive, conceptual ideas, for example "this is a table," "this is a good table," "I don't like this table," and so forth, these come subsequent to the direct perception of the table by the eye. Those who have no cultural experience of tables will never be able to generate the idea "this is a table" just from seeing the object. They will have all sorts of unrelated inputs, but they won't be able to generate that idea unless they have been introduced to it first. It is the person who has already had the cultural introduction to a table, who has it in their general vocabulary, that will be able to say "that's a table."

You can work backwards to the tone of your sense experience by looking at the different sorts of discursive assertions which it generates, definite knowledges which one feels one has. When you can say "that was definitely a table," that means that the earlier state of awareness was a direct one. Its ability to generate certainties is a defining characteristic. [This is actually a simplification of a formal argument concerning which types of statements are "definite."] On the other hand, I wouldn't say that the eye consciousness sees all of the atoms or parts of that table. At any particular time it can only see parts, you cannot say that at any time you are seeing all of the parts of a table. This explains why you cannot have that ascertainment, "Ah, I saw such and such an atomic structure." An eye consciousness cannot give rise to such certainties. You have the ability to remember and be certain of seeing a rough object, but you cannot from such consciousnesses have the remembrance or certainty that you saw less rough objects such as the atomic structures of the thing.

CONSCIOUSNESS IS NOT THE BRAIN

Using the same kind of model for ideas and general ideational states, they cannot be thought to be produced by the brain any more than is the sight, the eye consciousness, produced by the eye. It is a condition, one of a set of conditions which is necessary for an ideational state to come into being, but the consciousness is not produced solely by it.

CdC: Could you elaborate?

Rinpoche: Put it this way, the ideational state or the thought comes about from the brain. Based on the brain you are going to get certain types of good or bad ideas or thoughts, but it isn't the actual brain that is the idea. The thought is not the brain. Based on the brain you get thoughts, but the brain itself is not the thoughts.

CdC: I see, just as you were saying that the eye allows seeing, but the eye is not itself the sight.

Rinpoche: Exactly. The eye functions as a condition for eye consciousness, but you don't say that the eye is the seeing, that the eye is the sight. In the same way you don't say that the brain is the thought, is "the think." One should make a distinction here. I would say that the eye functions as a unique condition, the uncommon empowering condition for sight. It must be there for sight to come about, and it is common only to sight. The brain does not function for ideas in the same way. It is a help to them, but it is not the same in detail. They are not functioning in the same way.

The parallel condition to eye-sense when you are talking about a thinker, or thoughts, or ideas, is actually a thinker, or thoughts, or ideas. The brain is definitely a functioning thing to take into consideration, but it isn't a parallel to the eye. The eye is paralleled by the [technical concepts translated as the] "mind-sense," "non-sensory consciousness," or "mental faculty."

CdC: So, is it correct that the empowering condition for one moment of mental consciousness is the preceding moment of consciousness, so the mind is driven to the next moment by the previous moment in the way that it can be driven to the next moment by the sight consciousness?

Rinpoche: I don't know if you are confused about its being a power. It is a condition certainly. I am not sure if I would say by the power of the previous consciousness. You have to have many different conditions. It is not just the previous moment of consciousness existing that gives rise to the mental direct perception. You need conditions, always a set of them, and then it will give rise to perception.

THE ILLUMINATING ELEMENT OF MIND

Rinpoche: The comment that I wanted to make about the brain is that it is fundamentally like these hands [holding them out for examination]. These things are body, they are meat. This sort of thing does not see, it is not consciousness. Except that the brain is inside and the hands on the surface, they are the same. This sort of material in the universe is not a cognitive material. You need an *illuminating element*. The material of the brain, the meat of the brain as you might say, is not an illuminating element. It has the potential to generate those sorts of illuminating elements, probably (it seems to have), but looking at the makeup of anything in the brain, it is going to be material, not of the illuminating nature. Presumably there will be different pathways, different potentials for seeing one sort of thing and not another sort of thing, there will be all sorts of potentials in it for generating these illuminating elements, but there is no illuminating element in the brain itself.

CdC: We are getting close to issues that I feel are very important for scientists here, two in particular. In Western neuroscience I would agree that the brain alone does not have cognition, does not cognize, but it has the capacity to function, and its function is this illuminating element that allows consciousness. So, my question is exactly how this illuminating potential works, either with regard to the eye bringing in light, or to the eye empowering the mental awareness.

Rinpoche: Would you please explain to me exactly what you had in mind by your second example?

CdC: In the first example, about the eye, you have given the four conditions that have to be met for perception to take place, but these are quite broad. I wondered if you could give a more detailed description of the conditions that must be met, and also what is the chain of events that takes place during direct perception. As I understand, the Tibetan teachings suggest that it is possible through meditation to become very aware of the individual moments of consciousness, also described as the individual *lung's* or energies, and then to observe at each step in the process exactly what the detailed conditions are that give rise to the next step in perception, and then the next step, and so on. The first step seems to be just for the light to work through the uncommon empowering condition of the eye.

THE CAUSAL SEQUENCE OF THE MIND STREAM

Rinpoche: I should say what I mean when I talk about *sal rig*, the illuminating aspect or element. I see that element as having a continuum which goes back from itself to the moment of illumination which is the inner cognitive state. It is not related in that sense to the outer light. I see them as unconnected.

From the perspective of Buddhist logic, if you connect the inner [mental] and the outer [physical] illuminations, then the knowing would be somehow related to the table [taking this as an example of a visual object]. You earlier described the light functioning relative to an object and then hitting the different parts of the eye sense and functioning in that way. But, if you imagine that perception is connected to the physical light, if *that* illumination somehow connects in a causal sequence to the mental illumination which is the illumination that we experience as knowing, then the knowing would be related to the table. In formal logical terms, it would go back [to the table], and you would have knowing related to the table because you are relating the two illuminations. That illumination of knowing would then go back and have a relationship to the table. In a formal and literal sense the knowing would be *on* the table. You would have knowing on the table in the way that you can have knowing on a knower, because you have a causal stream or continuum leading back to the light which is on the table, whereas the light which is the light which is knowing is of a different breed.

CdC: Could Rinpoche say a little more about the logic of this causal continuum?

Rinpoche: In fact, it has no beginning, it goes back and back and back and back and back and back and back....It is something of which beginning is not an issue. Sometimes it is in a latent form, not actually manifesting. This is knowing, *sal rig,* the illuminating element. *Rig* is knowing. *Sal,* well, you open your eyes and there is the *sal,* otherwise you wouldn't be seeing anything. There is also "seeing things" or *sal rig* together—being with the thought "it's a table." That is an inner thing and that inner thing, that "being illuminated," has a continuum going back forever. It is not always manifesting, it can be in a latent state. Its continuum can be latent. When you are deep asleep it might be latent.

CdC: So do the four conditions for perception bring about the change from the latent state to the active state, or do they change the continuum when it is already in an active state to a state of apprehending an object? Again, how exactly are the individual moments of consciousness leading this to take place?

Rinpoche: When the four conditions are not met the continuum is indeed in a latent state. When the four conditions are met then it manifests from the latent state. For example, if you don't actually have as an objective condition a table, you are not going to have the awareness of a table. You have to have the conditions in order for it to actualize out of its latent state. That is what I mean by condition, you see. Based on the conditions we get a perception of a table coming from its latent state.

Initially, that condition causes the state of awareness which is defined as an eye consciousness to come about. The eye consciousness as a condition then causes the pearl of awareness which is the conceptual thought "that's a table" to come about, and so on.

I understood the content of the second thing that you were talking about to be the electricity, or the neurological activity in the brain functioning, and that giving rise to illuminating states.

THE FLOW OF BODILY ENERGY AND THE ILLUMINATING ESSENCE

CdC: What I imagine to happen is that for the state of direct perception, the function of the corresponding pattern of activity in the brain, would be to be this illuminating essence. There are many theories about how the neural pattern of visual direct perception can lead through specific connections and specific flows of the neural "energies" to the arising of a broader pattern that would be a cognitive inference like "this is a table." Again, it wouldn't be the hardware or even the energy that would be the inference, but the process taking place.

Rinpoche: It is interesting what you say, because you find a similar statement in Tantra. It is said that as the *lung* [energy] moves in the left and right main neural channel it does generate conceptualization. Even though that is true, I would still want to say that the major force or condition for the arising of the thought "this is a table" would be the earlier moment of awareness. I would like to give that a capacity for itself. You are right in talking of the energy or the *lung* as causing conceptualization as you are saying, there is indeed a reference to a causal relationship. Nevertheless, I still prefer to give causal weight to the perception which gives rise to another "drop" of knowing, to illumination.

CdC: Perhaps that is similar to the neuroscience view that the perceptual activity and the energy movements and so on involved in visual perception later somehow give rise to a broader activity pattern that corresponds to the cognitive inference "this is a table." Similar, I think, to what Rinpoche is saying, the particular cognitive inference that will take place, and whether it takes place as "this is a table," will depend entirely on the experiences of the person, the state of the brain hardware, and the previous functioning at the moment that the perception arose. If there are pathways to allow the generation of a pattern corresponding to the cognition of the table as a table, then that cognition is possible, but if there are not—if those memories or pathways are not present (we would say)—then it is not possible to have that particular cognition of the object. This sounds similar.

Rinpoche: It is certainly found in Buddhist scripture that the movement of energy through different pathways has a relationship to the arising of the different states of thought, to different ideas and different conceptualizations. It is also said that the movement of energy through a certain pathway, only one I might say, does in fact quiet thought. The movement of energy through this pathway quiets all ideation. It is certainly said in Buddhist writing, what you are saying. The cause of perception or ideation is not ever one thing. I was just pointing out the main areas of conditionality which have to be met in order for it to come about. It is never just one, there must always be quite a lot.

The earlier moment in a continuum of awareness has always got to be the main causal factor for the arising of the next moment of awareness. I use the word "main" in terms of a Buddhist presentation of the kinds of material causes, as distinct from conditions, which must be met for it to come about. In this sense, the main cause must be the material cause of the continuum. I say main condition with the thought that you can have all sorts of specific conditions present or not there, but without the material cause for awareness it will never happen. With the material cause for it, then specific conditions can give rise to a change in awareness. Without the material condition you just don't have the main necessary cause of it.

If you look at emotion from its negative aspect, which is to say emotions which don't function to the benefit of the person because of the behavior that they cause, such emotions as those won't come about, regardless of the conditions that the person meets with, if the material causes of those emotions have somehow been stopped. [This is, of course, one of the major themes of the Buddhist meditative practice.]

CdC: The two understandings of the need for material causes seem to sound quite similar.

Rinpoche: Yes, they *would*. It would seem to me that this is where thought leads one to. Also, our sacred scriptures say as much. So our sacred books, spoken by an enlightened being, meet with your ideas?

CdC: [Laughs and bows to end this discussion.]

SECTION V
IDEAS OF REALITY

There is no end to the formation of conceptualizations. It is infinite.
Let us examine ourselves. In a day alone, how many conceptualizations
do we form? In any one moment, how many conceptual thoughts do
we produce? There is no end to it.

—Lati Rinpoche

10 Concepts in Tibetan Abhidharma and Western Neuroscience

In this section our focus will shift from the simple or "bare" perceptions of reality that we experience to the complex thoughts and images that we create. The section as a whole addresses the question of how we can form concepts, thoughts, ideas, and reactions, and what effects they have upon us. From the scientific and philosophical standpoint this is a perennially captivating question: What is the real nature of thought itself, and how might thoughts be created within the physical machine of our brains? How can our thoughts grasp the true realities of the world when thought itself is merely subjective, does not seem to directly contact the physical world, and is ultimately created by the human mind? From the Gelugpa's viewpoint this issue is central because the Gelugpas teach that through correctly guided conceptual training, coupled with meditative observation, the student can ultimately come to grasp the truth of experience, and thereby transcend ignorance and limited views. This is a particularly interesting point in the Gelugpa presentation of mind, as it holds that the mind can use conceptuality to come to grasp truths which are considered to be completely inexpressible in words and inaccessible to thought.

THE USE OF CONCEPTS IN TIBETAN BUDDHISM

The role of conceptuality is very different in the Gelugpa tradition from many other presentations, even within the Buddhist worldview. In some Buddhist meditative traditions thought is considered as a primary source of confusion, not of understanding. Conceptuality is

very nearly reviled as the deluded cause of suffering itself, and meditation is seen as anything but a conceptual enterprise. In the Gelugpa
tradition of scholasticism and debate the emphasis is very different.
Here conceptuality is taken to be an important basis of understanding, even though conceptuality itself does not ultimately grasp what
is realized experientially.

How do the Gelugpas reconcile this seeming contradiction? Using
an elaborate presentation of how conceptuality leads a mind to realize a nonconceptual object, the Gelugpas teach that a correct conceptual understanding is a necessary prerequisite for many kinds of understanding and for many types of meditation. The Gelugpa presentation of the functioning of thought contains a detailed presentation
of types of minds, types of objects, the modes of action of conceptual
thought, and finally a prescription. The Sautrantika school's presentation of concepts is central to the Gelugpa curriculum largely because
it presents the position that a concept is a "non-affirming negative," a
particular form of object of the mind which can clear away misunderstanding, leaving no trace, as we will see.

The question of how concepts and thoughts arise is very complex
and has been the subject of countless theories. Here, I will present two
versions of answers to this question in a simple form, again with the
hope that they might inform one another. The first version will be the
presentation of Sautrantika, with all of its detailed definitions and categories, and the second version will be based on ideas from brain science, which are far less definite regarding this matter but contain a
wealth of detail. In the end I will present ideas on how some of the
difficult problems of understanding the nature of thought might be
addressed using pieces from each of these two approaches. Following
this chapter will be interviews and discussions of this matter with
experts of Tibetan Abhidharma. First, I will present in summary the
formal Tibetan view of the nature of thought.

WHAT CONCEPTUAL THOUGHTS ARE—THE
SAUTRANTIKA PERSPECTIVE

Definition of a conceptual consciousness

Within the Sautrantika system thought is defined in terms of a particular type of mind; a mind of conceptuality. As in the case of perception, a conceptual mind should be understood as a particular mental
moment of conceptuality, not as the long term character of a particular

person's mind. Also as in the case of perception, a conceptual consciousness is defined principally in terms of the types of object which
it takes. The formal definition of a conceptual consciousness within
the Gelugpa presentation of Sautrantika is

> a consciousness that takes a meaning generality [that is, a mental
> semblance, for example a visual mental image,] as its apprehended
> object.[90]

In other words, a conceptual consciousness is a mind apprehending an object which the mind itself has created, based on past experience and perception. A concept or thought is taken to be a mental
semblance of a specific, real, physical object, an object that the mind is
"looking at." The object of a conceptual mind, then, is "merely imputed by thought"[91] according to Sautrantika, in that it has no independent existence and is created or shaped by the process of
conceptuality from prior experience. This definition of conceptuality
is presented in direct opposition to the definition of a perceptual awareness, which cognizes its object directly from experience and does not
mentally impute it. Since a conceptual mind cognizes its object by internally constructing a mental semblance of an object, the understanding which it has is necessarily only a general rendering. It does not
contain the object's full richness of detail nor does it give a completely
correct understanding of the object's true nature. Conceptual thought
just forms a semblance of an object which is the best that the mind can
do, and this is what appears to the one who is thinking.

Although what appears to the thinker is a creation of the mind, is
imputed by thought, it is still related to the object that is being "thought
of," and this relationship is the basis of the understanding of how
conceptuality can be used for understanding reality. Conceptuality
does not just randomly create notions. It functions by mixing together
a "meaning generality," which is a mental semblance, with a perception of a real object. This mixture is what appears to mind. The meaning generality is the general rendering of an object created by the mind,
and is what is added by thought, in a sense, to a bare object of experience. The meaning generality is formally defined (taking the standard
example of a pot) as

> that superimposed factor which appears like a pot to the thought
> consciousness apprehending pot although it is not a pot.[92]

So conceptual minds always *add* this superimposed factor, which is
like the object but is not the object itself, and they cannot distinguish

between this object which appears to them and the real object itself. In this sense conceptual thought is always said to be mistaken. Within Sautrantika a mentally imputed understanding can *never* fully reflect fact, it is always something general which acts as a superimposed factor. This is in accord with common experience. When we think about a person, for example, we often (and perhaps always) select which aspects of the person to think about, and we may add quite obvious forms of "touching up" to our mental notions of them. We certainly do not capture them in our minds in all of their detail—our mental semblance is not so perfect that we would be fooled into believing that they are actually present. This is the meaning of the idea that conceptuality is by its nature "mistaken."

We can also be plain wrong about something: for example, if we imagined someone to be our uncle who is really just a friend of the family. In formal terms, in addition to being mistaken or limited, conceptuality can also be counterfactual with regard to its object of engagement. In these cases the mental semblance which conceptuality forms is not only general but also factually non-concordant with the engaged object of mind, and thereby incorrect regarding the world.

Jam-bel-sam-pel illustrates these two types of mistake or misunderstanding in his *Presentation of Awareness and Knowledge* by making the following three divisions of consciousnesses:

1. Conceptual consciousnesses that take a meaning generality as their apprehended object.
2. [Direct perceivers that are] nonconceptual non-mistaken consciousnesses that take a specifically characterized phenomenon as their apprehended object.
3. Nonconceptual mistaken consciousnesses that take a clearly appearing nonexistent as their apprehended object.[93]

A logical fourth category which I will add would be:

4. Conceptual consciousnesses that take a meaning generality as their apprehended object that is not factually concordant with respect to the object of engagement.

So there are two types of consciousness, direct and conceptual, and two ways in which a consciousness can be incorrect: it can be mistaken with regard to its appearing object (because what appears to the mind is only a general semblance of the real object), or it can be factually wrong regarding the object that it is engaging. These distinctions and terms will be further clarified below.

WHAT CONCEPTUAL THOUGHTS ARE FOR

The purpose of conceptual thought is to understand what is not at first perceived

Before pursuing the details of concepts, we need to consider what concepts are thought to *do* in Sautrantika thought, because this will give content to many of the definitions. This section therefore considers the purpose of conceptuality, rather than its functioning.

Within Sautrantika conceptual thought is posited to have an indispensable supportive role to the direct understanding of particular aspects of reality which cannot normally be perceived directly by ordinary observers. Aspects of objects which are described using a term translated as "hidden phenomena," meaning phenomena which may not be readily observable, must initially be grasped through conceptual understanding. There are many types of "hidden phenomena," which can be basic properties of normal objects, that are not normally accessible to direct perception. For example, "hidden phenomena" include phenomena like the underlying microscopic or atomic structure of an object, the causal relations of an object, or its subtle impermanence. These are basic properties of objects that are not in general ascertained through simple perception, yet they can be understood when explained conceptually. Phenomena which can only be experienced once they have been grasped conceptually in this way form a crucial part of a full understanding of experience within the Sautrantika view.

In the Buddhist view, it is taught that by experientially appreciating that all matter and even the self have the subtle nature of being impermanent and constantly changing, one will cease to cling to them, a fundamental aspect of the Buddhist presentation of enlightenment. For this reason, the explanation of how the mind is able to grasp these subtle features is of central importance to the Buddhist explanation of mind in general, and to the Sautrantika explanation of the role of conceptuality in particular. Experiencing reality with a full appreciation of its subtlest features, which are not readily observed directly, is a primary goal of the Sautrantika system. In order to explain how the understanding of these subtle features of objects can take place, Sautrantika provides a broad description of how conceptuality functions in general.

Within Buddhist systems overall, it is generally accepted that concepts themselves cannot *fully* grasp phenomena directly, for conceptuality is always limited and lacks the richness of direct experience. In this sense, simple and bare experiences of reality are understood to be conceptually unreachable, and verbally inexpressible. Our memory or description of the taste of a ripe raspberry are a far cry from the taste of the fresh fruit itself.

Within the Gelugpa tradition of Buddhism, conceptuality is nonetheless considered to be essential because it is what paves the way to the direct perception of the subtle nature of experience by preparing the mind. The Gelugpa order asserts that meditation in the absence of a correct conceptual understanding of the object being meditated upon is useless and even counterproductive because it will not lead to a full direct experience of the object which ascertains all of its subtle features. This is the reason that the Gelugpa order supports its strong emphasis on debate and scholarship as bases for meditation. The Gelugpa masters clearly set out that although conceptuality can never attain nor express the full truth, it is nonetheless absolutely necessary to have a firm conceptual understanding which can lead one's mind towards direct experience or realization. Among other Buddhist perspectives, this unusual view of the central role of thoughts and words for realizing the full and inexpressible nature of reality is underscored by a remarkable quotation from the Dalai Lama, who remarked of the inexpressible truth of experience:

> After all, it is not *that* inexpressible.[94]

HOW CONCEPTUAL THOUGHT GRASPS REALITY

It is clearly central to Sautrantika thinking that mental concepts have the power, and the purpose, of leading one to experiential knowledge of the physically manifest world. The details of this functional view of conceptuality are intricate, and they will be discussed below in detail because they are basic to the Sautrantika view of mind in general, and to the Sautrantika understanding of the path to wisdom. In short and very simplified form, what *appears* to a conceptual consciousness is explained to be only a "meaning generality," a fusion of a general mental semblance and an actual object, but what is *realized* by a conceptual consciousness is the actual object itself. Putting it in different words, correct conceptual thought is said to "get at" its actual object, not only the mental semblance which appears to it. This makes clear that conceptual thought actually has two closely related objects, one of which "appears" to the mind and the other of which is "realized." The point of this terminological distinction for Sautrantika is to clarify that through becoming more and more acquainted with a mental sem-blance of an object, the mental semblance becomes more and more like the object itself, so that in the end the mind can directly realize the subtle features of the object and experience the object in its fullness. When the object becomes sufficiently familiar to the mind it becomes possible to be aware of all of its subtle features without the mistaken mental semblance being present at all, to fully cognize and appreciate the object directly.[95]

This position regarding the distinction between what appears to conceptual thought and what it is realizing is described through ex-amples that illustrate the purpose of conceptuality. One example that is frequently given is that if one is aware of the light from a jewel (the light being a metaphor for the concept that appears to the mind), then one would be mistaken to take the light to be the jewel itself, but one could still correctly follow the light and find the real jewel.[96] Another example is that if one grabs one's leg while wearing robes, one does not actually touch the leg but just the cloth—one has only an indirect understanding of the leg underneath that has the "feel" or appear-ance of the cloth above. Nevertheless, although all that one can feel is the cloth, one can still correctly realize that there is a leg there beneath it.[97] These metaphors of conceptuality clearly highlight the difference between the perceptual and the conceptual capacities of mind, to which we will now turn.

TWO TYPES OF THOUGHT AND THEIR OBJECTS
"Conventional" and "ultimate" minds

Starting from this very general definition and purpose of conceptuality within Sautrantika, we will now consider the presentation of conceptuality in greater detail. It is clear at the outset that conceptuality is explained in Sautrantika in a counterpoint to direct perception, and that each one is ascribed a corresponding form of awareness which takes a particular type of object. A mind which takes a mental image or thought as its object is defined using a term translated as a "con-ventional mind." This designates that the abstracted objects of thought are largely matters of mental, linguistic, or societal convention, rather than objects of direct experience in all their fullness. Conversely, the term designating a mind involved in perception is translated as an "ultimate mind," indicating that during perception the mind has "ultimate," or direct, access to its perceived object, without any

interpretation based on past experience or "convention" being explicitly necessary. This severely loaded terminology reflects the overall
Sautrantika pedagogical aim of cultivating directly experienced understanding, rather than merely conceptualized views.

From this viewpoint then, the distinction between the two cardinal
types of awareness becomes a difference in the types of objects which
they take. A mind of direct perception is an ultimate mind in that it
has direct access to the "ultimate truths" which are the simple, specific, and richly detailed objects of our direct experience.[98] The mind
of conceptuality, in contrast, is a conventional mind, a mind who's
appearing object is a conventional (or general) rendering taken from
actual experience. This distinction begins an emphasis on the kind of
object that is taken by a mind, which will be considered in some detail. The description of the several types of objects of mind which I
present next is initially quite complex, but I hope that it will begin to
become more clear once the mode of action of conceptual thought is
presented, which follows.

The objects of conceptual and directly perceiving minds

Within the Sautrantika system, every awareness is described as having several types of objects intimately associated with it. This list of
rather difficult distinctions is made in part to further the Sautrantika
position that both conceptual minds and perceptual minds engage with
experienced reality in a definite sense, but that neither one necessarily
leads the mind to grasp the reality of its object fully. This maintains
the necessary logic of the Sautrantika view as follows: Direct perception must be able to directly access experienced truths by reflecting
them or true understanding of experience would be impossible, yet it
cannot fully ascertain these ultimate truths in all individuals, because
then there would be no need for a path to understanding. It is taken as
an axiom that we do not already have a full ascertainment of reality.
On the other hand, direct perception can *present* a full understanding
to the mind, so in this sense we *do* have a full experience of reality that
we can learn to access. Conceptual minds only observe mentally imputed objects, since this is the nature of their conventional understanding, yet they must still have some connection with ultimate truths or
else reasoned action would be impossible and conceptuality would
have no validity at all. The difference between direct perception and
conceptual awareness, then, is that for direct perception all of these
terms refer to the same object—to the real, impermanent object being

perceived, whereas conceptual awareness can be engaged with a real object, but only a meaning generality (mental semblance of that object) appears to the mind and is apprehended by the mind.

The description of the types of objects of the mind allows a delineation of conceptual from nonconceptual awarenesses. Unfortunately, several systems of translation of the relevant terms have been used, none of which convey the meaning of their Tibetan equivalents with ideal clarity. Even after considerable discussion I find these translations and their explanations somewhat problematic, but the following table summarizes the translations of these terms used here and elsewhere:

OBJECT NAME USED			WHAT IT CORRESPONDS TO	
Tibetan	Here	Elsewhere	Direct Perceiver	Conceptual Mind
'jug yul	Engagement	Operation	actual object	actual object
zhen yul	Determined	Referent	not used	actual object
snang yul	Appearing	Appearing	actual object	mental semblance
bzung yul	Apprehended	Apprehending	actual object	mental semblance

The four entities on this list should not be thought of as four separate objects which the same mind is taking at once; they each describe a facet of the single object which is engaged by a mind during direct perception or conceptualization.[99] For both types of minds the first two terms on the list correspond to what the mind is realizing—they correspond to the real object, while terms three and four correspond to what is appearing to the mind. Unfortunately, there are no concise definitions of these terms available, so they are defined through use and example, and their translation is difficult at best. Nonetheless, although they are difficult, they become useful in understanding and distinguishing the Sautrantika view of the different types of awareness.

OBJECTS OF A DIRECT PERCEIVER

In the case of a direct perceiver, the three relevant terms (*zhen yul* is not used in this case) refer to the bare, external object itself, but from slightly different perspectives.[100] The object of a perceptual awareness, a physical form for example, is formally said to "share a common mode of abiding in place, time, and nature" with many ordinary features, such as its color and so on, and also with its subtle or "hidden" features, which are not so easily ascertained (as described above), such as its impermanent nature (that it is non-static or always changing), that it is produced from causes and produces causes (and hence has an interdependent nature), and others. Since all of these features are formally considered to be of "one entity" with the object, the object formally must cast an aspect to the directly perceiving mind which inseparably contains all of these elements—they are all part of the same bundle.[101] However, the directly perceiving mind of an ordinary individual can only ascertain, or distinguish, the more general, or coarse, features of the object, not the subtler ones (again, as described above).

This distinction between the features that an object of experience contains and the features that are ascertained leads to a distinction among the terms listed above. The subtler features of an object are held to appear to the mind or be reflected by it, and hence to be included in the object of apprehension and the appearing object taken by that mind, but they are not normally ascertained or "engaged" by the same mind, and so they are not included in the object of engagement. The terms for appearing and apprehended objects are nearly synonymous, they refer to the same object, but the perspective of the two is slightly different. The appearing object refers to the aspect which is cast to the mind itself, whereas the apprehended object is the thing which the mind "grasps onto" in order to get at the main object.[102] Despite these formal distinctions, for a mind directly perceiving a form, each of these objects still corresponds to the form itself.

OBJECTS OF A CONCEPTUAL MIND

In the case of the conceptual mind this need not be so; the object that appears to the mind does not correspond in detail to an actual experiential object. In the case of a conceptual mind there are two types of terms used to designate a mind's object. These two types correspond to the object that actually "appears" to the mind, and the real object that the mind is "thinking about." The first two terms of the table still refer to a real object which the mind is considering, indicating that conceptual thought is believed to engage with an actual object, although indirectly. These first two terms are subtly distinguished by the perspective upon the object which they imply. The object of engagement is described as being what the mind is "entering into" or "getting at," while the determined object refers to what the conceptual mind is judging in a particular way. The term translated as "determined object" does not apply to a mind of direct perception because it corresponds to the type of conceptual, categorical determination between objects of the form "this is that," which is a part of conceptualization but not of bare perception. This term implies a kind of attachment to the object as being something in particular, or existing in a certain way—a type of believed certainty about the object or its nature.[103]

The principal distinction between conceptual minds and directly perceiving minds is made on the basis of the final two types of objects which refer to the object which is actually appearing to the consciousness and not necessarily what it is comprehending. Since what appears to a conceptual mind is something that it creates, it does not take a physically existing, specifically characterized, real thing as its object of appearance or its object of apprehension. Instead, for a conceptual mind these latter two terms refer to a "meaning generality," a mental semblance which is used as a medium to get at the object, as will be described. This is the chief distinction between conceptualization and direct experience of an object: perception apprehends its object directly, without the use of any intervening structure or notions which are "imputed by thought," while conceptuality apprehends its object through a mental semblance which serves as a medium. The appearing and apprehended objects are nearly synonymous for conceptuality (as well as for perception), with the distinction that the apprehended object is what the mind "grasps onto" as the medium, whereas what appears to the mind is the meaning generality or mental semblance.[104]

THE MISTAKES OF A MISTAKEN MIND AND THE TRUTH OF CONCEPTUALITY

If conceptuality bears some definable relationship to reality, then it is pertinent to explain what this relationship is and to consider again, in more detail, how thought can be led astray. Again, there are two classes of errors that a mind can make in the Sautrantika view: a mind can either be obscured in the sense of taking a meaning generality as its appearing and apprehended object; or it can be factually incorrect with respect to its object of engagement and determined object. In other words, the concept can be mistaken because only a generality appears to it, or it can be simply wrong in what it is getting at. For direct perception there is never any mistake; the appearing object, the apprehended object, and the actual object of engagement are always the same, which is in part why a direct perception is called an incontrovertible knower and an ultimate mind.

Mistakes of what appears to the mind

For conceptual thought the appearing object and the apprehended object are not a real, impermanent thing; they are described as mixtures of a mental semblance and an object of engagement. The conceptual mind is said to be mistaken, obscured, or deceived[105] because "it erroneously apprehends a fusion of the actual object and its image [to be the object itself]." This does not necessarily reflect a flaw in reasoning, since a conceptual mind does not necessarily *conceive* the image and the real object to be mixed, they just *appear* that way.[106]

For a metaphorical example, "a reflection of a face in a mirror appears to be a face but is not usually conceived to be so. Thus, a correct intellectual consciousness is mistaken with regard to its appearing object but not with regard to its [determined] object."[107] Although one cannot grasp the face reflected in the mirror, one can learn from it and come to understand it. Once again, this distinction of two types of error is preserved to allow the claim that while concepts cannot actually attain experienced truth fully, they can nonetheless lead one to grasp it in a definite sense. This first type of error might be called epistemic in nature: it reflects the properties of the conceptual knower rather than the truth or falsity of what is known.

Mistakes of what the mind ascertains

The second type of error might be called an ontologic error: it reflects whether a given concept is concordant with factual reality or not. This class of error regards the engaged or determined object of consciousness, the impermanent object which consciousness is getting at or realizing. Whether one apprehends an object through perception or through forming a concept, one can understand the object correctly or incorrectly. "Counterfeit" perception can result from various flaws in the perceptual system that lead one to perceive the world in a skewed way. A common example given is that one might perceive that a snowy mountain is yellow if ones eyes are yellow with jaundice.

There are certainly many other examples that demonstrate the flaws of our perception, which come from the scientific literature. One of my favorites is the fact that all people are actually blind in one section of each eye, but most people have never even noticed it! If you close

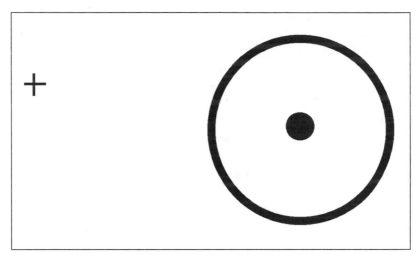

Figure 3. The Blind Spot Illusion

Each of our eyes actually has a spot where it cannot take in light, where we are totally blind, but most people have never even noticed it. Hold this image about one foot away from your face, close your left eye and fix your right eye on the cross. As long as you keep your eye fixed on the cross, you should see the large circle clearly but be completely unable to see the spot. If you can see the spot, move the image closer of farther from your face or tilt it slightly, while fixing you right eye on the cross and keeping your left eye closed. You should be able to trace out the area of your blind spot. As long as the spot (or anything else) is within the area of the blind spot, you will not be able to sense its presence, but you will probably not experience the "hole."

---

one eye, you will almost certainly experience what appears to be a full field of view through the other eye. You will probably not notice that there is actually a rather large hole in the middle of what you sense of the world. Figure 3 demonstrates this very convincingly, and the legend explains how to look at the figure in order to experience this effect. In the discussion of the physiology of sight I mentioned other examples of how the brain hardware itself seems to contain the flaws that lead to some counterfeit perceptions.

A concept can also be false. The textbook example of this given by Gelugpa teachers is that someone (perhaps everyone) might use false reasoning at some point to believe conceptually that they exist as a substantially existent self which has some permanent or inherent nature beyond the scope of its insubstantial parts. Simpler examples abound in the everyday experience of conceptual life and can be as tenacious as the blind spot illusion. If someone said at the time of the Buddha, "World sure is flat!", who would have argued?

In the Buddhist understanding both false perceptions and erroneous thoughts are epistemic possibilities, both are wrong consciousnesses which apprehend nonexistent objects. This type of error is more serious, in a sense, than the error of generalization presented above, because as long as someone is wrong with regard to an object of engagement then the determined object can *never* be correctly realized. In the standard Tibetan example presented above, although a jewel's light is not itself a jewel, if one correctly follows it one can get to an actual jewel, just as a mistaken conceptual mind can realize its apprehended object. However, if one follows the light of a butter lamp, thinking that it is the light of a jewel, then the jewel will never be found.[108] This again speaks to the need for valid conceptual education and training as a path out of ignorance, rather than merely trying to experience the world directly.

A presentation of the types of mistaken and wrong consciousnesses (the counterfeit direct perceivers) is enumerated by Geshe Jam-bel-sam-pel as follows:

1. mistaken wrong conception
2. conventional consciousness
3. inferential consciousness (conceptual)
4. conception arisen from inference
5. memory-conception
6. wishing-conception
7. dimness of sight[109]

From the above list of seven, all but the last type are conceptual and thus mistaken because they take a meaning generality as their appearing and apprehended object. The first and last are also wrong because they are counterfactual with regard to their object of engagement (and determined object in the case of the first one).

THE NEGATIVE MODE OF ACTION OF THE MIND IN THOUGHT

So the Gelugpas tell us that the conceptual mind takes a meaning generality as its object, which can be on the right track to understanding reality in a general way at best, or it can be completely wrong. These are all descriptions of *what* thought is doing. But the next question is *how* is it doing these things? What *is* a meaning generality? What is the *nature* of these objects that appear to our minds in thought? These questions are taken up in the interviews in the following chapters, and will be presented in expository form here.

In order to understand the answers from the Sautrantika perspective we will have to go into some detail regarding the kinds of objects that there are in the world, the kinds of objects that one can "have in mind," and the relationship between them. Particularly, we will have to explore the Sautrantika idea that the mind forms a concept by a "clearing away process," by excluding things from the mind rather than by collecting them. After considering this idea in detail it will be possible to address how this might be possible physiologically and what we can learn about this from studying the brain directly. Of course, when we are finished we will not have a complete experiential and physical description of the objects of mind, but we may have some interesting starting points.

Most basically, the Sautrantika school suggests that thought is a process of excluding from the mind everything which is *not* the object being conceived of. This is the starting point of their understanding of the mechanism of conceptuality. The mental semblance (or remainder) that is left behind is called an *isolate*. It is also possible to view some objects of thought from a positive perspective, but this is not the standard presentation.[110] All objects of conceptual thought are traditionally viewed as negative objects, as exclusions of other things.

This is another distinction between perception, which is viewed in the positive sense, and conceptualization, which is understood in the negative. Direct perception positively perceives all of the specific characteristics and details of its objects, while conceptualization excludes things which are not related to its object and thereby forms a mental semblance of the general features of an object that remain after other features have been excluded.[111] The Sautrantika description of the exclusions is said to be the most subtle part of this school's teachings and it involves a number of different types of negative (or exclusion) objects, which will be presented in brief as an introduction to how exclusions are used in an explanation of the process of thought.

Negative and positive phenomena

All objects of mind can be exhaustively divided into negative and positive phenomena, and this simple distinction will characterize the objects of mind which follow below. The distinction is not made based on any inherent properties of an object, nor by the verbal or logical means whereby the object is designated. It is made by the way in which an object comes into the awareness of a mind, the way that the object is "gotten at." A positive phenomenon can be accessed directly by the mind, as when someone perceives a goat in a field in their direct experience. No exclusion of anything is required to have this experience. A negative phenomenon is simply the opposite, it is something which *must* come into one's mind by the exclusion of something else. A formal definition of a negative phenomenon, or exclusion, is

> an object realized by the thought consciousness apprehending it in the manner of an explicit elimination of its object of negation.[112]

For example, to understand that one *lacks* a goat one must exclude goats from an understanding of those things that one possesses. One cannot have this understanding of lacking something except through an explicit exclusion. All positive phenomena can technically also be viewed as negatives, or exclusions, because they are held to implicitly exclude all objects other than themselves. For example, a direct perception of a goat excludes all other goats and all non-goats from perception.[113] Nonetheless, a goat is a positive phenomenon because it does not *require* this mental process of negation in order to be understood. These negative phenomena are then classified into several types of exclusions, as described below, and conceptual thought is explained in terms of these various types of objects.

Non-affirming negatives

Non-affirming negatives are exclusions which negate the existence of one thing but do not suggest anything else in its place. An example is the statement, "Brahmins do not drink beer," which excludes from thought the positive phenomenon of a Brahmin drinking beer, but does not suggest any other positive phenomenon instead.[114] Formally, a non-affirming negative is

> a negative which is such that the term expressing it does not suggest in place of the negation of its own object of negation another, positive phenomenon which is its own object of suggestion.[115]

In other words, a non-affirming negative can suggest another non-affirming negative, such as the implicit suggestion that Brahmins also do not drink malt beer, but it cannot affirm anything positive, such as what things Brahmins *do* drink. It can serve to delineate the range of excluded objects, but it still affirms nothing positive.

Affirming negatives

Most of our concepts *do* suggest something; they are affirming negatives. For example, the thought of a mountainless plain excludes mountains from the mind and affirms the existence of a plain in their stead. An affirming negative is formally defined as

> a negative that is expressed by a phrase indicating another phenomenon—either an affirming negative or a positive phenomenon—in place of its own object of negation.[116]

In contrast to non-affirming negatives, an affirming negative can suggest another affirming negative in its place, which in turn suggests a positive phenomenon. For example, the thought of "a lakeless, mountainless plain" suggests a mountainless plain in place of a lake (or a lakeless plain in place of a mountain). The conceptual mind operating by way of an affirming negative is not directly and positively aware of the suggested object as a directly perceiving mind would be, it has just allowed an isolate to remain and appear to it following a process of exclusion.

The distinction between affirming and non-affirming negatives is one of the most important parts of Sautrantika thought for the Gelugpa monastic curriculum, because once the idea of a non-affirming negative is clearly grasped this opens the mind to understanding the most important non-affirming negative of all for the Gelugpa, the understanding of emptiness. Emptiness is realized as a non-affirming negative by the process of excluding from the mind any idea of an inherently or permanently existing self or identity in something, which in fact *never did nor ever will exist*. This concept is a non-affirming negative, so the exclusion suggests absolutely nothing in its place.[117] In order to foster realization of this phenomenon, students must first have a firm grasp of the idea of a non-affirming concept.

Mental and objective affirming negatives

Affirming negatives are not *just* the objects of thoughts, the distinction holds for physical (impermanent) objects as well. This leads to another division into two types, in accordance with whether an object is imputed by thought or exists objectively, from its own side. In his *Presentation of Tenets*, Jang-gya Rol-bay Dor-jay defines the two terms thus:

> The definition of a *mental exclusion* is: An affirming negative exclusion with the status of a mere imputation by thought.[118]

The definition of an *objective exclusion* is: An exclusion that is an
affirming negative established by way of its own nature and is
not a mere mental imputation.[119]

There are thus two ways that the term exclusion can be used. It can
be used to designate a physical phenomenon which exists in the absence of being known, just as any other physical phenomenon does.
For example "the people of the world who are not men" have physical existence, whether or not they are being imputed, in the same sense
that positive objects like trees and rocks exist. The other sense of the
term exclusion designates something which is known by someone,
and in this case it must be imputed by thought, as when someone
thinks about the people on the planet who are not men. Obviously, the
referent is the same in both cases, but the actual scope, detail, and so
on of the remaining isolate is not. A central feature of the Sautrantika
view is that objective negative phenomena can exist as negative phenomena from their own side and that mental negative phenomena
must be imputed by thought, but nonetheless that both can share the
same referent.

It is important for the independent existence of each of these types
of negatives and the distinction between the two to be made clear. A
mental affirming negative exists only by imputation; it only exists in
the sense that it appears to a mind that has excluded something else.
Objective affirming negatives, on the other hand, are physical objects
which exist in the same way that positive physical objects exist, without requiring mental imputation. Something is thus not a negative by
virtue of being imputed by thought. In the same way that a pot exists,
everything else in the world which is *not* a pot also exists, independently of imputation. Of course, only an aware subject can designate
which things are a pot and which are not, but the ones that are not a
pot still exist in the absence of this designation in the same way that
the ones that are pots exist. The general *features* which are common to
all pots can also be viewed to exist without imputation in this same
way, by virtue of being the remaining features in the world beyond
features not shared by pots.

The importance of the distinction between mental and objective
affirming negatives is to set out the view that what appears to a conceptual mind is a mental affirming negative, which exists only by imputation, but what is realized by a conceptual mind is a real, specifically characterized object, which exists independently of imputation.
The appearing objects of conceptual thought are mental exclusions,

but the engaged and determined objects, which the conceptual mind is "getting at," are objective exclusions which are impermanent phenomena that are suitable to be directly perceived. Objective exclusions are impermanent, ultimate truths, specifically characterized objects, and they exists from their own side, rather than being imputed by thought.[120] Mental exclusions are permanent phenomena, conventional truths, and generally characterized objects which exist only by imputation.[121] The conceptual mind can exist in relation to both types at once.

Double-negative exclusion objects

Perhaps the most important type of exclusion object, and also the most difficult to grasp, is the double-negative exclusion, or self-isolate. The double negation process is one of the points where Sautrantika thought comes closest to a mechanistic analysis, and is perhaps the most interesting part of the presentation of concept formation from the viewpoint of cognitive neuroscience. Beginning with an example: if we can negate (or exclude) everything which *is* a pot, then we can obviously also negate everything which *is not* a pot. When everything which *is not* a pot is excluded, then what remains is, simply enough, pot. The difference between double negatives and positives (as with single negatives and positives) does not arise from a difference of inherent properties of the objects that they refer to; it does not arise from the way in which they are verbally designated; and it does not arise by virtue of a necessity to be imputed by thought. It arises from a difference in the way that the object comes into a mind's awareness. The distinction between double negatives and positives is used to explain *how* the mind is arriving at its object.

THE MODE OF ACTION OF CONCEPTUAL THOUGHT IN TERMS OF ITS OBJECT

Having defined the relevant types of negative objects, we can move on to how Sautrantika posits that conceptual thought uses these objects in its functioning. Meaning generalities are the objects of the mind during conceptualization, and they are presented as being mental exclusion objects as described above, double negatives imputed by the mind.

What might it mean to say that we think by using double negative objects? Here is how I envision it. When I "see an image in my mind's eye," the image is not nearly so real as I might at first think. I would certainly never confuse it with my direct experience. But it also doesn't seem to be wrong about anything, it doesn't seem to suggest anything that is obviously not part of the object (or at least sometimes it doesn't). On the other hand, it does seem to leave a lot out. And it also seems quite general. If this isn't your experience, explore this exercise: Try to form a detailed mental image of a tiger and then see if there is anything added or anything missing. If nothing seems to be missing, try to count the stripes, or to see if the tiger blinks. Does your tiger have any unusual markings, or is it a quite "general" tiger? It seems to me quite plausible that when I think of a tiger I am not creating a tiger in my head, I am just removing whatever things don't apply. This seems to me a reasonable explanation of why I don't *really* seem to see something, but I get a notion of it anyway. Naturally, with practice this mental semblance can become more and more like the real object itself.

This suggests a clear mechanism for the functioning of thought, and it suggests some details regarding how thought is explained to be related to the objects of the physical world. The meaning generality, which is the object appearing to the mind during thought, is described as being "general," as in the preceding example. It generalizes over a class of objects rather than focusing on the particular specific details of a single experience. There is a corresponding objectively existing double negative which is also general in precisely the same way. It does not exclude everything except for one particular, specifically characterized object with all of its features. It excludes everything except for a general rendering of something. For example, it is possible to imagine an exclusion of everything which is not a feature of "pots in general," as opposed to excluding everything except the features of a particular pot. In the former case what remains is a self-isolate that contains only the general features of pots, like having a flat base, a round belly, and holding water. These general features *exist* "objectively," in the same way that any physical object exists, but in order to be *known* conceptually they must be cognized by an excluding mind.

THE OBJECTS OF A CONCEPTUAL MIND: MEANING GENERALITIES AND DOUBLE NEGATIVE EXCLUSIONS

Presenting the objects of a conceptual mind again in more formal terms, the appearing object of a conceptual mind is a meaning generality, which is a double negative exclusion imputed by thought. The actual object being engaged by a conceptual mind is an objective self-isolate, which is an objective double negative.

Returning to our example, both the meaning generality and the objective self-isolate exclude things not common to "pot," and leave an isolate of "pot" (they have the same referent), but they are not the same. The objective self-isolate is a double negative which exists from the object's own side, that is, it is an impermanent and functioning thing, whereas the meaning generality is a double negative which is merely imputed by thought, so it is not a functioning thing. Again, impermanence should be taken here as a criterion of objects which discriminates that "objectively existing" phenomena are in continuous physical flux, both due to the ongoing processes of physical aging and degradation and also at the atomic level, whereas a mental phenomenon need not share these types of change. Similarly, how something can function is a criterion for the status of the object; physical objects are taken to function in a sense in which mentally imputed objects do not. Together, the critical point being made is that although the meaning generality is imputed by thought and the objective self-isolate exists objectively like any other object, both share the same referent. This is the relationship between thought and objective phenomena.

The meaning generality is a conventional approximation, in a sense, of the self-isolate. A meaning generality and a self-isolate are not exactly the same because the "isolate exists on the side of the object as a natural predicate of its being one with itself [whereas] the meaning-generality is what appears to the conceptual awareness [and is thus imputed by thought]."[122] The meaning generality is an isolate which is formed by mental exclusion in the mind, so it is a conventional truth, and it is a mental semblance since it exists only by mental imputation.

Since a mental exclusion is merely imputed by thought, it can only exclude from mind those objects which the mind selects to exclude, and it leaves remaining those that the mind encompasses, which is only a general assortment. A meaning generality is only *general*. It focuses on a general exclusion object, an isolate, understanding an abstract rather than a specific object. Most simply put, the objective self-isolate has all of the specific properties and functions of pot, whereas the mental exclusion or meaning generality has only general properties and is inert.[123] The objective self-isolate can perform functions, whereas the meaning generality is only a rendering, and can do nothing.

THE REASON FOR THE PRESENTATION OF EXCLUSIONS RATHER THAN POSITIVE PHENOMENA

The Sautrantika explanation of how conceptual thought can grasp reality relies on the relationship between the mental exclusion, which is the appearing object of thought, and the objective self-isolate, which is the real determined object and an "ultimate" truth (a simple, objectively existing aspect of reality). How does the mind come to realize the truth about something? The appearing object of a conceptual mind is the mental exclusion, all that the mind *conceives* as being opposite from not an object. The actual object being realized by the mind, however, is the objective exclusion, the specifically characterized opposite from non-pot in our example. Conceptual thought is held to realize its object because through continued reasoning, observation, and thought the mental exclusion becomes more and more like the objective exclusion until finally an inferential understanding is reached. Later, once this inferential understanding has been reached, a direct perception of the objective exclusion itself can take place, meaning that one can now experience the object in the light of a new-found entrance into one of its full array of properties and features that were not at first obvious.

It is possible to present many objects of conceptual thought as either positive or negative phenomena, although the traditional emphasis is on the negative sense. Only the presentation of Gomang College of Drepung Monastery goes further, to suggest that all permanent phenomena, and all meaning generalities which are objects of a conceptual mind, *must* be negatives.[124] Conceptual objects are normally considered from their negative perspective for a number of important reasons. First of all, as mentioned above, there are many types of objects which cannot be presented as positive phenomena, so the negative presentation must be used if these are to be included. These include the concepts of selflessness and emptiness, which are both non-affirming negatives, and both are crucial to the Buddhist viewpoint in general. Therefore, the presentation of negatives is particularly important for pedagogical reasons. This presentation is also favored because when a generic image itself becomes the main object of the mind (when one conceptual consciousness observes another conceptual consciousness) then the object of this mind is described as a negative phenomenon.[125] Finally, from a logical standpoint, the Gelugpas argue that if the mentally imputed properties of an object of a conceptual mind were inherent positive properties of the objectively existing referent object, then this would suggest that they have an inherently existing positive link between them, that there are absolute attributes which are positively linked between the conceptual mind and its object. The Gelugpas do not accept that there is an *inherent* link between the conceptual mind and reality, and instead posit an inferential link based upon exclusion.

PRESENTATION OF HOW A CONCEPTUAL CONSCIOUSNESS IS INDUCED

The idea that a conceptual mind takes a double negative meaning generality as its object leads us to ask how this object arises. The Gelugpas suggest that conceptuality can be induced either during a concurrent perception, or from a memory, or through reasoning, and discuss the causal sequence of moments of mind in each case.

Conceptuality in the presence of an object being observed

While one is perceiving an object, one can think about the object as well (in fact one normally does), and in this case the object of perception leads along a series of "mind moments" to conceptualization. Once again, new terminology is introduced and used to clarify the distinctions between the different sequential moments of mind and their objects in detail. In brief, during the first moment that one sees an object, one experiences a direct prime cognizer, a new, incontrovertible direct perceiver.[126] The following moments may also be direct perceivers but they are different in character in that they are no longer prime cognizers (since they cognize an object already known because the preceding moment of consciousness was engaged with the same object). Instead, they are termed subsequent cognizers, defined by Jambel-sam-pel in his *Presentation of Awareness and Knowledge* as follows:

> A subsequent cognizer is a knower which is not a prime cognizer [a *new*, incontrovertible knower] and which realizes what has already been realized by the former prime cognizer inducing it.[127]

So the first link in the sequence is that given the right circumstances a prime cognizer can induce subsequent moments of awareness which take a different type of object. At some point during this chain of subsequent moments of direct perception, one moment can lead to a mental direct perception of the same object. A mental direct perception uses the sixth of the gates to perception in the Tibetan system, the "mind door," which is considered in the same category with the traditional five perceptual senses. This moment of awareness is thus still a perceptual event, not a conceptualization, and its object is an impermanent, specifically characterized, objectively existing phenomenon, which the direct perceiver engages completely and in all of its detail. The mental direct perception lasts for just a single moment of awareness and is therefore normally too short to be noticed, but it is postulated to form the link between perception and conceptualization. Since the moment of mental direct perception is normally not noticed, the object of this mental direct perception *appears* to the mind but it is not normally *ascertained*, just as with other objects of direct perception which are not fully ascertained. This means that not only the five traditional senses but also the mind of an ordinary person has direct access to "ultimate" reality during this moment of mental direct perception (although this is not normally ascertained), and this is a quite unique feature of the Gelugpa Sautrantika perspective.

According to Sautrantika, the mental direct perceiver must arise from a preceding moment of direct perception, so this type of object of mind at the "mind door" is distinct from conceptual objects in that it cannot arise from memory directly.[128] The object taken by the mental direct perceiver serves as something of a liaison which conveys an object from the process of perception to that of conceptual thought. Exactly how mental direct perceivers arise is debated within Gelugpa Sautrantika and this debate will be considered in a section of its own below.

The conceptual consciousness which follows a moment of mental direct perception still engages the same object, which is why conceptuality can access reality in a certain sense, but in this case what appears to the mind is a mixture of the aspect of the real object and a mental semblance of that object. Since conceptual consciousnesses of sense forms follow direct perception, they are necessarily in the class of subsequent cognizers. After the induction of a first conceptual consciousness, additional moments of conceptuality can continue on into complex trains of thought. Sometimes streams of conceptuality go on seemingly endlessly, reflecting the mind's propensity towards conceptual thought.[129]

The next step in the process of conceptualization is a normative categorization of the object which has arisen in the mind. An integral part of this process is that the object is categorized as good, bad, or neutral based upon past memories and as a result a feeling (or affective component) which has become associated with the object. These normative judgments about an object do not arise from inherent properties of the object itself (technically speaking, they are not one entity in place, time, and nature with it), since different observers may react differently to the same object. Nevertheless, this judgment about the object (or this component of the meaning imputed to the object) arises from what the aspect of the object suggests, not in a random or haphazard fashion. This is largely based upon past experience, bringing up another aspect of the "conventional" nature of conceptuality. This normative judgment about the object is obviously critical in reacting to it, both mentally and behaviorally.

Concepts induced by perception, just described, are the first subclass of two types of conceptual consciousnesses, described by Jambel-sam-pel as follows:

> There are [only] two conceptual subsequent cognizers: those induced by direct perception [either immediately or at a later time through memory], and those induced by inference. An illustration of a conceptual subsequent cognizer induced by direct perception is a consciousness ascertaining blue which is produced subsequent to a direct perceiver apprehending blue; an illustration of a conceptual subsequent cognizer induced by inference is the second moment [and subsequent moments] of an inferential consciousness.[130]

The kinds of thought induced in the absence of direct sensory perception will be considered next.

Conceptuality induced by memory

The Sautrantika presentation also describes the mode of arising of conceptuality from the memory of a past experience, rather than the experience of a present perception. When a conceptual awareness is generated from a memory a meaning generality is recalled directly, with no intervening stage of mental direct perception as a liaison. Only conceptual forms of awareness can ripen from memory of the past; "directly perceived objects of the mind" (mental direct perceivers) cannot be generated directly from memory, and arise from sensory events only. When mental objects arise from memory, they appear immediately as members of the class of "conventional" objects, which are technically characterized as permanent, generally characterized objects of conceptual thought. These designations are intended to place these mental objects into a particular class of phenomena, distinct from objectively existent objects of direct perception.

While our mental semblances appear to dance and change before us, the Sautrantikas posit that in fact they should be regarded as permanent in the technical sense of being static, non-decaying, non-produced, and unable to produce effects.[131] I take this assertion to mean that a given mental object does not change in the way that a physical object does, but that another very similar mental object can immediately follow it. For example, my idea of my mother does not by its nature tend to get older while I think about it (although my real mother does get older during the same time span). I might in a following moment of awareness have another idea of my mother that is older, but this idea would be distinct and would also then be static. Similarly, an idea such as a triangle can exist timelessly in a sense and does not arise from or produce physical causes in the same way that a particular physical triangle does.

In my view, the Sautrantika presentation asserts that there are fairly static boundaries between conceptual categories within which mental objects fall (as has been shown for many types of object categories in the scientific literature), and that as long as a particular mental object exists, it has fixed allegiances to particular categories and designators. In the next moment, the mental object does not slowly drift into new characteristics, it makes an abrupt transition to a new (but perhaps closely related) mental object.

Since objects "ripen" from memory directly as meaning generalities, all objects of memory are necessarily incomplete and only general renderings of previously perceived reality. As is common experience, memories are often factually wrong as well; this is said to happen because the way that a potentiality, or seed, laid upon the mind ripens into a new conceptual consciousness depends heavily upon the circumstances at the time that it ripens. The consciousness of one object can later ripen into the memory of a distorted form of that object, or even a different object altogether, depending upon the circumstances.[132] In an example used to draw out the details of this process, if one creates a potentiality to remember a pot by seeing it, it is possible that this potentiality will actually ripen into the memory of a pillar at a later time. Memory is fallible because it leads past objects to arise to the mind only in the context of the fluctuating circumstances at the time of recollection. These circumstances, particularly the details of the preceding moment of consciousness, serve as conditions that allow memory to arise. This is explained as another reason that conceptuality is inherently fallible, and why Buddhism in general values conceptuality and memory decidedly less than direct perception.

Conceptuality induced by reason

A particular moment or object of conceptuality can also be induced through a process of thought or reasoning. Conceptual consciousnesses induced by reason (correct ones) are named inferential cognizers, and are defined by Jam-bel-sam-pel as follows:

> An inferential cognizer is a determinative knower which, depending on its basis, a correct sign, is incontrovertible with regard to its object of comprehension [determined object], a hidden phenomenon [which cannot be seen directly but must be understood by reasoning].[133]

The correct sign upon which an inference is based is simply a reason, a proof, or a process of analysis. An example typically used to explain this type of conceptual thought is a student's realization of the impermanence of sound following reasoned debate with a teacher.[134]

An awareness based on reason can be a prime cognizer, meaning that it can be one's first understanding of an object which one has not previously perceived directly. There are many objects which one can only gain first access to through this sort of inference or sign, not through direct experience. For example, one can only first grasp the elementary constituents and physical laws working within a perceived object when they are explained, not by viewing the object very carefully. This is something which is "hidden" to ordinary direct perception; the object does not come to mind originally from direct perception, but it can be realized for the first time through conceptuality induced by sequences of logic, reason, and discussion.

To summarize this section, the Gelugpas posit a central role for conceptuality as a way that the mind can be led to a true understanding of the experienced world. The mind of conceptuality is held to take objects described in two classes, the objects that appear to the mind, and the objects that are realized or engaged by the mind. The appearance to the mind is a general rendering of a real physical object which is heavily colored by past experience and other effects of our conventional understanding of reality, but the object which the mind is engaging can be a part of directly experienced reality itself. The

Gelugpas explain this relationship between mental semblance and physical object, and how the mind forms conceptual objects through a process of excluding from the mind all aspects which do not pertain to a particular object. The presentation of conceptuality ends with the prescription that through the proper use of reason one can come to directly perceive the truth of experience, and (crucially) its emptiness of any type of inherently or permanently existing nature or conceptual characterization beyond the real world objects of direct perception themselves.

CONCEPTS IN CONTEMPORARY NEUROSCIENCE

The understanding of the nature and process of formation of concepts in cognitive neuroscience is not nearly so unified or well agreed upon as that found in Sautrantika, and there is considerable debate regarding even the most basic issues. This is an area of increasing contemporary research interest with many competing theories. Moreover, the question of concept formation is often considered using very different language and concepts in the fields of psychology, cognitive science, artificial intelligence, and neurophysiology. I will focus here on the perspective which is arising out of the data which are being taken directly from the brain.

The vision in neurobiology regarding thought and concept formation is completely mechanistic, inviting us to consider our own mental life and trains of thought as the functioning of an elaborate but completely impersonal machine. This theme obviously shares a certain general resonance and compatibility with the Gelugpa presentation of mind, centering on selflessness, but it leads in a somewhat different direction. The view of concepts from neurobiology starts with the machine, starts with how the concepts might work and what they might do. It then tries to stretch upwards towards what they might be like experientially, rather than moving in the opposite direction by starting with subjective experience. It suggests things about how thoughts might function in terms of their detailed mechanisms. It also holds out the prospect that certain aspects of a system for understanding thought might be verified or rejected by experiment, that at least some of the ancient debates about the mind might come to have essentially final resolutions based on empirical observations.

The field of neuroscience has traditionally laid its emphasis decidedly on perception in favor of conceptuality, a bias very similar to that found in Gelugpa Sautrantika. Within Sautrantika this bias reflects the view that perception is more directly linked with a true and direct understanding of experience, whereas within neuroscience this bias has arisen principally for the practical reason that perception has been more easily studied empirically. As a result, the contemporary understandings of concept formation and many other aspects of consciousness are often outgrowths of the understanding of perception, and they share many of the same metaphors in their description. The mechanisms of conceptual thought and mental imagery are now being sought as the mechanisms of perception have been sought in the past, with the approach being to try to understand these more complex processes in the same ways and using the same methods that have been used on perception before. It is still not completely clear whether the brain does use similar mechanisms to conceive and to perceive, but the data thus far accumulated suggest that this assumption is a valid starting point, and may well be largely correct.

Since there is currently no veridical understanding of how concept formation takes place within the brain, one is forced to piece together an understanding of conceptualization that is consistent with available data and seems intellectually appealing—at present one must extrapolate available data somewhat in order to imagine how the brain produces concepts. This speculation should not be taken as solid fact, but it can be useful in presenting new perspectives and putting ideas to the test, and often it is backed up by data which can serve as an anchor to independent confirmation. The theory that is presented below as a comparison with Sautrantika thought should be considered in the critical light that it is still being formed by a comparatively new field, but the scientific findings and details which are presented and used to contradict other possibilities are all soundly established and can be taken as reliable.

Conceptuality as a neural engine—metaphors from physical science

Concepts in general are considered to be brain processes that operate following physical laws implemented in neural systems. This does *not* necessarily entail as a consequence that people just function as simple machines, that they just follow orders, or that they just live out genetically predestined programs. The hardware of the brain is extremely subtle in its ability to adapt creatively to new situations and produce novel solutions in changing circumstances. As I have argued elsewhere, the brain is extremely plastic and is constantly being shaped and reshaped by experience.[135] The choices that one makes in each moment cumulatively determine what shape one's brain and one's mind will take from that point onward. In a machine with literally trillions of interconnected parts and a constantly changing connectivity, simple metaphors about the properties of deterministic systems seem very unlikely to be relevant.

The current overall view of how this engine might work is taken from computational neuroscience and from artificial intelligence.[136] Let me try to distill this entire conceptual framework into one very impoverished example. Imagine an agrarian city of people, all of whom are only out for their own immediate best interest, with no concern for anyone else and only a very limited scope of knowledge that comes from their experience of their immediate surroundings. The city has no overarching central administrator or government. If we consider this city as a whole, many types of complex information would be taken in, processed, and reacted to at a global level not appreciated by any of the members. For example, the city would constantly process information (and in a sense "know") about where food was coming from. It would continuously deploy its agents to (in a sense "decide" in favor of) these areas, even though no one individual might see the global pattern. In other words, complex information about the local conditions in many areas would be transformed into a "command" to move the cities resources and workers in new directions. This analogy lacks key components of a neural system, particularly complex organization and the ability to learn and plan globally, but I hope that it conveys the idea that many individual "dumb" elements can have the ability to produce complex and somewhat intelligent global states and behaviors.

Imagining the mind as the product of a neural mechanism is in some ways compatible with the starting point of the Abhidharma, which is that minds can be explained in terms of simple and selfless processes operating on matter in defined ways. The chief difference is that the laws described by biology are of a simple sort that have arisen from empirical measurements that are readily observable and understandable by anyone, although they are sometimes cloaked in difficult language. If we start from the mechanism rather than from the experience, then we find that we can make predictions about how the mechanism will function in new circumstances. The advantage here is that since these laws are simple and observable, their consequences can be readily understood and tested in the flesh.

If we view the process of concept formation as a neural engine then there are definite conclusions which we can draw about its mode of functioning, and thereby about thought and experience. The neural engine is built of trillions of individually functioning elements and their changing connections, and the processes of mind must necessarily reflect this fact in important ways. Taking this perspective, we see from the start that the system which generates subjective experience is not a single, unified process with a single "self" controlling it, but a process which runs in parallel and by the cooperation of many subparts. One of the challenges to neuroscience is to come to understand the neural origin of our subjective experience of self, of a sense of unity of experience, and of our belief in ourselves as a controller or an experiencer.

Understanding that the brain is a physical machine also makes clear that this engine must be run by some form of energy, and that it might be described well as a system with various energy states and a tendency to run in the direction of lower energy states, balanced by a source of energy which allows it to be replenished. There have been many models of the brain based upon this type of very general physical analogy.[137] They give us the notion that a persistently active mind state might be thought of as a particular state of the brain with a particular energy, and that a mind state will tend to lead on to another mind state if there is a path between the dense web of elements that allows it to relax to a state of lower energy. If there is a block, or lack of connection, then the higher energy mind state will not be able to be discharged, and may continue on and on in this state until a connection can be made. If there is a very ready path of connections from a mind state then this path will readily be followed, and the brain will change its content along this path. If the path is well worn by memory then the mind may tend to follow it over and over again, backwards and forwards perhaps. If the path is circular, then the mind has the opportunity to continue around a sequence until another alternative presents itself. Finally, if the mind sinks into a state where there is little activating it then it may be quite difficult to disturb by energy from outside input.

This is meant to demonstrate how physical analogies taken from other systems that have come to be understood in detail by the sciences can be used to try to explain mental processes in the crudest fashion, by rough metaphor. This particular analogy is a persistent one in neurobiology and seems quite similar to one found in Tibetan

Buddhism (see the interview with Kamtrul Rinpoche). In general this type of broad analogy is not the main objective of neuroscience; the main objective is to find detailed and verifiable descriptions and mechanisms, but it can be quite helpful in forming intuitions nonetheless.

The parallel processing hierarchy in brief

The search for a detailed understanding of the brain has sought first to chart out the connections within the system which are used in any given mental phenomenon. It has also tried to measure the activities of the different parts of the brain during mental processes in order to understand what their roles might be. This process has led to an overall current picture of the brain as a set of separate but interconnected "maps," or abstract images, which process information in defined ways that lead to our behaviors. Thoughts are understood as a form of processing within this system, a form of activity in between sensory input and motor output.

A main organizational feature of the brain's wiring that draws one's attention immediately is that it seems to be designed as a physical hierarchy, with processing of perceptual details taking place in many specialized "lower" areas which feed information "up" (or onwards into the brain), and processing of global abstractions taking place at the "higher" areas. The standard view of this hierarchy was discussed in the chapter on perception, but to summarize, an object of awareness is posited to be represented by the activity of a large number of heavily interconnected brain areas, each of which is involved in the representation of some feature of an object. Different types of features of the object are represented by the activities of neurons in different localized areas of the brain which are specialized for representing that particular aspect of objects, and the different areas are interconnected so that the object as a whole can be unified. These areas are organized into a parallel hierarchy, meaning that many lower areas together feed into higher areas. These areas can be imagined to correspond to a hierarchy of the details of our mental lives, with simple details of many types at the bottom, building up into more complex and abstract experiences at the top.

The most extensively studied example of this hierarchical process as it takes place during perception is the case of what happens when we see something. The information from our eyes is quickly carried to the backs of our heads and then onwards in two main parallel pathways, each of which proceeds through a number of areas of the brain, with processing of the information taking place at every step from the eye onwards. One pathway moves information predominantly about form and color, and another moves information about perceived motion and spatial relations.[138] The details get processed first, and these are slowly put together into more complex and abstract representations of whole unified objects, and the relations among objects, and so on.

Each of the areas of the brain which is in this hierarchy functions as a map by representing a semblance of one feature of the object. Each semblance represents a particular separate kind of information, such as information about which colors are found at each place on the object, about vertical and horizontal lines, about movement, and so forth.[139] These can be thought of as many images designating particular features of the object, like many world maps designating political borders, mineral deposits, and climate of the earth. The whole object is completely understood by the information from all of the maps and the relations between them. As was mentioned previously, these separate maps seem somewhat related to the many small "aspects" of the object of awareness posited by Sautrantika. It should be stressed that this idea of parallel processing of information through interconnected maps is not just a hypothetical or philosophical idea of how the brain works; the connections and image maps found in this hierarchy have all been physically observed within the brain.

This brain activity is believed not to present a perceptual or mental image to an awareness, but in fact to *be* the awareness itself—just as many drops of water and their motions *are* a river. During perception, a whole object is represented by a combination of maps which contain global, abstract features, and lower level maps which contain underlying fine details. These representations of objects are distributed in a highly organized, hierarchical fashion across many neurons in different areas of the brain. For perception, this process has been verified many times by experiment and these representations can be physically observed to exist.

Where is the mental semblance?

A starting point in the issue of how concepts are represented is the question of where in the brain a mental semblance, or meaning generality in Tibetan terms, might be found. Where in all of these maps is a mental image represented? At present this issue is not resolved, but data increasingly suggest that mental semblances are created in the same places within the brain as percepts and using closely related mechanisms,[140] which suggests that the brain uses some of the same hardware to imagine a face as to physically see one. Although this seems the simplest way for things to be done, there are a number of other alternatives that are equally plausible in the absence of neural data.[141] Fortunately, there are now a growing number of experiments which are starting to shed light for the first time on the issue of how mental semblances are formed at the physical level. I will consider a few examples of the search for the mental image in the brain as illustrations.

Martha Farah and her colleagues have made recordings of the brain's electrical activity (which is what conveys information between neural elements) from the head surface of conscious people who are imagining a visual picture, and they have found that the electrical patterns change in predictable ways over the areas of the brain used for vision (near the back of the head). This is considered suggestive evidence that the areas used for visual perception are also active during visual mental imagery, a clue to the location of the mental image.[142] Similar studies have also taken place more recently using brain scanning techniques in people during mental imagery.

There have also been a number of studies which have recorded the activity of single neurons in the visual areas of the brain during very simple tasks involving memory of concepts or mental images, and these seem to suggest that some of the neurons involved in perception are also involved in concept formation. The most well known example of this was discovered in the early 1970's by Joaquin Fuster, who showed that some visual neurons which are active when an animal sees an object remain active when the animal actively remembers the object, or maintains a mental image of it, even after the object has been removed. He suggested that these neurons are maintaining the memory or mental image of the object after the percept has ceased.[143]

A number of similar studies carried out by other labs have indicated that the higher, more abstract portions of the perceptual hierarchy are more strongly activated by conceptualization, memory, and mental imagery, which may explain why it often seems easier to maintain a general mental image of an object than to visualize all of its fine details.[144] The issue of concept formation is far from solved, but these studies and others currently support the idea that concepts (at least visual mental images) may be formed as images across the same maps that are used in the hierarchy of perceptual processing. This is a central question to neuroscience which remains to be verified and understood in more detail, but the prospects seem encouraging for being able to find the physical mechanisms of this process and thereby finally laying to rest many age-old debates.

The standard theory—generating concepts from positive features

The *de facto* understanding of concept formation in terms of neural mechanism, then, might be that concepts are represented in a similar way to percepts. It is likely that the most general aspects of an idea might activate the most global representations in the brain, while the simplest features of a given concept activate lower level maps of detail. The additional feature that is needed for concept formation, as opposed to perception, is that we seem to be able to form our concepts "top down," starting with the most abstract of ideas and working out the details as needed. This poses a real problem for the hierarchical model, which has a tendency to funnel details in towards abstractions, because a given abstract thought can correspond to many sets of details, many different "views." When we imagine, how does the brain fill in the details? How does it decide how many stripes on our imagined tiger? Does this process happen through active, positive association, or (in accordance with the Gelugpa view) through exclusion?

A SOURCE OF THE GENERALITY OF THOUGHT

At each successive level towards the top of the representational hierarchy, neurons represent not only more complex and abstract features, but also more general features—features common to a greater variety of objects. For example, let us consider the high level neurons that respond to a particular face as an abstract object.[145] These neurons are able to recognize views of the same face that are visually very different, and they can recognize the same face after a haircut and when it is wearing glasses. They might even be able to recognize the face twenty years later when it belongs to a very changed person, or be able to recognize a family member who is a different person altogether. The point is that they are responding to general features of the face, rather than responding to a specific pattern of details. They are not responding to the specific characteristics of the face that abide in a given moment, to use the Buddhist terminology. This is one way that the generality of thought is believed to be created, and it may be necessary for all thoughts which form associations between different objects.

If one is to think about the image of a person, to take an example, as being the same person on different days and from different visual perspectives, then it is necessary to be able to find common, general features shared between these different views, and neurons at the higher levels of the visual hierarchy seem to do this. These neurons become active when a particular face is seen, but not otherwise, and they will respond to (or "recognize") the general features of the same face even if it is presented at a different angle, upside down, or with some of its parts hidden.[146] Some of these neurons are more general in their responses than others; while some will respond to many kinds of objects, some will respond only within a more narrow category. Even lower level neurons generalize somewhat—no neuron has only one precise object that will activate it during perception. The brain, therefore, has neurons at different levels that are able to generalize over particular instances to differing extents, and thereby to look for members of increasingly general and abstract categories.

When an object is perceived, and probably when it is thought about, many of these neurons are activated, some of which are more specific and some more general. This neural ensemble represents the object and spans the processing hierarchy from bottom to top, simple to complex, specific to general. This is believed to be how we recognize the general features of an object that allow us to call it the same even though it has actually changed, and also how we recognize the details attendant upon a particular experience. This is also thought to be how we recognize the similarities among categories of objects, even though the individual instances are different. Obviously the activity of these sorts of neurons, which have the ability to form associations and to generalize over instances of objects, is a tantalizing candidate for a neural correlate of the Sautrantika concept of a meaning generality.

CONTRAST WITH THE SAMKHYA VIEW

The view just presented is one of positive recognition and correlation of features, but it is not similar to the logic of the non-Buddhist Samkhya school's view that positive general properties inhere in objects, a perspective often refuted by Gelugpa scholars.[147] This point seems important as it came up in a number of discussions. The Samkhya view, in brief, is that an object is an instance of a general class, and that a general nature is inherently found within each object of that class. From this viewpoint it can be argued that consciousness merely needs to positively recognize this inhering nature, or defining feature, in order to recognize its object. The many Gelugpa refutations of this position center around the point that there are no general qualities or nature which substantially inhere within objects—that these qualities must instead be imputed by the observer.[148] The view of neurobiology just presented does not fall prey to this argument.

Although the understanding from neuroscience is positive rather than negative, it still accepts that an object's nature must be imputed by an observer. The standard neuroscience approach suggests that the general qualities which are observed and aggregated from an object by consciousness depend upon the conscious mechanism itself, and cannot be held to exist inherently in the object. For example, although a table does have positive physical attributes (as in Sautrantika), in order to be recognized as a table these attributes must be noted, aggregated, and judged by the perceptual process. There is no inherent "tableness," only a positive process of building up more complex, abstract, and general features from simpler ones, of "imputing them by brain processing."

Concepts as descending exclusions

How might the brain solve the problem of getting from general notions to precise detail? At present it is tenable that conceptual objects are formed based on negative exclusions being propagated *down* the processing hierarchy from abstract levels to the fine details, in a fashion similar to that suggested by Sautrantika. This view is based upon the notion that while perceptual information ascends the processing hierarchy in a positive fashion, conceptual information can descend the hierarchy in a negative fashion and thereby become mixed with the incoming sensory percept. [149]

ASCENDING PERCEPTUAL INFORMATION

In this understanding, perception functions as described already, but concurrently with conceptualization. In other words, there is perceptual information being propagated up through the hierarchy in its normal way while conceptualization is taking place. Each level is therefore posited to contain some information that has arisen from direct perception, and some from conceptualization. The perceptual information spans from the most detailed representations, such as points of light, to the most complex, such as faces or spatial relations, just as described above, and the conceptual information covers much of the same span.

DESCENDING, NEGATIVE CONCEPTUAL INFORMATION

The different aspect of this view is that conceptual information is proposed to be projected back *down* the processing hierarchy from above in a negative, exclusionary, or permissive fashion. For example, the meaning generality or mental semblance of a pot would be represented at the highest levels, and this would exclude inappropriate details at lower levels, leaving only appropriate features to manifest. So, in this example, flat objects, square objects, and so forth would be excluded from the image without actively selecting particular positive features in their place. These features would be allowed to manifest by a permissive mechanism rather being forced into place by a positive necessitating mechanism. Neurally, at each level in the hierarchy the information in an abstracted image map would actively exclude inappropriate details at the next lowest level by simply turning them off, leaving all of the possibilities of appropriate details remaining.

One of the nice features of this model is that it poses a solution of the question of how a mental exclusion can seemingly negate an infinite number of things (all of the things that do not correspond to it) in the finite period of time that it takes to have a thought. Unfortunately, this question does not seem to arise in the Gelugpa tradition, which does not tend to consider mechanisms, and I had a great deal of difficulty in explaining it to Tibetans. If we imagine the exclusion process as a machine, then we need to know how the machine can exclude so many things at once, and this hierarchical model suggests that it does it recursively, by having each step exclude the inappropriate subdetails below in parallel and at the same time. This also allows that only the *relevant* sub-details actually need to be excluded actively, not all possible sub-details.

INSEPARABLE MIXING OF THE OBJECT OF ENGAGEMENT AND THE MEANING GENERALITY

This understanding of hierarchical exclusion accords closely with the Sautrantika position regarding the intimate mixing of meaning generality and real object that characterizes conceptual thought. When conceptualization takes place at the time that an object is present there are two processes going on simultaneously in the same physical space:

there is a positive, ascending perception which is working its way up through successive levels from the sense organ, and at the same time there is an exclusionary, negative, descending conceptualization. Since they are using the same physical space, clearly the two will interact. The idea is that the two processes flow through the same areas of the brain in a simultaneously ascending and descending cascade, and that the two cascades become thoroughly mixed at each level where they meet. At each level the information is mixed because it shares the same maps and the same space for its images, and only this mixed information is then left to flow onwards to further levels, either upwards or downwards. In this way no clear distinction remains between the information derived from the object and the information derived from the concept, the two are inseparably fused.

Putting this another way, the concept selects the percept and the percept shapes the concept until a unified whole is formed. If the concept of reality and the perception of reality do not match, then an interaction will take place so that the appearing object of consciousness will tend to be a composite of the two. Because of the cyclic relationship suggested here, concept and percept are mixed in the sense that they affect each other's very creation and development—they arise and cease together.

COMPARING THE TWO SYSTEMS AND CONSIDERING UNANSWERED QUESTIONS

Now that we have gone over the presentations of these two traditions in brief, it is possible to consider how they might interact and what can be learned from this interaction. For now, I will consider a few central points which are debated within each tradition, with the hope that some new insights can be gained by inspiration from the other tradition's perspective.

Some debated points within the Gelugpa presentation of Sautrantika

TERM AND MEANING GENERALITIES—SEPARATE OR UNITED?

What is the relationship between thought and language? This age old question has expressed itself in the form of a set of detailed debates in the Gelugpa scholastic tradition, but there are now some powerful new arguments to be added based on what has been learned about the structure of the brain. These debates center around the exact definition of conceptuality and the object of a conceptual mind. Does a concept necessarily contain a separate verbal component and nonverbal comprehending component or are these two united? This debate stems from difficulty in translating the Sanskrit word *shabdartha* (Tibetan *sgra don*), or term-meaning, from the original texts.[150] Some scholars assert that this word's referent has two separate components, a term generality and a meaning generality, whereas others maintain that this is a cumbersome and misleading distinction and that a concept is best thought of as a "meaning of the term," which includes both aspects of the word *shabdartha*. This issue obviously has strong implications for how thought in general is posited to function, and these will be discussed in terms of brain function below. The different Gelugpa standpoints are summarized here.

Separate components of concepts
The Gelugpa scholar Jam-bel-Sam-pel defines a conceptual consciousness as

> a determinative knower that apprehends a sound [or term] generality and a meaning generality as suitable to be mixed.[151]

This definition is also shared by Jam-yang-shay-ba and Pur-bu-jok.[152] The definition states that the term and meaning generalities are suitable to be mixed, instead of stating that they actually *are* mixed, because:

> According to Pur-bu-jok [and others], there are consciousnesses that apprehend only sound and meaning generalities, for example apprehending just the sound generality 'pot' without associating it with its meaning or just the meaning generality of pot without associating it with its name. Thus all conceptual consciousnesses are not necessarily cases of the association of a sound [or term] and meaning generality.[153]

Jam-yang-shay-ba concurs and adds that

> not all conceptual consciousnesses are cases of the association of a sound and a meaning generality....When conceptual consciousnesses are divided there are two [separate kinds]: those affixing names and [those affixing] meanings.[154]

This definition of conceptuality also solves the problem of animals and children untrained in language, both of which are presumed to use conceptual thoughts but not terms. It is noted that:

> A child untrained in language does not associate the term 'pot,' for example, with its meaning but does have a thought consciousness apprehending a pot.[155]

This presentation of concepts stresses the separation of terminological designations and semblances related to meaning. It is suggested that one starts out with a mere term generality which describes or names some phenomenon, and gradually one builds a meaning generality until the term is no longer needed; ultimately full understanding of the meaning of the term, and thereby full understanding of the determined object, can take place.

A united "meaning of the term"

Other historical scholars, notably Jang-gya Rol-bay Dor-jay in his Presentation of Tenets, suggest that a mental semblance should not be considered as two separate parts but as a united "meaning of the term." Jang-gya Rol-bay Dor-jay cites Tsong-kha-pa as explaining that

> *shabdartha* is not to be interpreted [as a compound structure] and divided into "term generality and meaning generality" [because the sense that an internal image is what is expressed or referred to by a term would be lost].[156]

Jang-gya Rol-bay Dor-jay suggests that it is more important for the definition to convey an understanding of conceptuality than to cover all possible cases, and he believes that it is important to maintain an understanding of an integrated image because errors can result from trying to break this image into two separate parts.

SEPARATE REPRESENTATIONS OF TERMS AND MEANINGS IN THE BRAIN

If a concept has two separate components, one verbal and the other nonverbal and comprehending, then is it possible to find these two parts within the brain? Surprisingly enough, the simple answer seems to be yes. The brain is known to have separate areas for processing language and processing other types of information, such as visual images, tactile sensations, sounds and so forth. Current understanding shows that the visual areas of the brain seem to hold an image of a pot, for example, and that this is physically separated from the linguistic representation of the word "pot," which exists in language areas.

In most cases these two representations are intimately associated and one conceives of both together, but in some cases they can be temporarily or even permanently separated. Since these two aspects of a concept can be physically located within the brain, they can also be physically separated, and this has been done experimentally, providing a strong argument that they are best considered as independent entities which are intimately associated. There are patients who have undergone a major surgical procedure which severs the normal link between the left and right sides of the brain in order to control otherwise intractable epilepsy. Fortunately, these patients are amazingly unimpaired by this drastic surgery. By allowing themselves to be psychologically tested after their surgery, these patients have led to most of the understanding of the different characters of the two sides of the brain which is now commonly known. The left side of the brain is normally most involved with language representations, while the right side contains some forms of nonverbal or "meaning" representations (among many, many other things), and in these patients the two have been permanently separated.

Although these patients seem in most ways surprisingly unimpeded by this drastic procedure, it is possible to create special circumstances that allow one to demonstrate the permanent separation of different aspects of their mental lives. This is possible because the left side of the perceived world is mostly processed by the right brain and vice versa, so information which is presented on the left side in the correct circumstances will only be processed by half of the mental and neural system. In particular, since the language areas are normally on the left side of the brain, when these patients are presented with an object on the left side of their face they will often not be able to name it, describe it, or show verbal understanding of it, because the verbal sector of their brain never really experiences the object and can't get the message from the part that did. However, the patient may still be able to use the object in many other respects (writing with a pen, combing their hair with a comb, etc.), showing that the right half of their brain has certainly recognized the meaning of the object in some sense. Conversely, if the object is presented to the other side of the same patient, the patient might be able to name it and talk freely about it but not know what it is for.[157] There are many other examples of the kinds of dissociations of function which this surgery creates, all suggesting that different aspects of the mind are truly subserved by different parts of the brain which can act somewhat independently but are normally strongly linked together.

There are also patients who have had either the predominantly language parts of their brains or the predominantly non-language parts of their brains permanently damaged by some form of injury (usually a stroke). Some of these patients have essentially no language under-standing remaining but are able to manipulate objects normally, sug-gesting that the correlates of term generalities have been stripped away leaving the correlates of meaning generalities behind. Others show the opposite syndrome of being able to describe objects but not use them. There are also cases of patients who have lost particular parts of each of these capacities, like people who fail to recognize certain classes of objects (perhaps living things for example) while being able to rec-ognize other kinds of objects.[158] The many studied patients that show these types of phenomena strongly support the notion that term and meaning generalities are best considered as separate entities which can be acquired and lost individually, but are generally used in com-bination and strongly related.

THE MODE OF ARISING OF MENTAL DIRECT PERCEIVERS

Another commonly debated point within the Gelugpa regards how concepts arise; what actually happens between perception and thought that serves as the liaison between the two. There are three views within the Gelugpa formulation of Sautrantika regarding how mental direct perceivers which cognize sense objects are produced, and these three theories are called alternating production, production of three types, and production at the end of a continuum.[159] These were set out by Prajnakaragupta, the Brahmin Shankarananda, and Dharmottara, all commentators on Dharmakirti. These will be outlined here, along with some of the philosophical arguments regarding them, in preparation for a discussion of this topic in the light of cognitive neuroscience.

Alternating production

The proponents of alternating production assert that following one moment of sense direct perception there is a moment of mental direct perception and following this the two types of awareness alternate in succession. The Gelugpa position argues against this because if there were a moment of conceptual consciousness intervening between suc-cessive moments of direct perception then the first moment of direct perception could not cause the next one because of the time lag. This contradicts the Gelugpa view that the second moment of direct per-ception, a subsequent cognizer, has as one of its substantial causes the preceding prime cognizer.[160]

Production of three types

This position of the production of three types posits that three different types of consciousness take place immediately in the wake of direct perception. Following the moment of sense direct perception there
is one moment of three simultaneous consciousnesses: a second moment of the sense direct perceiver, a first moment of a mental direct
perceiver apprehending the form, and a self-knowing direct perceiver
which experiences both. This position is argued against by the
Gelugpas for two reasons, both based on how many consciousnesses
are possible at once. The first reason is that if there are two consciousnesses directed outwards, apprehending the sense object and the mind
object, then there would need to be two inwardly directed self-knowers
to experience these, making a total of four consciousnesses, not three
as suggested. This contradicts the notion that there is only one moment of a given type of consciousness at a time. Consciousnesses are
explained to take place in a series, not more than one at time. It is also
argued that since even the three consciousnesses posited in this explanation take the same object, they contradict the Buddha's statement
that "each sentient being has only one continuum of each consciousness."[161] This point in particular will be argued against from a scientific perspective below.

Production at the end of a continuum

The mode of production posited by Tsong-kha-pa, the founder of the
Gelugpa sect, and followed by most Gelugpa scholars, is that a single
smallest moment of a mental direct perceiver is produced at the end
of a continuum of sense direct perceivers and shares the same object.
This position is supported by the authoritative Gelugpa texts of Pan-
chen So-nam-drak-ba and Jam-yang-shay-ba,[162] and also seems most
commensurate with the present understanding of the brain.

CONCURRENT PERCEPTUAL AND CONCEPTUAL THOUGHT

The model of the arising of conceptuality that seems most concordant
with current brain research, as I hope is clear, is that conceptualization
and perception take place together, with each percept having the
opportunity to evoke a concept in its wake. There is no obvious analog
to the notion of a mental direct perceiver in this presentation; it is sup-
planted by an understanding of a continuum from perception to conception. As a perception arises and ascends the hierarchy a conceptual

understanding is posited to be superimposed as part of the very same process, as described above.

In this model a single continuum of moments of awareness taking place through time is replaced by many simultaneous continua of processes ascending through a hierarchy which spans across locations in the brain, across levels of complexity, and across the time that these processes take to become complete. Whereas Tsong-kha-pa suggests that mental direct perception and then conceptualization take place at the end of a temporal continuum of many direct perceptions, the idea here is that conceptualization takes place at the far end of a representational continuum of what appears to consciousness. Conceptualization is still suggested to take place in the wake of direct perception and at a later time, but, in addition, it is also suggested to explicitly involve greater levels of abstraction and generality and so to take place at the end of a continuum of generality as well.

The ideas of brain function presented here do not accord well with either of the other two presentations of the formation of mental direct perceivers and conceptual consciousnesses. There is no evidence for alternating production of conceptual and direct consciousnesses; in fact the evidence available suggests just the opposite, that the two take place concurrently. There is also no reason that I am aware of, from a scientific standpoint, to posit the need for three simultaneous moments of consciousness together. Conceptualization can take place directly as a result of perception (or memory, or reasoning); one does not need to suggest that there is a duplicate second moment of perception, another duplicate which is a mental direct perceiver, and a third duplicate which is a self-knower. Although I know of nothing which explicitly contradicts the existence of these three moments of consciousness, it seems unnecessary and cumbersome to posit them. The mode of Production of Three Types also clings to the notion that moments of consciousness are separate and unitary which has now been repeatedly undermined. In short, an enlargement of the Gelugpa position on the production of concepts that was posited by Tsong-ka-pa regarding the production of conceptuality seems most satisfactory from the standpoint of brain function.

SPANNING THE TWO TRUTHS—GENERAL AND SPECIFIC OBJECTS

A fundamental tenet of Sautrantika is that there are generally and specifically characterized objects, which are the objects of thought and of perception respectively, and it is possible to consider what is known about the brain in a similar light and perhaps gain some detail in the process. As has been mentioned, it is well documented that the lower levels of the representational hierarchy are involved primarily with specific detail and have little ability to generalize, while the higher levels tend to be more abstract and general in their representations. These higher level representations do indeed seem to generalize according to "convention" or "imputation" in recognizing the similarities between objects or in representing one object as being the same from day to day. They also seem more susceptible to the effects of attention and expectancy and the like. They seem excellent candidates for the brain correlates of the "conventions" suggested by the term conventional truth, and for the generalizing capability of imputation by thought.

Conversely, the lower levels of the system represent fine detail and have less ability to generalize or be affected by attentional effects. These representations are much less affected by the observer and more closely mimic a mere reflection of the aspect of the object, without involving inferences about it. Thus they can be said logically to be "not merely imputed by thought." The lowest levels of the representational hierarchy thus seem a suitable neural substrate for the appearing objects of direct perception.

This speculation suggests direct correlates in the brain of the "two truths" of Sautrantika, correlates which presumably must exist somewhere in the brain if the Sautrantika presentation is correct, and it also suggests the idea of a continuum between the two, as opposed to a sharp division. Traditional Sautrantika certainly posits a firm distinction between the two truths, but this itself leads to problems of marginal cases. For example, mental direct perceivers are held to be impermanent, ever-changing phenomena completely unaffected by the conceptual mind, while mental images are held to be permanent, completely static, and to contain no specific details. There is no middle ground posited, which poses a real difficulty for the notion that conceptuality can gradually induce the formation of directly perceiving awarenesses. It also seems counter-intuitive to posit that all mental images are completely static when they seem to change from moment to moment, as even some Gelugpas have noted.[163] Perhaps the idea of a continuum existing between directly perceived truths and concepts solves some of these problems, and suggests how a person might shift their mode of awareness from the conceptual to the perceptual end of the continuum during the process of realization of an object, the goal of this entire presentation for the Gelugpas.

Gen Damcho (Photo: Christopher deCharms)

11   A Discussion with Gen Damcho—Objects of Thought

Gen Damcho received his Geshe degree from Drepung Loseling, studying first in Tibet and then in India. Until his untimely death in February, 1997, he was the principal of the Institute of Buddhist Dialectics in Dharamsala. He was particularly noted for his expertise in Abhidharma and buddhist epistemology. Sherab Gyatso, who kindly translated these interviews, is also a teacher at the Institute of Buddhist Dialectics and a superb translator for difficult technical material such as this. In this interview, we discussed many aspects of the Sautrantika presentation of conceptuality. We particularly focused on the objects taken by the mind during thought, and on clarifying the definitions within the Sautrantika system.

THE MEANING GENERALITY OR MENTAL SEMBLANCE OF AN OBJECT OF THOUGHT

CdC: I am very interested in the Tibetan presentation of the precise nature of the mental objects that arise to the mind during thought, and I wonder if Genla would like to speak about this from the Sautrantika perspective. In the Sautrantika view, what is the object that appears to the mind during conceptualization?

Gen Damcho: During thought, the meaning generality, or mental semblance, is seen as the veil that obscures the mind from direct awareness. It is the veil that comes between. The meaning generality is likened to a veil in the sense that it is the medium that lets us get to the mind's conceptual object during thought. You do get at the object, or engage with the object, but it is not through seeing the object directly. What you see is a type of appearance which arises in the mind which is similar to the object. It is similar to the object to allow you to understand the object, to get at the object.

CdC: So the meaning generality is likened to the veil itself or to the appearance in the veil?

Gen Damcho: The meaning generality is likened to the appearance of the veil. The meaning generality is the appearance, not the object itself.

If my hand grabs my leg through my robe, we certainly cannot say my hand is not grabbing my leg. If we ask whether my hand is grabbing my leg directly, well, not exactly, because there is something between. The hand is not directly holding onto the leg, but it is holding it nonetheless. In the same way, the mind does get at its object, but not directly. It has to go through an intermediate.

The thing which comes between is a medium which we must rely upon and which will necessarily come between oneself and the object. That is something which appears very similar to the object, but is not the object itself, the meaning generality. It is something similar which arises to that mind.

REALIZATION OF AN OBJECT THROUGH CONCEPTUALITY OR DIRECT PERCEPTION

It is said that a different sort of process can occur or can be used in the Buddhist practice. There are certain objects which are not simple objects of sense perception, they are not that gross or manifest in their form. (These are objects which can only first be understood by explanation, not by perception, like the atomic structure of matter.) One's initial access to these can only be by way of a mental image. Those mental images are formed by reading texts and so forth and gradually getting a clear understanding of what the object is. It is said that eventually, after a very long process of practice, the clearer one's understanding of the object becomes the less need there is to rely upon the generic image. Eventually the generic image fades away, and then the mind is directly experiencing the object without the need for the medium of the generic image. This is a conceptual mind which is transformed into a direct state of mind, translated as a yogic direct perceiver.

When we see something directly, the object is presenting itself directly to us with all of its features. We are not simply seeing just the cup; *all* of the features are appearing or arising to the mind. Even the subtle features of the cup, things like its being impermanent, and a functioning thing, and a product, and so forth, are appearing to the eye consciousness. That does not mean that a person will be aware of those or understand them. For the specifically characterized phenomena, such as a cup, when they appear to the mind, then all of the features must appear to the mind also.

OBJECT NAME USED			WHAT IT CORRESPONDS TO	
Tibetan	Here	Elsewhere	Direct Perceiver	Conceptual Mind
'jug yul	Engagement	Operation	actual object	actual object
zhen yul	Determined	Referent	not used	actual object
snang yul	Appearing	Appearing	actual object	mental semblance
bzung yul	Apprehended	Apprehending	actual object	mental semblance

Table of terms used in this interview, with comparison to other sources, taken from previous chapter.

THE FOUR TYPES OF OBJECTS OF A MIND

CdC: These different features of an object which appear to mind are described in some detail in terms of the types of object appearing to consciousness. I wonder if you could give a presentation of the four types of objects of consciousness which are used to distinguish directly perceiving minds from minds of conceptuality. I have not been able to understand exactly what the distinctions among them are, and I have also found differing translations of the terms themselves. [See the above table for the translation used here.]

Gen Damcho: In order to describe the objects of consciousness we need to establish some standard terms. The exact translations are not perfect, but to not have confusion we need to be consistent. The usual way of translating is as the object of engagement, object of appearance, apprehended object.

CdC: I have heard the terms referent and determined objects used also in relation to conceptual minds.

Sherab Gyatso: We will use determined object for now.

Gen Damcho: Yes, so then we have four: the object of engagement, determined object, appearing object, and apprehended object. Of those four terms, then, only three can be talked of as regards direct perceivers. The term "determined object" does not apply here.

OBJECTS OF A CONCEPTUAL MIND

The main distinction between conceptualization and perception is that with the direct perceiver the object is coming from "out there," it is presenting itself to the mind. With the conceptual mind that is not the case. There is no object which is coming towards the mind. The action is more coming from the side of the mind itself. In this case there is a generic image in the mind. The term used for a generic image, we could almost use representation in English, is something which is similar to the object which represents the object for the person. The person is not actually directly getting at the object itself, the generic image acts as a medium for them. In that sense it has to be something, from the point of view of the person, which is *similar* to the object.

CdC: Shall we say a mental semblance?

Sherab Gyatso: Yes, that term is fine.

Gen Damcho: So we use an analogy. If we consider the difference between the two objects, it is like the example that if you have the cloth between your fingers and then you hold the table, you are holding the table in a sense, but you are not. There is something between you and the object. When the cloth is not there then you are holding it directly. [When the cloth is there], instead of the object of engagement, you are still getting at the object, you are still getting at the table, but you are doing so by means of a medium. The medium is sometimes described as an obscurer because it obscures the object as it exists for a direct perception. Even though it is a medium for one's understanding, it still stands between the mind and the object as compared with a direct experience.

Once you get a direct experience, then there is no need to depend upon the medium any more. If we are experiencing form directly, if we are looking with our eyes, and then if we close our eyes and then recall the form, then it seems as though someone throws a veil over our understanding or experience of the object. Our conceptual experience is nothing like as clear and lucid as in the direct experience.

So, to relate this to the objects of the conceptual mind, because the conceptual mind is not getting at the form directly, because it has to rely upon a medium, the form itself is not said to be the appearing object. You can also say that it is not the apprehended object. The form is the object of engagement and the determined object. Even though the mind is not getting at it directly because it is relying upon a medium—something which is similar to the object, something which represents the object to the mind—still the mind does get at that object. Because it does still get at the object or ascertain it, then it is called the object of engagement, the determined object.

CdC: So can we also distinguish the difference between the first two types of objects and the difference between the second two types of objects?

Gen Damcho: Let us start with the first two. Direct perception is a bare perception. With a conceptual mind there is no longer a bare perception of the object, one can no longer get at it exactly as it is, one has to get at it by means of a medium. Now with those two objects, the object of engagement and the determined object, there is no difference from the point of view of what they are talking about. If you talk about a conceptual mind apprehending form, then what you might give as examples of either the object of engagement or the determined object could be the same. The reason for having the two is that they represent two slightly different ways of the mind looking at the same thing. From the point of view of the action of the mind, the object of engagement has this property of...the word is something like entering into or getting at the object. This is one possible perspective of the mind relative to the object.

The perspective that one takes in looking at an object as a determined object is this: the conceptual mind has the ability to judge something, such as the judgment "this is a form," "this is not a form," and judgments like that. In terms of their ability to see or realize something as form, then, the direct perceiver and the conceptual mind do not differ, they can both realize form in this way. But it is only the conceptual mind which is able to judge one thing as being something, and distinguish it, saying this is a form, this is something else. That distinguishing is what the determined object means in this case, and this is why the term determined object is not used in the case of direct perceivers.

CdC: Could you say a little bit more about exactly what sort of judging is taking place in the case of the determined object, but not the object of engagement?

Sherab Gyatso: They are terms that describe the same object, but are different ways of looking at the object. The object for the conceptual mind is the object of engagement, or it is the determined object. In describing why an object is the object of engagement, you will be talking about a particular feature of the mind at that point, the engaging feature. When you talk about the feature of referring to something then you talk about the determined object, but in fact both point to the same object. We shouldn't say that the object is different, but that they are different perspectives on the same object, on the same mind. These are just slightly different features of the same mind.

CdC: And that is why, since they are both one, they can both be considered as the realized object.

Gen Damcho: If we are talking about the object realizing minds, then yes.

CdC: I would still find helpful a bit of distinction about what it is that is referred to or judged in the determined object.

Sherab Gyatso: The word actually means some form of attachment. It is translated as determined but in Tibetan it actually means some form of attachment to something.

Gen Damcho: In this sense, once we attach to something, then there is a sort of certainty in the mind. One holds on to it as being a certain thing, having a certain feature, or just existing in a certain way. This is also true with the conception. From the point of view of describing these things as the determined object, there is a sort of confidence. We are able to say, "this is form," and in that way distinguish it from other things. There is a certain confidence or thinking, that is just the way it is. You get it right if you have a particular object and you are able to distinguish it correctly. For example, saying "form is form," one thing is another. The understanding can act as the basis for acting in accordance with the way things exist. You are not going to make a mistake. If you get it wrong, however, if you think that something is one thing when in fact it is not, then the conceptual mind sort of latches onto that understanding, even though it is incorrect, and in latching on there is a sense of making this mistake concrete. If you then do something on the basis of that, you make mistakes.

CdC: So is this referring or judgment the idea that is gotten across by the phrase "this is that?" That is a phrase that I have heard often about conceptual minds, which I take to mean that they equate one thing with something else by using categories.

Gen Damcho: Yes, they are the same thing.

CdC: Could you give a distinction between the appearing object and the apprehended object?

Gen Damcho: Again, they are synonyms. The example of either is the same, but again they are slightly different perspectives on what the object represents for the mind. When you say appearing object then it is the thing which is appearing to the mind, the aspect which is appearing to the mind. The apprehended object is the thing which the mind grasps onto because it is the medium. It is the thing which the mind has to hold onto to get to the object. From that point of view it is called the apprehended object.

Sherab Gyatso: Again, I don't like this translation here as it is not actually ascertained.

Gen Damcho: It is the thing which the mind is holding onto.

CdC: Does this distinction apply to direct perceivers as well as conceptuality?

Gen Damcho: Yes.

CdC: So it sounds as if a similar distinction is being made between the first two objects and the second two (for the case of conceptual minds).

Gen Damcho: Yes, that is right.

OBJECTS OF A DIRECTLY PERCEIVING MIND

Gen Damcho: The appearing and apprehended objects are said to be synonymous for direct perceivers. They both describe the same object. You can also use another term, translated as the explicit object. So for direct perceivers there is *no* distinction between the two terms translated as appearing object and apprehended object. We must distinguish which objects share which types of features.

There is a technical term used to explain those types of features which are of the same substance as the object in place, time, and nature. This is often translated that they share the "same mode of abiding." These things which make up part of the substance of an object, which share its same mode of abiding, you cannot ascertain unless you do it conceptually. You cannot ascertain that a form is a product, and that it is impermanent and momentary and so forth directly through perception. They are things which come together as one bundle with form itself. They also come bundled together for perception of any direct experience of form. When you have a direct experience of form, form is casting its aspect toward a directly perceiving mind. Because an object casts an aspect of form, the aspect of the form's impermanence and other subtle features which share the same mode of abiding with form have to be cast as well. Although they appear to the mind, say the eye consciousness of a direct perceiver, they are not apprehended. One does not ascertain these different subtle features.

This is the basis of the distinction between the engaged object of the mind and the appearing or apprehended object of the mind. When we are just looking at form, then form itself is the engaged object. These other things which necessarily come along as part and parcel of a direct experience of form (i.e. its impermanence and so forth), make up the appearing and apprehended objects.

Sherab Gyatso: This is the problem with the translation "apprehended object," it in fact refers to an object which is not ascertained at all.

CdC: So it is possible that the object can be "apprehended" but not ascertained?

Sherab Gyatso: Yes. Apprehended is a poor translation because there is no sense of any apprehension or understanding of it at all, it is just appearing. Nonetheless, as this is commonly used, we will continue with it.

Gen Damcho: So the things like the impermanence of the form and the other subtle properties which share the same mode of abiding with the form but are not ascertained are features of the appearing object and they are features of the apprehended object. They are not the engaged object. A normal person cannot ascertain those from direct experience. [They *are*, however, ascertained through direct experience in more discerning perceivers, according to the Sautrantika view.]

Why do they always come together? If you look at these two cups, for example, they are different substances. One does not depend on the other in any way. They are completely separate. On the other hand, when you have something like these different qualities of form [which share the same mode of abiding with the form itself], then from the point of view of form casting an aspect towards consciousness they are together in a sort of bundle. You cannot have one without the other.

Just because the object is there, just because the object is form, then it is also impermanent, for example. Because form itself casts an aspect towards the consciousness, then the impermanence of it and these other subtle things such as it being a product and so forth, they are also part of that aspect which is cast.

Those things that we mentioned, like impermanence and so forth, they *must* arise as part of the object in terms of experience. So they are indeed appearing to the mind, but there is no way that a normal person can ascertain or distinguish those subtle features. The difference with the mere form itself is that it is not only appearing to the person, but the person can distinguish it, they can ascertain it. So, as well as being the appearing object, the mere form is also the object of engagement.

Everything which is appearing, the form and all of these different subtle qualities which I mentioned earlier, are appearing to the mind so they are appearing objects of the mind, and also the apprehended objects because these two terms have the same meaning for direct perception. Of those, it is only the form which the person is able to really ascertain, not these subtle characteristics. Because it is the form which they are able to ascertain and really understand, this is called the object of engagement.

CdC: So the object of engagement of the mind does not include things like subtle impermanence. It does not include all of the subtle things which share the same mode of abiding with the object. It doesn't include emptiness or any of those things. The object of engagement is only the simplest aspects of form which the mind is getting at and ascertaining.

Gen Damcho: Yes. To put it the usual way: if, for example we take an eye consciousness apprehending form, then the object of engagement is form. In one sense, the main object which the mind is understanding is the object of engagement, the object it is getting at, and it is only what is ascertained, nothing more.

The impermanence of the object is there, as part of the form. One cannot separate them in terms of the experience, so it does cast an aspect towards the consciousness. They share the same mode of abiding in place, time, and nature. They all appear to the mind. However, a person normally cannot ascertain them. Since the person cannot ascertain them they are said not to be included in the object of engagement. They are the appearing object and the apprehended object. That is the division between the two.

The distinction of the objects of the mind of direct perceivers should be clear now. There are only three types of objects which are used in this case. Of those three, the thing which is the main object, which is not only appearing to the mind but which the mind is able to ascertain is the engaged object, in our example, form. The other aspects of the object, which one cannot separate from the object itself in terms of a direct experience of it, do appear to the mind but are not ascertained, and they are the appearing object and the apprehended object. Because one cannot ascertain them from the experience, they are not the object of engagement.

THE REASON FOR POSITING EXCLUSION OBJECTS (ISOLATES)

CdC: Now I would like to ask about the reason for the presentation of double negative exclusion objects. First I wanted to just mention why I think that this is important. I am excited about the idea of double negative exclusion objects in terms of its implications for understanding the brain, because I think that it has the possibility to add some insight into a number of unsolved problems in my own field. I wanted to very briefly present what the standard idea in neuroscience is, and that I think this idea may be leading to some problems. That is why I am interested in learning to understand about exclusions.

First of all, although the standard neuroscience perspective today is one of positive building up of features, I want to distinguish that it is not equivalent to the refuted Samkhya view of an inherent positive nature that can be found within an object. Taking the example of a table, the neuroscience view is that the way that one understands a table is not through recognizing an inherent "tableness" which is posited to exist [which would be analogous to the Samkhya position], but by aggregating different features. To give a very simplified idea, if you see vertical lines of light, the simplest aggregation is to put the points of light together to form lines. These lines are then aggregated to form the idea of a vertical pillar or leg, and then all of these kinds of objects are aggregated together by the brain to have the understanding of a table. The features exist positively and are aggregated positively, as opposed to being aggregated negatively through exclusion as they are in Sautrantika.

I think that I have some degree of understanding about what the different kinds of negatives are, but, especially as regards mental exclusions/affirming negatives, I was wondering if you could present what the reason for having this double negative viewpoint is—why this understanding is superior to an understanding of building up positive features.

Gen Damcho: When we see an object such as a vase, which is the usual example, obviously just by seeing it we do not gain the understanding that it is a vase. We are not able to say in each case that we see a vase, "this is a vase." This relies upon someone helping us to make the connection between the essential features of a vase and the name. There is a definition of a vase, and we talk about three characteristics for this example: it has a round belly, a flat base, and it is able to perform the function of holding water. What one relies upon to conceptually understand what a vase is and then to apply that to other examples, is someone else's help to make the connection between the name (the term), and the object. So another person helps to know how to use the term correctly. They will use a specific example and draw the attention to certain features. Something which has those features, in which those features are present, is called a vase. Now if the person has understood correctly, then at a subsequent time, when they meet another object which has the same features, then they are also going to be able to see that and judge that it is a vase.

At the time when a person initially learns a new term, are the objects which are not essential features of the term excluded, from the point of view of the person learning the term? The answer from this person's perspective is yes, these other features have to be excluded. It is only those features which are essential to understanding the vase in that situation, and which can later be applied to other situations, which have to be carried through in memory. Only those features are going to be understood at that point. In that sense, the mind has to be excluding the other features which are not those features, which are not essential to that understanding. In that sense the mind is engaging in its object in a negative or negating fashion.

The question is, from the point of view of the person learning the new term, at the time that they initially have this other person help them to learn how to apply the term correctly, are the objects which are not essential features of the vase excluded from that person's point of view. The answer from this person's perspective is yes, they have to be.

One has to make a distinction between the way that a direct perceiver engages in its object and the way that a concept does. One is said to be by way of the reality of the object, in the sense that all of the features of the object, whether one ascertains them or not, are part and parcel of the object. For example, its impermanence and so forth are part of the object, though not ascertained. You cannot separate those different features, including subtle features, in terms of how the object exists. A concept does not engage in its object by means of that reality. Rather, it takes only certain features; it can distinguish only certain features. If you have a number of objects before you on a table, then you can just pick one out. That is the way that the conceptual mind works, in the sense of picking out a certain feature. Even though the feature, for example the impermanence of the object, or its being a product, does not necessarily exist separately from the object in reality, still, from the point of view of a conceptual mind, the mind is able to distinguish those features as separate. When it does distinguish those features, it only takes a single feature to mind.

I am talking about the conceptual mind, in comparison with direct perception. With a directly perceiving mind you have the object of engagement. Along with the object of engagement you also have the appearing object to that mind with all of these different features arising, different features of the same object. Even though all of the features appear to the mind, it does not have to ascertain them all, they can just be appearing. That is not the same with the conceptual mind. For the conceptual mind all of these unascertained features do not appear. The only way that the conceptual mind gets at its object is by distinguishing a certain feature and taking that as the thing which it is paying attention to. In that sense, conceptualization is a process of exclusion. Just by choosing a certain object, choosing to pay attention to that object, the other objects which are not appearing to that mind are being put aside. The mind is able to discard those. It is obviously not a process in which the mind thinks, "I am not going to pay attention to these." Rather, just by paying attention to one object, the other things, like for example the form of the object, the impermanence of form, the product feature of form, and so forth, don't enter into that mind. It has only taken that one single feature to mind. In that sense it is a process of exclusion, it can discard those other features.

For the direct mind the object is out there, form. The object and generic image do not exist as separate things. When the direct mind engages in those forms there is no sense of its choosing its object. When the aspect is cast by an object to the direct mind, all of the features come together to that mind. With the conceptual mind, the generic image or terms *lead that mind into* the experience of the object. They act as a *medium*, the thing which the mind has to depend upon to get at the object. So, there is a certain amount of choosing that must take place in the sense that the mind is drawing out one particular feature of the object which, in reality, if we think of reality "out there," does not exist separately from the other features, or from the object. You can only do that, make that separation, by mentally distinguishing them. That is the way that the conceptual mind works, by mentally distinguishing them, taking one thing out and discarding everything else which is not essential to the interest of that mind or its understanding of the object. One does say that the form, for example, casts an aspect. It is only that which the mind is actually engaging in, it is only that which the mind is interested in or wants to get at, and because it is able to discard those other features which are not essential to that understanding, because in reality out there they do not exist as separate things, then there is a process of exclusion, because you are drawing one out and excluding the others. The others are excluded from that point of view. From that perspective you talk about conceptuality being a negative process.

CdC: Why do you choose to describe that as negative, the process of choosing one aspect of the object and pushing the others aside? It seems like you could either talk about the positive choosing of some aspects or of the negative pushing away of others. Why is it important to talk in the negative sense instead of in the positive sense?

Gen Damcho: What you are saying is true. If you have the example of the vase apprehending concept, from a negative point of view, a point of view of exclusion, it does get rid of those features which are not essential to that object, which are not the vase. In the end, you have just vase itself. But "vase itself" represents a positive feature to the mind, an affirming negative. You can talk about it either from a positive sense or from a negative sense. In terms of the experience, or getting at the experience, both of those features are necessary. You cannot talk about that as applying to all objects, because in that case we have to go into another explanation of some things being negative phenomena and some things being positive phenomena. "Vase," for example, is a positive phenomenon. When one generates a conceptual mind apprehending it, there is a sense of exclusion. You do have to get rid of those features which are not the vase from the point of view of that mind. It is not a direct excluding or negating process. When you have some other types of objects, like for example "opposite-from-not-being-pot," which is an example object used for the sake of discussion of this point, the way that that object arises to a conceptual mind is by directly excluding or negating. The way that it is going to appear to the mind is explicitly negative. If you take any other negative phenomenon, the way that it has to be understood by the mind is by directly excluding something else. In general we can say that for conceptual minds there is a process of exclusion. Dependent upon the main object of understanding we may or may not be able to also talk of a more positive sense in which the mind is engaging positively in the object. There are cases where objects are classed as negative, in the sense that the mind excludes those things which are not the object—the understanding of that object is by a process of direct exclusion. That is the way that the mind gets at the object.

CdC: I still do not understand why for the positive case objects—which seems like most objects (like the vase)—it is better to talk about conceptualization in terms of the negative sense instead of the positive sense. I can understand why you need to talk in those terms for something like an overtly negative object. For most objects, which have this positive sense, I do not understand why it is best to describe them in this somewhat confusing negative language.

Sherab Gyatso: Please let me interject here that what you might be coming across is that when Western interpreters have described this aspect of Abhidharma, they have principally said that the Buddhists talk about a concept, or the conceptual process, as being a process of exclusion. The emphasis is laid upon that. However, when the question was posed directly, Genla said that it is also true that there is a positive feature there. What it means for one to say that conceptuality is a process of exclusion is that one excludes all of those features which are not the object. What you may have is a difference in the stress. That is, the Western interpreters have chosen to stress this idea of conceptualization being a negative process. All that represents, as Genla has explained, is that it has to get rid of those features which are not the object.

CdC: Let me try to summarize this point and see if I understand it correctly. For objects like a table or a pen, it is in fact equally valid and equally helpful to describe one's conceptual understanding in terms of a positive process or in terms of a negative process, and the negative understanding is really only necessary for overtly negative objects.

Gen Damcho: What you are saying is true. If the object is a positive object, the distinction of positive and negative is just on the basis of the way that they arise to the mind, the way that the mind engages in them. The mind is led into experience of them by means of their terms and so forth, but from the point of view of positive objects, then yes, there are two features, there is the excluding process going on, but the object itself is casting a positive aspect upon the mind. There are two features.

CdC: Which of the objects of conceptuality is it that is casting the aspect, and can that aspect be either positive or negative? Can the meaning generality be cast in either positive or negative terms? I am asking a sort of two-pronged question here. First, which of the four objects is said to be the one which casts a positive aspect, and can this positive aspect then be mixed with a positive meaning generality for a conceptual mind?

Gen Damcho: The object which casts the aspect towards the conceptual mind is the first two objects, the objects of engagement and the determined object. Those two represent the aspect for a conceptual mind.

Even though that is the case, that aspect is not said to be the appearing object of the mind or the apprehended object. The aspect is the object of engagement and the determined object, but not the other two. Even though the object does cast an aspect to the mind, the way that the mind gets at it from its side is through the use of a medium. So the use of a medium is the thing that is actually relevant. The medium is said to be the appearing object. But, they do cast an aspect.

CONCEPTUAL AWARENESS OF A MENTAL OBJECT

Gen Damcho: In general a generic image is said to be a negative phenomenon. Negative objects are negative from the point of view of the way that they cast their aspect to the mind which apprehends them, the mind which they become the object of apprehension for, not the mind that they become the object of engagement for. If I think about a vase, I am doing so by means of a generic image which is appearing to my mind. The object which I am getting at is not the generic image, it is the thing which the medium is the medium for, that is the vase.

I can think about generic images, and then they can become the main object of my mind. In this case there is a generic image of a generic image. At that point the *engaged* object is a generic image. That mind will necessarily have a negative aspect cast towards it. The generic image which is being taken as an object will cast a negative aspect towards the mind. When it is not the main object of the mind, when it is the appearing object, then it does not have to be a negative object. It depends upon what is the main object.

CdC: I think that I understand. So, the meaning generality always casts a negative aspect when it is itself the object of engagement, but when it is the appearing object then it can have a positive aspect.

Gen Damcho: Depending on what the main object of the mind is.

CdC: It can be either positive or negative?

Gen Damcho: Yes. If someone asks in general, "What is the mental image?", then it is best to answer this question from the point of view of the mind which understands it. The mind which understands it is not, in general, the mind which it appears to. It is going to be a mind which holds it as the main object of its interest, the main object which it wants to understand. From that point of view it must appear as something which has a negative aspect.

A REFUTATION OF THE ULTIMACY OF PERCEPTION BY NEUROSCIENCE AND PRASANGIKA MADHYAMIKA

CdC: To end, I would like to talk about the neuroscience perspective in relation to the Prasangika Madhyamika refutation of the ultimacy of perception.[164] From the neuroscience perspective there are many reasons to say that the same or similar processes are taking place in perception and concept formation, and so for a number of different reasons it is possible to argue that they share the same status, in the sense that they can both be mistaken. There are examples like optical illusions where it can be shown in the brain that the mistakes of perception can be found to have a physical basis. In a sense, it seems a matter of subtlety whether one wants to call percepts fundamentally different from concepts or not. My understanding is that Madhyamika also draws out the issue that perception can be mistaken, and in that sense it is not an ultimate mind, and so is of the same status as the conceptual mind.

Gen Damcho: Maybe from a Western technical point of view it becomes difficult to say that there is a real distinction between perception and conception. From the Prasangika point of view there are two ways of analyzing things, these are translated as "conventional" analysis and "ultimate" analysis. In terms of conventional analysis there is a difference between the two, a quality difference. When you get down to making a more ultimate analysis, there is no clear distinction between the two. You are not going to be able to say that they are definitely different. You are not going to find a certain central feature to either one. You are not going to find anything at the end of the analysis which is going to be a direct perception or a conception. I wonder which of the two types of analysis you are talking about, conventional or ultimate. If you say the second one, then ultimately there is no distinction between the two, that is the answer.

CdC: In what sense is there no distinction between the two? How is it that through that analysis it becomes clear that, ultimately, there is not a distinction between them?

Gen Damcho: When you find the ultimate nature of them, they are both things which are imputed from the side of the mind. From that point of view they have the same nature, the same level of existence, the same type of existence. You are not going to find some intrinsic difference because the distinctions have to be made from the point of view of the imputing mind. Because those distinctions cannot stand up to an ultimate analysis, those distinctions are going to be dissolved from the point of view of an ultimate analysis. The distinction does not stand up to that sort of analysis.

12 A Discussion with Lati Rinpoche— Ideas, Concepts, and Terms

In this second section of discussions with Lati Rinpoche, we discuss the details of the Tibetan presentation of concept formation. This raises the general issue of the mechanism of the arising of concepts within the mind, and we particularly focus on the issue of how concepts arise through the exclusion from the mind of features which do not pertain to the object which is being contemplated. We also consider the role of verbal designation in conceptual thought—is it possible to think without words? This section is taken from several discussions in which we tried to come to terms with the differences and similarities between our two perspectives regarding this issue.

CAN A CONCEPT EXIST IN THE ABSENCE OF A TERM?

CdC: Perhaps I will give Rinpoche a thought teaser from my own tradition. In science there is a great deal of emphasis on language, as in the Tibetan system, but in addition we have a notion of concepts that are not directly connected with words. There is great debate about whether it is possible to have a concept which is not connected to a word, but there is accumulating evidence that this is possible, and this is my belief. Many scientists believe that some complete concepts may be made up of one part which is like a word and one part which is like an image or some other kind of understanding of something. For the case of mental images these have been described as a descriptive (word-like) component and a depictive (picture-like) component. It is possible that these two parts are closely connected but are nonetheless distinct, so one can in principle imagine each part of the concept existing independently of the other. There are some fascinating examples of this which have been shown to exist both using psychological tests and in patients with neurological problems.[165]

[In the Gelugpa tradition there is a long-standing debate, discussed in the accompanying text, about whether a concept is best thought of as a unified "meaning of the term," or as a two part object which contains a separate "term generality" and "meaning generality." This is clearly related to the question of whether verbal and nonverbal aspects of a concept can be imagined to be distinct.]

For example, there are some patients who have undergone a severe surgical manipulation which cuts the main connecting pathway from the right to the left sides of the brain. This has sometimes been done to treat people who have severe epileptic seizures which cannot otherwise be prevented, and it is often successful in preventing their seizures. Amazingly, these patients seem remarkably unaffected by this procedure unless one carefully tests them. In fact, if I met one of these patients on the street and talked with them for a while, I might not notice anything out of the ordinary about them. Nonetheless, what is interesting is that they seem to have a separation of two component parts of concepts, a separation of words from some forms of nonverbal understanding.

The overall idea here is simply that the word part of a concept exists primarily on the left side of the brain and the nonverbal part of the understanding on the right, and in these patients the two are separated and can be used completely independently in special circumstances. This is done by presenting an object, for example a pen, to each side of the patient's brain separately, by allowing the patient to view it only in one half of his or her field of view. If the pen is presented to the left side of the patient's brain, by showing the patient the pen in one half of his field of vision, then the patient will be able to name the pen immediately, showing that he has accessed his verbal understanding of the concept, but he will not know what to do with it, showing that this verbal recognition has been disconnected from his general understanding of the object and its use. On the other hand, if the pen is presented to the other side of his brain, he will know what it is for and may immediately pick it up and start writing with it, but he will not have any idea of its name. The clear implication of these examples, and many others, is that it is possible to have and use a concept which is mostly verbal, or one which is mostly nonverbal, and that a single concept need not encompass both of these aspects.

[This type of research is the basis of most of the popularized ideas about the different functions of the different sides of the brain. The idea that one side of the brain is more logical or linear and that the other is more spatially abstract, pictorial, intuitive, or nonlinear come from experiments of this sort. In these patients many kinds of problems can be posed in a way that accesses mainly one side of the brain or the other, but not both, and thus it is possible to see how the two sides function differently. The idea that within one brain, one organ of consciousness, there are different parts which use different ways of knowing at the same time, and can even compete with each other, has arisen from these studies.]

Rinpoche: Though that may be, there is still nothing anywhere but it has a name. Before the brain was severed, someone told the patient that the object was a pen. What I am trying to say is that until one person tells another person "this is the name of that," there is no way that the awareness "this is that" will ever come into being. An awareness of the type "this is that" is called a "language awareness," or "linguistic awareness."

We Buddhists have a category of manifest things and a category of hidden things. All physical objects are manifest things. However, even though they are manifest and there are awarenesses relative to that manifestation, still, before we will ever have an arising of an awarenesses of the sort "this is a table," we must have been taught the term by someone. Such awarenesses can have relationships to as many languages as may exist.

I would like to make a parallel. In your field you have two sides of the brain, and you divide those two sides. We have these two categories of conscious objects, manifest, and non-manifest or hidden. Hidden objects are brought to awareness based on language. You can only bring a hidden object into consciousness through language.

CdC: Could you give an example?

Rinpoche: Something which has to be thought about before it is understood or known is something which is hidden. For example, if you take the forces inside an atom, they each have to have a thought and a name in order to be understood. Your two sides of the brain seem similar to this understanding of ours. The language function seems to parallel the group of hidden objects which must be understood using the language function related to them, whereas the other side seems to parallel the objects which are immediately apprehensible, which do not require an inference or process of reasoning.

The hidden objects have to be apprehended through a thought process. In the Buddhist presentation the table is self-evident but some of its features are hidden and must be understood through a process of reason, such as its transitory nature, impermanence, or the fact that it has no essential essence to it. It is similar for the elements of material things. There are incredible energies within them which are not apparent but have to be thought about and can only be brought to mind through thought. Science, through thought and observation, has been able to talk about many of those energies and so forth. It is only through a process of reasoning that one can come to identify the different forces and so on that were originally hidden from the people who were investigating those objects, but the objects themselves, even at the beginning, seemed self-evident.

CONCEPTUALIZING OBJECTS THROUGH EXCLUSION

CdC: I hoped that we could speak about how perceptions turn into ideas. I wonder if Rinpoche could discuss the Tibetan perspective on this issue.

Rinpoche: Let us approach this issue from the perspective of conceptualization, of ideation. I will discuss the idea of inference within the larger framework of ideation in general. Any inferential knowledge which is true knowledge, as opposed to superstition or false understanding, can be discussed within the more general framework of conceptuality or ideation. When you look at how the mind is functioning—at how conceptualization goes on—what is it that you are looking at? In other words, what is your object? What is the idea? In this endeavor you are not thinking of the idea as the thing known, but thinking of the idea as the mind itself. When you have an idea that you are contemplating, what *is* the idea that is being looked at? That idea is actually a negative thing. It is simply an appearance. You are only going to get at the idea through, literally, the direct object of everything that it is not.

The technical word which is used to refer to that negative object is *dön chi* [*artha-samanya* in Sanskrit]. *Dön* means content or object, and *chi* means something like generality. So, this is an object generality, or a meaning generality.

The meaning generality itself is negatively framed. Its generality comes from its being negatively framed. That negativity is how it will get finally to its content. If a meaning generality is just an idea with no substance to it, and there can be all sorts of ideas like that, then although the process will be the same, it will never have any contact with reality.

So now some more terminology concerning "exclusions," in Tibetan called the *zhan sel*. *Zhan* means "something else." *Sel* means "eliminating other things." So these *zhan sel's* describe how this mind, this conceptualization, is coming at what it knows by eliminating something else. It is coming at *what it knows* through eliminating something else that it is ultimately going to find that *what it knows* is not. [In simpler language, the exclusion is arriving at an understanding of its object by eliminating all irrelevant or incorrect understandings and all understandings of other objects.]

There are different sorts of these eliminations talked of. The first of the *zhan sel* can be called content elimination, or real content elimination of other. The second is called the awareness elimination of other. The next is called the non-affirming negative elimination of other. These three terms are found in this presentation of concept formation. [These distinctions are made in greater detail in chapter 10.]

So, what is it that is appearing to the awareness? By awareness here I mean the idea, the concept. Let's take for example a book. You look at a book and have the idea, "that's a book." Now, in that process, you have the mind elimination of other, you have a mental exclusion. The mind elimination of other is *appearing* to that thought, although you cannot see it. In other words, if you have the thought of the book, the exclusion is appearing to you, but you cannot see it because it is, as it were, behind the curtain of the ideas. That book appearing to thought as the reverse of what it is not, *is* that book. The book itself *is* that. It appears to thought, to the thought, "that is the book." It appears to thought as the reverse of what it is not.

We are talking here about the thing which is closest to the awareness that is still an object, although that seems an odd way to put it. That object is called a *meaning generality*. The meaning generality also has the name "the mind exclusion of other," in Tibetan "*lo zhan sel-wa*." In other words the *dön chi* or the meaning generality, the *lo zhan sel* or the mind exclusion of other, are in fact what is *mediating* the thought.

You see, the meaning generality, the mental elimination of other, is made up. It is absolutely created by the mind. It is a figment of the imagination. To that extent it is permanent, in the sense that it is not a real, degenerating thing. [Here permanent is best thought of in the sense that an idea like "triangle" is permanent, the idea itself will not cease existing in the same way that a physical triangle will.] It is a mental figment, whereas that book on the table is not a mental figment in that sense. So do you follow what I mean by the real exclusion of the other?

CdC: I don't think so. Could you say a bit more?

Rinpoche: An idea can only look at one thing. So that locus around which an idea is forming, in other words the remainder which is being converged upon or realized by the thought, the "that" of the expression "this is that," relative to this locus of the idea which is being formed, it can be said of all of the other loci that each of them is not there. Not in the locus of the idea which is being formed.

[The point here is that the mind is forming an exclusion object by removing all objects contradictory to the object which it is thinking about. In other words, in thinking of a book the mind excludes all thoughts of things which are not books, and what is left is the semblance of a book, which is our thought.]

All three of these exclusions are objects, objects in the sense that the book is the object of the thought. The three of these function as objects when there is the idea "this is a book." When you have this sort of conceptual inference all three of these function together at the same time, although they are not all thought of. They are hidden—you are not seeing them in your mind. They are all functioning there together at the same time. They are all functioning as part of the idea. All of them have to function as objects. They function together as objects whenever you have a thought of the kind, "this is a book."

The object and the meaning generality in the mind appear absolutely mixed up together, which is why there is a distortion or a mistake in an idea necessarily. Mistake is perhaps too strong a word to use, distortion gives a better understanding. All of these are also reasons that a conceptual mind is also called a mind that excludes something else, a mind in possession of an exclusion object.

This is a difficult subject to talk about. It is difficult to explain and to understand.

HOW CONCEPTUALIZATION ARRIVES AT ITS EXCLUSION OBJECT

CdC: I agree [laughing]. I would like to ask specifically about how this negative inference or negative "mask" of all other objects takes place. When I see the book, the sensation of the book, as Rinpoche has said, comes upward, and then it seems that it is as if a mask comes down which excludes everything that is not the book. [This interpretation is an expansion of what is found in the traditional Buddhist texts, which seems in accord with some ideas from neuroscience, as is explained in detail in chapter 10.] In the case of the first exclusion it seems that it comes from my memory—that it is my own reaction—and it excludes everything which I imagine to not be the book. In that sense it is incomplete or general. My question is this: How are those things which will be excluded selected from all of the other things in my mind? In other words, how are the proper memories which are going to be excluded selected from the ones that are not going to be excluded?

Rinpoche: What comes to my mind is the comment of Dharmakirti [one of the main founders of Buddhist epistemological theory in India] in his text the *Pramanavartika*, that you can only process one idea at a time. This is the reason why only one idea comes at a specific time instead of two. Why do you only remember one thing at that time? The answer is because you can only process one thing at that very time. The mind cannot think two thoughts at the same time.

CdC: Okay. How is it that it is the "proper" one that arises? So that when I see the book the negative inference says "it's not a circle, it's not a tea cup, it's not a person," but somehow it doesn't say "it's not a book," and it doesn't even say "it's not rectangular"?

Rinpoche: Because the earlier reality that, as you put it, appeared in the sense of its coming up and causing the thought. That [earlier] one is superior to the thought, to the remembrance. The two appear mixed up together. That is the reason why the relationship between what is coming up and the negative inference coming down is always going to be the proper relationship. Because always their appearance will be mixed together. So, the earlier one, the sense of the object coming upwards, the appearance of the object looked at just as the object, just as a sensory input, and the descending negative inference, will always happen together. One might say, "but it couldn't, because the sensation happened before," but it is not thought of in that way.

CdC: In my memory I have had many different inferences of many different kinds of objects, so how is it that when the sensation of the book arises all of the other ones that are not the book are negated out, or masked out in this negative inference, but the remaining proper ones are left? I am sure that this has to do with how clear a memory we have of what a book is, because I am sure that as our understanding becomes better, what is left becomes more and more precise.

Rinpoche: Whenever you have an ascertainment (where ascertainment and memory are very similar) of the sort "that was that," in a certain sense, this is remembering. Whenever you have an ascertainment you will always have the process of exclusion involved. But, having the process of exclusion does not mean that you have ascertainment. This exclusion is an extremely swift process by which an awareness comes into being. Your questions are coming from associating the process of exclusion with the process of getting to be able to ascertain that it was "that and not that." In fact the process of exclusion is merely an extremely swift process by which awareness comes into being. This process of exclusion is almost instantaneous, happening whenever awareness comes about. [It is not a matter of taking time to reason out in a slow thought pattern which things need to be excluded and which do not.]

CdC: So, somehow when the awareness of the book comes up, of all of the memories and all of the past conceptual consciousnesses that I have had from my life, all are excluded except for a very small few, and those are in a sense selected. So, I then have an awareness of the things that are in the nature of the book, for example pages and a rectangle. My question is, how is it that some of these memories are in that sense selected or activated, and where do they come from, and how are the other ones selected against or pushed away?

Rinpoche: Because it was explained to you at one point. Seeing the book, someone said, "That is a book." At that point the awareness was of a different sort, it was a conceptual awareness. That conceptual awareness came into being with an object, an eliminative object, and that sort of object is not lost. And therefore that eliminative object can keep going through that object to find that thing that was being referred to at that time. It can therefore get back, through the same object, to the same one.

CdC: Okay. I am starting to understand.

Rinpoche: The naming has to happen in a way that is related to the sensory input. When the naming is related to the sensory input, the sensory input becomes related to, and tied up with, a whole concept, including a name. The concept here means the eliminative object. They are mixed together.

CdC: And this happened in the past sometime when someone said "this is a book" and pointed to the object?

Rinpoche: If that had never happened then you could never have a remembrance of it. That is the reason for having this whole presentation. The reason for having this whole explanation is to explain how you can have that conceptualization. Without such an object.... Well, let me give an example, the color blue. Even something as basic as that, although every time you see it there will definitely be an input, until somebody says "That is blue," you are not going to have the ability to say, "Oh, there is blue again." Until someone actually gives you that exclusionary thing, you will not be able to give rise to those inferential consciousnesses.

CdC: So after that happens there is a direct link that is in some sense permanent, permanent in the sense of not immediately subsiding, between the very object and this one group of ideas, or conceptual consciousnesses.

Rinpoche: Yes, that's very interesting. They become the same. In that person's mind they are now the same. In the mind you cannot get to the real object except through that link, that previously formed connection between a mental semblance and a real object.

The person imagines that what they think *is* the object, even though it is not. Without that thing that they think is the object, they cannot think of the object at all. They need to make something, they need the *dön chi*, they need the meaning generality, or the mind exclusion of other, which is stuck together with the object in the mind, completely stuck together with it, inseparably mixed with it. That meaning generality is indeed something which is said to be permanent. It is not something that degenerates.

CdC: I wish that you would have the opportunity to explore the ideas of neuroscience fully, because I think that you would be fascinated at the relationships between our ideas and the Tibetan understanding.

Rinpoche: [Deep laughter.]

OBJECTS OF THOUGHT—DOUBLE NEGATIVES

A view from neuroscience

CdC: I have thought about the idea of double negative inference and I find it very exciting. Perhaps scientists can begin to rearrange some of our ideas in this way and see if we find anything new.

I will try to give the Western ideas that I think bear the most resemblance to the Tibetan understanding, and then I will try to explain my understanding of the Tibetan view so that we can compare. I will try to explain how I think that concepts and percepts might be formed in the brain, with the hope that Rinpoche might find this interesting. Some of what I will say is known fact, and some is my own speculation about how thought might work.

First of all, there are different areas in the brain which are thought to be responsible for our awareness of different aspects of objects of perception, as I have mentioned before. For example, there are some areas that seem to be responsible for keeping track of motion, and others that seem to be responsible for keeping track of color. The first question that arises is whether these same areas that are used for perception are used for concept formation also. Without going into the details, this is an unsolved mystery, but the data seem to be suggesting that concepts are in fact processed by the same areas of the brain as percepts.[166]

The next question is how this might come about, how it could be that the same areas of the brain perform these two functions and how they interact. The idea that I would like to put forward is that perception works basically by positively activating these areas in particular ways, whereas concept formation works by activating them in a negative way roughly analogous with exclusion. In order to consider this I need to go into at least a few of the details.

These many areas can be understood to be arranged in something of a hierarchy, as I have mentioned before. At the bottom of the hierarchy are the areas that are thought to be involved with awareness of simple details, like lines or colors in a visual image. In the middle of the hierarchy are areas that are involved with intermediate aspects, like the local complex features in a visual object such as which areas share similar colors and so on. Finally, at the highest levels, the most complex aspects of our awareness are represented, such as our recognizing someone's face or understanding an object within a given whole context of experience. In the case of perception all of this machinery is thought to work in a positive fashion. The information enters through the "sense door," to use the Tibetan term, and then activates the lowest areas, which contain the most detail but the least general abstraction. These in turn activate the higher areas on up the hierarchy until in the end (in about a tenth of a second), the whole hierarchy is activated and our percept of an object is complete from the details to our abstract understanding.

In the case of concept formation this obviously cannot take place because there is no external object to activate the system, so the question is where this activity might come from. The position that I would like to put forth is that the activity trickles down from the most abstract ideas to the more detailed in a negative, or exclusionary fashion. In this way, if we have a very general idea at the highest level, which might just arise in the mind by a very global memory getting activated by circumstance and by chance, then this abstract concept excludes details at the levels below it which do not "fit" with it. It turns off the details in lower parts of the brain that do not match in some sense. In this way it does not positively "impute" all of the details at lower levels by specifying which ones must be active, it just excludes the wrong ones and permits others to manifest. Now, if there is perception going on at the same time as concept formation, then both processes will use the same spaces in the brain, and what appears to mind will thereby be a mixture of a concept and the percept of a real object.

Although there are actually more descending connections in the brain's perceptual system than ascending ones, people still have very little understanding of what they are for. That is why I find very exciting this idea of the negative or exclusionary inference projecting downwards.

As I understand the Buddhist view, using this same spatial and hierarchical metaphor, the first step is the direct perception of a sense object rising up, and then this leads to the coming down of the inferential, conceptual consciousness which overlays on top of that.

Rinpoche: Downwards to where?

CdC: Yes, that becomes a complicated issue. Let me try to explain it. In current Western thinking "up" usually means towards the parts of the brain involved in complex understanding of the global features of a whole object, like recognizing a person as one's mother, and ultimately to decision making and behavior. "Down," on the other hand, usually means a movement towards the parts of the brain involved in perceiving smaller, simpler details, such as the small individual lines and colors that make up an entire visual object, and ultimately down to the "bottom" at the sense organ. The difficult conceptual question, as Rinpoche clearly grasps, is "to where?" Where does all of this information lead, and where is the point where consciousness happens? Our answer is everywhere. The idea is that the consciousness is not being presented by this complex system to a "self" somewhere that is aware of what is going on; the awareness is taken to be the activity of this system.

My question though, is what is the nature of the kinds of objects that the conceptual mind has to represent, perhaps using this system?

A view from Tibetan Buddhism

Rinpoche: When you have this *lo zhan sel*, this mental exclusion, it has the *appearance* of a similar real object. Here the mind has only the apparently similar object, not the real object. So the appearance is not the real object itself. Take for example a vase. In the place of it an object appears to the mind which is other than the object itself. The consciousness gets a clue about the object, but mixed with a general picture of the object, because through a conceptual appearance there is no way of the object itself, alone, appearing.

CdC: So, what exactly are the entities which are mixed?

Rinpoche: Two things appear to the mind and are indistinguishably mixed as one in the appearance of the aspect (or perspective) of a conceptual understanding. What appears mixed is the generic image of the object and the object itself. The consciousness is a conceptual understanding, so the object cannot appear to it bare, alone, as it is. The object appears along with the generic image of the object.

CdC: So the mind has the real, bare perception of the object and also, mixed together with that, the meaning generality. They are mixed together so that someone cannot be aware of one or the other.

Rinpoche: The object itself and the generic image of the object are indistinguishably apparent. To give you an example so that you understand what is meant by the generic image of something, say for instance that you are here and you have a car in America, you have your family members and so on. So as soon as you give or project a thought, right at this place, all of them can appear to you. But they do not appear to you barely, do they? Not at all, right? They appear to you in their generic image form. In other words, they appear to you in their form of images.

So, therefore, at this very moment, as your house, your car, your family members, and so on appear to you, the mode of appearance is not as if they are really here with you. But, you do not perceive that you have their appearance mixed up with their images. You don't normally understand this. In fact, it is them that actually appears to you at this moment, not someone else, but they appear mixed up with their images. That is the real mode of experience, although we may not understand it. All conceptual understanding or perception has the appearance of the real object, only mixed up with the appearance of the real object is the generic image. That is to say, mixed indistinguishably with the generic image. But, we do not normally have that understanding. We do not understand that this is the mode of appearance for a conception.

So, therefore, to all conceptual understandings, the real thing that appears is the mental exclusion, in other words, just the image of the object, not the object itself in its reality with all of its details.

FORMING A CONCEPT BY INTRODUCTION AND VERBAL DESIGNATION

Let us take the example of someone introducing you to our translator, Tsepak. He introduces you to Tsepak because you are seeing him for the first time. He introduces you with a thought because he already has an image of Tsepak. First, that image of Tsepak arises in him. Using that image, confirming that image with the real Tsepak that he sees himself, he expresses the word, saying, "This is Tsepak!" to you. Now, similarly, you build up an image of him: this is his facial appearance, this is how he appears. You build up an image within you, and at the same time you remember the notion which is Tsepak. Using that image later on, when you see him as Tsepak, through your memory, upon that image you can express the word Tsepak. At that moment of recognition, you are reminded by the image that you built up when you saw him for the first time and were introduced to him. This is how conceptual thought recognizes its objects. This is the mechanism.

For this reason, if you see him later in other circumstances, as soon as you see him, unless you have forgotten him, you will immediately be able to recognize him. This is because at the point that you were introduced by means of his image and using the expression which is Tsepak's name, you generated an image of Tsepak. With that notion you were introduced to him and your memory has settled there. For that reason, later on in other instances, whenever you see him you will recollect him by using that image of him and that is how you will recognize him. This is how you conceptually recognize him.

The Buddhist schools say that a concept introduces itself only through the introduction of a mental exclusion. A mental exclusion is the meaning generality of the object which is formed by generating a mental image of the object. The mental image of that object can only be built by excluding the non-characteristics of that object. Unless you mentally exclude those things which are *not* the object you can't get the image of the "is-ness" of the object, that *being* of the object. So, conceptual understanding is generated through mental exclusion of the characteristics that are not that object, that do not qualify that object. Only in this way can you build up the image of the object. This is how you are introduced to an object in your process of thought mechanisms.

THE NECESSITY OF A TERM FOR A CONCEPT

You have to understand this very basic principle, that in order to understand things being "so and so," "this is this and that," you must rely on certain signs. These signs, signals, may relate somehow to the signals that reach the brain and so forth. Fundamentally, what we Buddhists say is that you must rely on being introduced by a term.

In reality, in order to be able to generate a conception, a thought, of course we must rely on the wind energy (*rlung*) that flows. In that respect you can say, of course, that this must have relevance to the signals that reach or that are given from the brain. That perspective is to be considered also, it is not to be negated.

From another perspective, we say that in order to be able to generate a conception, a thought in yourself, you must rely on a term. Without relying on that term one cannot conceptually understand or recognize anything. Though there is relevance of the flow of the energy, of course this is relevant too, but, nonetheless, a term denoting the object of conceptualization, introducing that object, is definitely a requirement to be able to conceptually generate an understanding of things being "so and so."

Take, for example, Tibetan words for colors. For you to understand that this [pointing to yellow fabric] is yellow in Tibetan, you have to know the Tibetan word for yellow, *ser-po*, otherwise you will not be able to generate the conceptual understanding, because you do not know the Tibetan word. You will be able to understand that being yellow only in terms of your own cultural background denoting the name for that object being yellow. So, if you use the word "yellow" in your own cultural sense, in your own linguistic terms, then you will be able to understand that being yellow, or it being blue or white or so on, as in America, because you are familiar with those terms, yellow, blue, white, and so forth. But your understanding would not be the way that a Tibetan would understand [the same objects, because the terms used are different and carry different connotations for the Tibetan].

So, it is our parents who initially introduce us to things. They introduce us to a thing by naming it. Later on, when you grow up, you don't need to have your parents introduce you to things because as your mind broadens; as you grow older, as you study more, your vocabulary and your capacity to understand things will increase, because your capacity to understand or comprehend the names and terms denoting things increases. Therefore, it is said that unless there is a term or a name denoting something, a conception cannot be generated in its fully characterized manner.

Unless there are names, or we are mainly meeting the object with the sense power or sense faculty, we will not be able to generate a concept or an idea of the object being this and that, being so and so. In order to broaden the horizon of our conceptualization, our conceptual understanding, we need to be introduced to these concepts through terms—through names—and through signs denoting them. That is why, although we spend twenty years or more in schools so that we understand these phenomena, so that we understand reality more, understand the things around us more, there are still hundreds and thousands of objects that we encounter each day for which we are not able to generate a proper conception of these things being "so and so." They simply remain abstract for us. Either we are not able to reach the objects because we do not have physical contact with them, or mental contact with them, or we do not have an experience connecting them. That is why even though we know lots of terms denoting them, we are still not able to generate a proper idea of knowing the things as being "so and so," because the horizon of knowledge is so vast, as vast as space itself. As space is endless, similarly the possible objects of the mind are unlimited.

Take for instance using the word "watch." Someone who doesn't know "watch," doesn't know the term or name "watch," will not be able to generate the conceptual idea of this [pointing to his wrist] being a watch. For that person who does not know the term "watch" being the name for this object, we need to teach him. Just because he has been introduced by using that term, "watch," that probably immediately sticks in his mind, in his mental process, so much so that he builds up an image of it. He immediately builds up an image of it through the propelling or movements of the energy winds within himself. That is how the process might be working.

ARE CONCEPTS POSITIVE OR DOUBLE NEGATIVE?

CdC: I would like to ask about the understanding that forming a concept is a positive act, is putting together the positive aspects of the object. The question that I am trying to get at, is why is it better to understand conceptualization in terms of exclusion, or differentiation? Why is it better to think of differentiating an object from everything else by saying it is not not all of these other things, as opposed to saying it is some group of positive features? Why is one a better understanding than the other?

Rinpoche: What we feel is that unless a conception understands an object being itself by negating those qualities that are not not the object, that conception might be a misconception, might be incorrect, because there is no way that you can get a correct conception of things.

CdC: Because it will always be incomplete?

Rinpoche: Yes. It might lead you to generate a misconception of the thing. It might lead you to misidentification of the thing. According to Buddhist formal logic, there is always room there, room for suspicion of it.

CdC: So only through the negative negative can you come to the real, full understanding. The positive qualities will never be completely, exactly and in every aspect the same as the object.

Rinpoche: Using exclusions is better in the sense that once you identify something conceptually by repelling, abandoning, and eliminating its negative qualities as not being so, then it will lead you to a conceptual understanding which is more stable. Later on, in the future, when you see that object, identification will come up. Stability. This does not mean that you have to eliminate all that is not it, but, at least, you have to eliminate the opposite of not it.

[This addresses the question of what the range of exclusion must be, as addressed in the chapter on conceptuality above. Does an exclusion need to negate an infinite range of other possibilities, or only the relevant ones?]

When you were introduced to a person as being a Tibetan, immediately you built up within your conceptualization certain features—so on and so forth being "Tibetan," and although those features may not be complete, at that moment you had automatically repelled a few characteristics that do not make up "Tibetan." They have automatically been eliminated. There are certain features that you do not think make up "Tibetan," and these have automatically been expelled or eliminated in the thought process.

A STABLE MEMORY IS DEPENDENT ON THE USE OF A TERM

CdC: I was wondering if we could talk about memory of these conceptions, how it is formed and how it is maintained and how it arises. This is one of the central questions in neuroscience today.

Rinpoche: Generally, you have to understand that conceptions, conceptualizations, conceptual ideas, are two kinds of things: those conceptual ideas that are generated by the force of a direct perception, and those conceptions that are not generated by a direct perception.

Take for instance a person who doesn't know the word "watch." For him, when he sees a watch with his sensory direct perception, his eye consciousness meets with this object but he is not able to generate an idea or conception thinking, "Oh, this is a watch." He just generates a conception, "This thing I see is such and such." Later on, as he sees the same thing, given the fact that he still doesn't know the term watch, he might generate a recollection in his thought process, "Well, this is the same thing I saw before," but he still will not be able to generate a conception, "This is a watch." Or he might generate a dubious conception, thinking, "What might this be called?" He might think, "Oh, this is the thing that I saw," that much conception he is able to generate, but he is still not able to generate a confirming conception saying that this thing that I am seeing is a watch. This can only be based on the fact that he has seen a watch as being a watch attentively. If he has seen it inattentively, he might not be able to recollect it later on.

The kind of conception thinking, "Oh, this is what I have seen," may not remain for long in memory. It may disappear. In order to generate a conception, "Oh, this is a watch," the term "watch" is something that must be understood, that must have been introduced to the person. Otherwise, he will not be able to generate the concept later on through memory or recollection that "this is a watch," because he doesn't know the term.

To understand anything being so and so is to rely on a term or a name to be introduced to that thing. Taking the example of obvious, manifest things, in order to generate a concept of such and such concrete thing being so and so, you have to first be introduced to the thing with a name, along with the coming of that object in contact with the senses.

With the non-physical, non-manifest, concealed, hidden things, where you don't have that chance to ascertain the object directly through perception, there is no way of talking about it and meeting it as a sense object. In this case, from the very beginning, you have to be introduced to that object conceptually by an idea.

There are two ways to understand the concealed phenomena, hidden phenomena, non-concrete, non-physical phenomena, in order to generate a conception of a hidden thing being so and so. Either you have to understand it through your own analysis and investigation, or you have to understand it through an introduction or instruction or advice from someone else. They are thereby inculcating that introduction or instruction into your own thought process. Then, you analyze, investigate, examine, and find out for yourself. Then you are able to recognize that hidden thing being so and so, conceptually only.

CdC: I would like once again to express my deepest thanks to Rinpoche for these wonderful discussions that we have been having. I greatly look forward to making these teachings available to others as well when they are published.

Rinpoche: That is a very good way. It is very good that you are thinking of sharing these discussions. One thing that I would say that might be common between us, no matter that the approach may be different, science or Buddhism, is that when we study, contemplate, and even meditate, we see our investigating nature. Even in meditation we are investigating. We analyze and try to understand things in their proper perspective. I believe that scientists are also analyzing things, examining things, observing things. They are doing research. That is what I value very much.

So, in fact, they come to a common ground. I feel that in this way we complement each other.

SECTION VI
MEMORIES OF EXPERIENCE

Mind is something which needs some earlier residual impressions, some sort of inputs, which give rise to it. Of itself it has no reality at all. You need some sort of earlier impression to give rise to a state of awareness. Then you would have a remembrance.

—Kamtrul Rinpoche

13   A Discussion with Kamtrul Rinpoche: Memory and the Freedom of the Mind

In this chapter, Kamtrul Rinpoche and I discuss different metaphors for memory. I discuss an empirically based understanding of how memory is thought to be laid down in the physical structure of the brain. Rinpoche presents a traditional tale of the nature of remembrance and its use and misuse.

A WESTERN VIEW OF AWARENESS AND MEMORY BASED ON NEURAL ACTIVITY

CdC: Although there are many subjects that I would be interested in speaking with you about today, I have selected one in particular that seems especially important, and that is the understanding of memory. If you are interested, I can begin by explaining some of the Western understanding of memory and then perhaps we can discuss the Tibetan view. It appears to me that the Tibetan understanding of the mind has a particularly broad and deep conceptual basis which is very much missing in my own field, which comes more from a biological tradition. I hope that over the years we will be able to bring small pieces of the Tibetan understanding back to share with some of the scientists and others in the West, and that also we will be able to bring to the Tibetan tradition some pieces of the very detailed understanding of the construction of the nervous system that we have in the West.

First, allow me to describe a bit about the Western understanding of the "channels"—to use the word that is used in the Tibetan understanding—that are thought to be involved in mediating the function

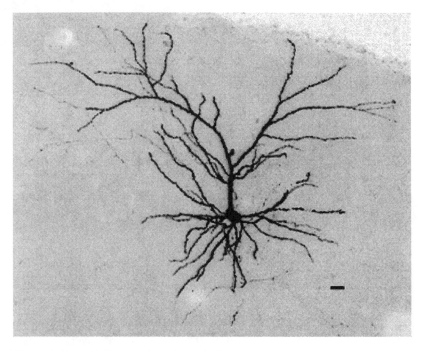

Figure 4. Pyramidal neuron from the cerebral cortex

The many branches of this neuron represent the many input elements (dendrites). A single fiber emanating from the cell body is the output element (axon).

---

of consciousness, and then I will describe a bit about how memory is thought to reside or be maintained in the connections between these tiny channels.

In an understanding that may be somewhat similar to the Tibetan view, we see major channels of the flow of neural energy, or information, which mediate conscious awareness that goes through the nervous system. We see those channels as being made up of very, very tiny channels that are made up of individual parts which we call neurons or nerve cells. So these pathways, or large channels, are made up of small channels, and the small channels are made up of individual neurons or nerve cells which we think are what constitute the channels.

Similarly, I believe, to the Tibetan understanding, we do not see the channels as being the consciousness, but as doing it. That is, they are thought by many neuroscientists to create the function which itself is conscious awareness. I have brought a couple of pictures to try to demonstrate this. If you look inside the brain, you can see many, many small pathways and the ways that they course. This diagram (see figure 4) represents a single neuron. This one was drawn by looking through a microscope, so it is possible to physically see from the outside where each of these tiny, tiny processes or channels goes.

Rinpoche: So, for example, the energy would be going in here [pointing to the neuron's dendrites, or input elements], but not in here [pointing to the neuron's axon or output element], is that what you are saying?

CdC: Yes. It can come in through any one of these small input fibers, move toward the center of the neuron, and then come out these other ones over here. So, making up the big channels of the brain are these tiny neurons. It has been found that there are about ten trillion inside a person's brain. For comparison, that is more than one thousand times the number of people who live on the earth.

So, to explain briefly how this is related with memory, Rinpoche can imagine that the function of the flow of energy through these channels is what gives rise to conscious awareness. Again, it is not the channels, and it is not the energy, but it is what these two things create together, what they do.

Each type of consciousness, each moment of conscious awareness, is going to involve energy going through many of these channels—through particular ones. So, if Rinpoche can imagine, these fibers here (at top of figure) are connected to the other channels of another cell that would be connected, and so on. There are many connected together, so there are thousands of connections from this cell to thousands of other cells, and these are the ways that the energy can flow, through these many connections which we name synapses. The way that a particular consciousness—a percept, or concept, or idea, or any sort of awareness—takes place is based on exactly which pattern of connections is used, and thereby which tiny channels, which neural processes the energy flows along. It is possible to measure the flow of energy through the very tiniest of these individual channels using modern electrophysiology equipment.

The understanding of memory that is most common now is that memory corresponds to which of the many connections are strong. The connections that are stronger will lead the energy to flow in particular pathways and will lead particular pathways to be activated. This is what corresponds to a particular type of awareness in our view.

Rinpoche: I like that.

CdC: In the very best of cases, where things are quite simple, it is possible to actually measure the strength of the connections between these tiny channels, and this strength of connection between channels is what guides the neural energy or activity along certain of these micro-pathways. As you see, we think that we have the beginnings of an understanding of what constitutes memory at the tiniest level, almost down to the individual molecules. Unfortunately, we have a much weaker understanding of what the basis of memory on a more complex scale is, although there are many competing theories. In other words, we do not really understand the precise way in which whole memories or concepts of a particular object are stored. We have many tiny pieces of the puzzle but we do not know how to put them together into an overall understanding of the question of memory. This is where I am particularly interested in the Tibetan view. I wonder if Rinpoche would like to speak about the Tibetan understanding of how whole memories are stored.

MEMORY AND TAMING THE WILD HORSE MIND

Rinpoche: Let me use the example which is used within the tantric context in this sort of area. The nerve, the nadi, we exemplify with a road or a path. The horse we give as the example of the energy or the wind (*rlung*) of consciousness. For the mind we use the example of the person sitting on the horse. That was the traditional example to use in a tantric context when talking about these things earlier in Tibet.

So this example which was traditionally given in Tibet was drawn out as follows: Given that the *nadi* is exemplified by the path and that the energy is exemplified by the horse and that the mind is exemplified by the rider, let's see where we can get. Say that you have a main horse pathway—an artery going into a city. Of course, branching off of the main road there are all sorts of pathways going into this and that village and this and that place. And then you have this horse, which is actually like an absolutely unbroken, wild stallion, and the person who is on the horse is absolutely blind. For the person to hold the horse and keep it under control is almost impossible. It could go anywhere.

This example is brought to its fullness by noticing that within the human being, if this blind person cannot direct the unbroken stallion, then he or she is just going to be taken who knows where. The stallion is going to charge here, it is going to gallop there. Just as you say, the horse is likely to go down the avenues of experience that it already knows well, that are wide and easy to travel. This going who-knows-where is the metaphor that we use for how we move through experiential sequence after experiential sequence—in particular the experiences which are whole lifetimes. Who knows where we will go? Again and again and again and again.

To the extent that the mind cannot be controlled we will continue doing that running as we have since time immemorial. So then, for the blind person, the blindness is the fundamental ignorance which is at the root of cyclic wandering. The unbroken stallion is the metaphor for the emotions, the hatred and incredible longing and general confusion that dominate our personalities, causing a person to run headlong here or headlong there. All of the different pathways which it is possible to go down are the examples for the five realms of existence and all of the experiences and awarenesses which can be gone down.

The crucial teaching here is that the ignorance which is being exemplified by the blindness of the person on the horse is an ignorance the nature of which is not inherent. It is a blindness which is removable. It is just a cataract. It is not absolutely built into the eye. Therefore, it is possible to remove the blindness from this rider. Then there can be some direction to the choices of how to direct experience in particular directions.

Just as a horse is trainable and tamable, the strong and afflictive emotional states are seen as removable. To the extent that they are removable, it is possible to tame the horse. When tamed, we have a tremendous stallion beast. By holding firmly the bit and seeing where you are going, it can then be directed along the path.

So, similarly, the example goes on. What about *nirvana*? What about freedom for the human being? For us? That freedom is indeed a reality for us. Just like when the horse is trained, is tamed, the blind person, that person on the horse, can now direct the horse to the place where the person wishes to go, and the horse will quickly take the person there. Just like that example, freedom for the person caught in the situation that we are caught in is not far when this has been achieved.

CdC: That is a very beautiful example.

Rinpoche: [Laughs.] So then, let us talk about more specific forms of remembering. What about the two factors, a mind which is in a state of remembering something, and an introspection looking at what is going on? What about these two things? When you pick the former, a remembering mind, that is described by a word for mind itself. Mind here is something which doesn't have any *independent* reality. This mind is something which needs some earlier residual impressions, some sort of inputs, which give rise to it. Of itself it has no reality, no independent existence at all. You need some sort of earlier impression to give rise to a state of awareness. Then you would have a remembrance. The mind will have no reality otherwise.

If I have never been somewhere, the state of mind will of course never come to me of the kind, "that is America," not without the preceding conditionality. It is just exactly as you have said. My having gone to America, whether I live in India later on, whether I live in Tibet later on, wherever I go, I may still have the remembering awareness. What you say is really so correct, that the *lung* (*rlung*), that energy, finds its way. Once the way has been traveled, only then can you have the experiences of memory. The mind of itself has no sort of reality. Only when it has found those ways will it find its way back along them. Then it will always go those ways.

Especially what you say has such a ring of truth because of the reality of the ways of pure awareness—not only the ways of pure awareness in terms of the energy which would be pure, which would go down the way which would be pure, but also the energy which gives rise to the awareness which is pure. Obviously, the only pathways which it is going down are pathways which are impure. The only energy which is going is energy which is impure. The only awarenesses which are arising are the awarenesses which are impure. The pathways are all there, the energies are all there, and the awarenesses are all there. Indeed, what you say is so true.

[Here Rinpoche uses the word "pure," I believe, to derive the highest sense of the meaning that a pathway of memory can have. If his example is understood as an instance of how energy can move for the first time down various pathways of experience with freedom and control, like the horse first controlled by its rider, then the example above gives its full meaning.]

So indeed, it is a beautiful fit here. Truly a great opportunity for friendliness. Let me give an example coming from the middle. You have America, a country of fifty states; you have in each of those states groups of different people. Now, there is knowledge of the different states, of the different communities, of the different people, of the different interactions between the communities. Similar to that knowledge, you have in your neurobiology a knowledge of the intricacies of the total picture which is absolutely amazing. Really heartening and exciting. What do *we* have? We have, as it were, the government. We have the knowledge of the main thing which is controlling, of mind; the thing which controls this entire process, this is what we Tibetans have to offer. More of the specifics, this isn't what we have. What we have to offer is how to govern this entire thing. How to give real freedom to this entire thing. Therefore, there seems such a beautiful fit. Such a tremendous opportunity for friendship.

So, what then?

14   A Discussion with Lati Rinpoche: Memory and the Subtle Channels of the Mind

In this final section of discussions with Lati Rinpoche, we discuss the view of memory arising from the study of the brain, and that found within Tibetan Buddhism. I again present a view based largely on the physical structure of the brain. Rinpoche responds with comments based on the premises of Buddhist logic. Rinpoche's basic point is that memory relies heavily on naming. He also introduces the idea of a potentiality which can be left latent in the mind, a topic that will be considered further in the next chapter.

AN INTRODUCTION TO CHANNELS AND PATHWAYS WITHIN THE NERVOUS SYSTEM

CdC: I was hoping that we could continue speaking about how the energy of the mind and the previously existing state of awareness go together to bring about a new moment of awareness. Particularly, I wonder about how the state of the mind and the brain in a given moment can store memories of the past. I will give a brief account of the Western notion of how this works. Perhaps we can then discuss some of the similarities and differences in the Tibetan and Western ideas.

The neural basis of the storage of a previously existing state of the brain (that arose during a previous experience) is thought of largely in terms of connections—which pathways are now available for neural energy to flow through. With a good microscope it is possible to actually see these channels directly with the eyes. This is a picture of a neuron (see figure 5), the fundamental unit from which the pathways of neural transmission are made up. The neuron has many branches, and these serve as the tiniest of the pathways which make up the larger ones. Information to the brain comes in along neurons that originate everywhere from the tips of the toes to the top of the head. In the brain there are about ten trillion of these neurons, or about as many as the number of drops of water in a lake that is one hundred kilometers around and fifty meters deep. It is possible using modern equipment to measure the energy flow in a single one of these neurons, and this is what I do in my own research. The energy usually flows through the neurons in bursts (called action potentials) and these usually happen between one and one thousand times per second in each individual neuron. The number of individual bursts of energy in the brain is incomprehensible.

Rinpoche said once before, and we would also say, that it is not correct to think of the trillions of neurons as consciousness, and it is also not correct to think of the hundreds of trillions of electrical signals which are passing as consciousness. In my opinion, and that of many neuroscientists, it is the functioning of this entire apparatus that allows the process of consciousness to take place. In other words, consciousness is not the form, but the form allows consciousness.

THE FLOW OF MIND LIKE WATER IN A RIVER

The next thing that I will talk about is how the patterns of channels are formed and how the state of the system and a particular perception might bring up a specific mental image or conception. I will take an analogy that was made by William James,[167] who was one of the founders of my field, and expand it somewhat with my own interpretation. The energy and patterns of connection in the brain can be thought of as water flowing along small channels, and even as the small grooves that are worn along the floor of a river valley. This idea is based on the notion that the neural energy can leave a trace of itself when it flows, that it can make a path that will be easier to follow the next time.

If you start off with an empty plain, and then very slowly begin to bring water in at one end every wet season, in the beginning the plain has no tracks made by water, but it already has its own shape and slope, and this shape leads it to have some innate propensities for which way water will flow. Depending on where the water first comes to the plain, which corresponds to the early flows of energy through our nervous system during our earliest experiences, the water will start to form pathways, to wear away a valley, and then it will use the shapes that are already there to flow down the river valley. It will start to form small streamlets. As we have more and more experiences, more and more water can be imagined flowing down the tiny streams, making those streams a little bit smoother and a little bit deeper and easier for water to flow through them again in the future.

When we have a sensory experience later on, like when we see an object such as a table, the neural energy which flows in our brains can be thought of in the same way as the water which flows in a riverbed. It comes in at the top and it has to flow in one direction or another. If the connections between a given perception and the thought "this is a table" have been worn smooth over the years, then the energy of the perception of a table can easily flow in this direction and bring up this thought. If we have never seen a table before, then no pathway has been made before, and the water can go any of a large number of different ways, leading to many different understandings. The more familiar we have become with an object or idea, the more times we have put neural energy down this neural path and the smoother it gets. Eventually we easily recognize the object, like the table, from our perception. Sometimes it becomes nearly impossible for the water to go any different way, and then we necessarily recognize the table in a particular way after we perceive it, and may not be able to think of it in any other way. The water represents the neural energy. The streamlets on the valley floor represent the trillions of neural pathways. In this analogy consciousness is not the streambed and it is not the flowing water. It is the river.

Rinpoche: The river then, would be like consciousness. Are you taking that in an absolute sense so that when you get all of the streamlets of water moving through all of their channels, when you get all of those together, at that point, all of the different pieces of energy together would form the consciousness?

CdC: I think that I would say yes and no. [Deep belly laughs from Rinpoche.] If you have all of these things together, then in one sense they constitute the process of awareness. But, it is not really correct that if you have the energies and the pathways together, that those two *are* the consciousness. It is also what they *do*. It is not that they are the conscious awareness, nor that they do it, but both together. They form the physical and motive substrates for it together. Together they provide the potential for the conscious awareness, but the consciousness itself is neither one in isolation nor the sum of the two, it is the whole that comes about. It is the river.

Rinpoche: So it is not the same nor exactly different [laughing].

CdC: I have brought a very simple example. A neuron from the visual system at birth, before any visual experience, has many, many channels available for the energy to flow in—many different possibilities. In the beginning the energy is going in many directions. After there has been visual experience, after the energy has flowed many times, the neurons look different. There are now particular pathways that have become strengthened, and others that have gone away, so now the energy is channeled in particular directions.

The basic idea is that there are some innate patterns that are already present at birth—the river bed already has a shape—and also there is random chance taking place, so that the water can go any which way. What happens that strengthens some of the paths, but not the others, is that the water will more often go along some pathways than others because of the random chance and the preexisting state that was already there. The key point is that the mechanism involves the simultaneous passage of energy reaching the same point.

The coincidence of two simultaneous patterns of activity can lead two mental objects to become associated. The simultaneous activities from two objects molds together the two pathways, as if water flowing in two small channels suddenly met to form into one deeper one. Ideas or percepts can be grouped together, or strongly associated, in the same way that if water came from two streamlets into one they would become joined and the water would have a greater force in clearing its path than either streamlet could have alone. Later, the water would flow only down the often used channels. Therefore, the number of channels that are activated by a perceptual object will converge down to a much smaller number. The idea is that the concept of each object will be the flowing of energy through this reduced set of channels.

There is not a prefabricated place which corresponds to the idea, "this is a table," but this concept is formed through use. It is formed by dividing up the world of perceived experience into categories of similar elements which we call our different concepts of objects, like tables and chairs and so on. These concepts are nothing more than the patterns of similarities and relationships between different objects. In fact, the idea is that these different concepts have been *created by the brain*. Reality has been divided into categories by dividing the paths in which neural energy can flow. Again, this is just present theory, but it is the best answer that I can offer in the light of present views.

In the end, when one object is perceived, only one group of pathways which have been formed will be predominantly activated, whereas when another object is presented another group of pathways will be activated. If there is some degree of similarity between the two objects, and hence similarity between the starting patterns of the way that the energy enters, then they will overlap somewhat. If they are very different then they will use very different pathways. In this way, depending on with what detail we have observed the two patterns, it becomes possible to make finer and finer distinctions between them, as well as finding their similarities. This is a very simplified view, but it is not too far from current thinking.

Rinpoche: By simultaneity here, what do we really mean? The analogy of the use of the common neural pathways by the two objects, I am not sure that I have grasped the importance of simultaneity.

CdC: For two ideas or objects to become associated, they must take place together. Of course, as in our analogy, the pathways that are strongly active together will enhance each other. This is thought to be the mechanism that underlies the creation of associative memory, because as two objects are presented together many times, we form associations between them and the pathways that they activate are simultaneously used, so they tend to merge together into one. The idea is that after learning to associate two objects they come to share some of the same neural pathways.

Rinpoche: Yes, I can see how that would be. Simply seeing a table, the very fact of the sight of tables, will not in each case lead the person to remember that table later on. Similarly, you may remember seeing someone but not remember who it was. This is a question that came up in my mind. I still do not see how what you are saying has answered my question, which was how some sort of force somehow moves the energy into the configuration that it needs to be in order to generate whatever the awareness is.

Gareth Sparham: What has happened is that the subtlety of your explanation has been lost in translation. What Rinpoche is trying to get to is, for example, you have two people standing right here, one sees a square and the other says its a table. Why is one seeing a table and the other not? He is trying to find out what is causing the energy to go through the channels such that one is seeing a table and the other isn't.

THE IMPORTANCE OF HAVING A TERM FOR HAVING A CONCEPT

Rinpoche: In this way I still have a problem: What about the very first time? What I had in mind when I was asking for the conditions for a concept to arise was the necessity to include language, which is described in specific Tibetan texts. It is actually the *name* which allows the person to generate the awareness of the sort "this is that." Without the introduction of that condition it isn't possible for those specific sorts of awarenesses to be generated. This is what I wanted to get to, that the naming process and passing on of words is a crucial element in this.

Here, we also have different languages. *You* will not generate from the sound of the Tibetan word for a table, the idea of a table. It doesn't matter how many times you hear the word, you will not have the thought, "this is a table." The naming process and the labeling process is crucial in awareness formation of the sort "this is that," for a conceptual awareness.

In other words, to answer my own question from the Tibetan system, the energy which is necessary for the awareness of the sort "this is a table" to arise in a person's mind, is in fact coming from the person naming the object. For example, we are taught by our parents what "a mother" and "a father" are, then we use that continually, based on the initial impetus given from them saying it. The communication of the name and then the name itself give the impetus for us to have the awareness of the type "this is that" throughout the rest of our days.

Words having shared meaning, so that the same understanding is shared in common throughout a community, so that you can have awarenesses of the sort "this is that," thus becomes an extremely important factor to think about. One of the schools of Buddhist insight (Prasangika) refers a great deal to the fact that things are simply labeled by a name. This starts to have a certain profundity from that perspective. In fact, it is the whole language learning process which is reflected in the importance given to the building of schools. What one is doing is introducing a person to more and more and more language, so that meanings, awarenesses one might say, can be put across. To the extent that the size of one's knowledge expands, the ignorance or confusion of names or terminologies leading to the ability to create awarenesses begins to decrease.

[This is reflected in the Tibetan monastic method of education, which relies heavily on memorization of texts as an initial stage in learning their meanings.]

Rinpoche: As to the function of the movement of the energy in the channels being consciousness, there are many other functions of it as well. The main function of the mental energy, or *lung*, is consciousness as you suggested. It is true that where you get the movement of the mental energy, the *lung*, through these channels, you do get the awareness coming into being. That is the function that this energy has.

Where you have an imprint which is left behind by the movement of the energies through the channels, one of the things left behind is called *bagcha*, or "hand mark," where you have the illuminating knowing. That is one of the things left behind.

15   A Discussion with Gen Damcho: Objects of the Mind and Memory

In this final discussion chapter I spoke with Gen Damcho about some of the details of how memories are thought to be stored, maintained, and reactivated, from the Tibetan viewpoint. This question is central to the current science of the brain, and there are volumes devoted to the explanation of it. The details of this presentation of mechanism do not form a central part of the Tibetan presentation of mind overall, which made it difficult to learn about how this mechanism is thought to work from the Tibetan perspective. In this discussion we touch on some aspects of the Tibetan understanding of the mechanisms of memory, and how it is related to direct perception and concept formation.

PERCEIVING OBJECTS AT THE "MIND DOOR"

CdC: I want to discuss the question of mind-door objects, or objects that are appearing to the mind consciousness, the sixth of the traditional Buddhist sense consciousnesses. I was wondering if you could present what these objects are, where they come from, and how they are related to memory. I am particularly wondering about objects arising at the mind door that are not coming from the direct experience that one is having at a given moment, but from memory. Later I would like to ask some more specific questions about how these relate to meaning generalities or exclusion objects that are to do with conceptual thought.

As I understand it, the objects of direct perception at the mind door are not exclusion objects. I wonder if you would say exactly what an object at the mind door is for a direct perceiver using the mind door consciousness, especially as this relates to memory.

Gen Damcho: Recollection, memory also, is said to be consciousness. It is always conceptual. You see something and then at a later date you call that to mind, and that mind is a conceptual mind. Not all conceptual minds are that type of consciousness.

The presentation in the Tibetan teachings is more in terms of what happens than how the process works. You see something, then you remember it, and what comes to mind is not just the object but the whole experience as it previously occurred. Memory is a recalling of the whole experience. There is no recollection of objects alone, but of experiences.

There is some discussion related to memory about whether there have to be two different consciousnesses which are responsible for the recording process, for memory induction. All of the schools accept that there is not only recollection of the object of previous awareness, but recollection of the subject who had the awareness at the same time. You don't see the object in isolation. When the original experience occurred there was a relationship of the object, and the subject perceiving the object. Also in the recalling experience there has to be the same sense. There are some differences among the different schools about whether or not you have to have a separate consciousness for the object and the subject. The Chittamatra school posits a second consciousness which is called the self-cognizer or apperceptive consciousness, which is a part of the mind which is constantly turned to the consciousness itself. In order to gain recollection, to recall the thought, "I experienced this," the thought of the subject, this type of consciousness is needed according to the Chittamatrin school.

CdC: So in other words, you have a re-representation of what you are remembering that includes not only the objects that you are remembering but the subject that was experiencing them at the time.

Gen Damcho: Yes. In that sense there is no disagreement between the schools. The question arises in terms of how that process happens, whether you have a separate type of consciousness to the sense consciousness. The sense consciousness is directed outward. When it is experiencing an object the object seems to be "out there." Some of the schools say that since that is the case, that type of consciousness which looks outward cannot be responsible for the induction of the later recollection, "I had this experience." That means that you have to have another type of consciousness which is also present at the same time, whose focus is turned inwards, looking at the mind itself. The highest school, the Prasangika Madhyamika, refute the need to posit such a consciousness. They say that just by recollection of the event, that is enough to bring recollection of the object and the subject.

It is possible to make a broad division between sense perceptions, sense consciousnesses, and conceptual minds. To explain exactly how perceptual consciousnesses engage in their objects is not an easy thing to do. When one's eyes are open and the sense perception is engaged in its object one has direct access to the object. If one closes one's eyes, one can still have awareness of the object, but the way that one is doing that is obviously different, since one hasn't got direct access to the object anymore. Something has veiled the object from us—something has come between us and the object. It is as if there is a veil, a piece of cloth between us. We still have the idea that there is something there, but we cannot see it directly. With the conceptual mind there is not the direct access, there is something between the object and the mind. While the object can still be experienced conceptually, it cannot be experienced to the same extent that it can be by a direct sense consciousness, with a very vivid, clear picture.

RETRIEVING CONCEPTS FROM MEMORY

CdC: If you have a single direct perception of an object, and you form a single conceptual consciousness, and then later you recall this object through memory, is there any difference between the first object of thought and what is remembered, or are they identical?

Gen Damcho: There is no real difference between the ways that the minds are getting at these objects, or the way that the objects appear, or what object appears, but there is a difference in terms of the clarity or how vivid the object is. Because the object that one has at the time that one has the eye consciousness can rely continuously on the direct experience of the eye consciousness, the image is more vivid. The recollection at a subsequent time is still getting at the same object, but cannot rely upon a constant direct experience, so it is not as clear. The concept that one has during the time that one is looking at the object is still not as clear as the object that appears to the direct perceiver, so the veil is still there even though there seems to be no veil.

CdC: How is it that this first conceptual consciousness that takes place when you are in the process of looking at an object is in some way stored or fixed, and then maintained over time in order to allow it to ripen later, and finally, when it does ripen, how does it come back? Maybe I should ask the first question first. At the time when someone is seeing a pot, when they form this conceptual consciousness, where does it go so that it can come back later? This seems particularly intriguing given the Buddhist refutation of a substantially existing self.

Gen Damcho: When you do not see the pot anymore, until the time that you call the memory to mind again in recall, it is not in consciousness. We do not say that the concept apprehending pot exists as a concept apprehending pot, as a consciousness, during this time. What happens to it is that it becomes a potential, a seed, for the production of something in the future. This term is used particularly by the higher schools. The term potential is used in a more general explanation.[168]

For talking about the consciousness, you have this "pot apprehending concept," for example. What happens to that between the time that it is manifest and the subsequent time that it manifests itself? It stays in the form of a seed.

CdC: Is there more that you could say about these two classes of things, these potentials and seeds? Is there more that you could say about what exactly these are?

Gen Damcho: We don't have to talk about conceptual consciousnesses, we can also talk about direct perceivers. If an eye consciousness is not present, then something can be present in the form of a potential for other eye consciousness. In the intermediate times it is not that the thing goes out of existence altogether, but rather that it is not consciousness any more.

CdC: So are you saying that when you have a direct perception, it also forms one of these seeds so that you can also have a direct perception ripen directly from memory? Is that what you are saying?

Gen Damcho: It wouldn't actually manifest as a direct perception. What I was saying was that if you close your eyes you do not have eye consciousness but it is still there in the form of potential.

MEMORIES AS POTENTIALS FOR FUTURE THOUGHTS

Gen Damcho: The conceptual mind is considered an object-apprehending mind. While it is not manifesting, we cannot say that it goes out of existence altogether, but we can say that it is not in the form of a conceptual mind anymore. Then we must begin to talk about a continuum of mind. The continuum must change its nature, it is not always of the same type. How it does this is to change into the form of a potential for a subsequent experience. In the potential form it is called a non-associated compositional factor. There are three different types of functioning things in general, one of them is consciousness, the second is form, and the third are the non-associated compositional factors. This means existent phenomena which are neither consciousness nor form. This includes all collections, like persons and so on. Potentials also fall into this category. Memories exist by these potentials being non-associated compositional factors upon the mindstream, which will manifest again when certain conditions arise. For that reason we say that they are not manifest consciousnesses.

Then there is another term which is translated as "substantial cause," which relates to the ripening of memory. For example, a plant's seed is the substantial cause of the sprout, in that the main substance of the seed is what goes into the sprout. The substance is taken up in forming the sprout. Things like sunlight and water are all helpful conditions. The imprints or potentials or seeds of memory are actually the substantial causes for the later consciousness. If you talk about a conceptual mind apprehending a pot, first of all the conceptual consciousness exists, and then it goes into the form of a potential, so it is not consciousness anymore at all, and then, under certain conditions, it can re-emerge as a consciousness.

CdC: You use the phrase, "upon the mind," does that mean that these compositional factors are existing as part of the mind stream, that they are part of what is composing the mind-stream during that intervening time?

Gen Damcho: The explanation now becomes somewhat difficult. I thought that you were only talking in terms of a continuum of one particular type of mind, relative to one single object. The imprint which a conceptual mind, say a mind apprehending a pot, places on the mind, the potential, does not have to ripen into the same consciousness, say apprehending a pot.

CdC: I do not understand what else it could ripen into.

Gen Damcho: The usual examples of material objects that are used in debate and so forth are pots and pillars. So, it could ripen into a pillar.

We have to say in general that there is a continuum of a particular consciousness, a concept. In subsequent times when it is generated it can then have a different object. The reason for this presentation is partly just logical, there is a fault with one's reasoning if one does not posit this. If one didn't posit this, then when one has a conceptual mind apprehending a pot, and when this is later regenerated, then it could only be regenerated as a pot. That would mean that if a new object came along, like a new invention or something, then one would have to say that it came from a conceptual mind of the same object, which is logically inconsistent. This would also not allow forgetting, or mis-remembering.

One has to say in general that one continuum of consciousness can switch objects, because there will be logical faults if one does not posit this. We do not have all of the concepts that we will ever have, so for that reason, they must be able to change.

CdC: So when a conceptual consciousness during experience creates a potential, creates a memory, then this goes on into this continuum of mind. During that time it can change somewhat so that when it ripens it can ripen in a way that is slightly different, or even quite different, from the way that it was originally experienced. Is that correct?

Gen Damcho: We cannot say that it is in between the two times that it changes. Becoming a pillar-apprehending consciousness is something which happens just at the moment of its production, again, because of certain conditions which turn the mind towards this object.

CdC: So the exact conditions in the mind at the time of ripening can cause it to ripen in a way that is different than the way that it was originally perceived.

What are the conditions and causes that turn the initial (now past) consciousness into one of these potentials, and exactly how does one of these potentials ripen and in turn cause a new conceptual consciousness to come about?

Gen Damcho: With respect to the second part of your question, the explanation is a mental one. A certain sense perception, a sense consciousness, is generated in the mind at a subsequent time. We talk about attention, the mental factor called attention. What one pays attention to or what one takes interest in has a chance of producing a consciousness. When I look back tomorrow I will only remember a portion of things, and this depends upon other factors than just what I saw. It depends upon this factor of attention particularly. The literal expression is "taking to mind," which things I choose to take to mind. Some things I give my attention to, some things do not make such an impression because I haven't given attention to them.

CdC: So this is the formation of the seed?

Gen Damcho: This is actually both, because if you are talking about a conceptual mind being reproduced apprehending a different object, then you can see a different consciousness, a different eye consciousness (or whatever type).

CdC: So when you are creating the potentiality, attention is one of the causal factors directing what is going to be stored. Only some of the conceptual consciousnesses relating to your perceptions are going to go into memory, and those are the particular ones that were holding your attention. Then, when you have experiences at a later time, again you are going to have attention and that is going to screen which of your perceptions you take the most interest in, which you take to mind. Those perceptions which you take to mind are then going to affect the way that the previously formed potential ripens into a new consciousness. Is that right?

Gen Damcho: The explanation is more related to the second part of what you are saying. This is a difficult thing to think of in physical terms. What the interest does at the time that the potential is placed upon the mind, is that it will affect how someone (or even whether someone) will be able to generate a mind of recollection. There are many things that appear to us, that are happening around us and that we are partially aware of. Awareness of them does also go to form a potential on the mind, but if there was not interest in them at the time, they are not likely to generate recollection.

CdC: They generate weaker potentials?

Gen Damcho: Yes, that is the second part.

SECTION VII
CONCLUSIONS: WHAT CAN BE LEARNED?

You have in your neurobiology a knowledge of the intricacies of the total picture which is absolutely amazing. Really heartening and exciting. What do *we* have? We have, as it were, the government. We have the knowledge of the main thing which is controlling, of mind. The thing which controls this entire process, this is what we Tibetans have to offer.

—Kamtrul Rinpoche

As space is endless, similarly the possible objects of the mind are unlimited.

—Lati Rinpoche

16   The Mind from Inside and Out

Buddhist philosophy and meditative insight and modern brain science are in many cases complementary—with the result that they often take very different approaches to the mind, and what one system lacks the other considers in detail. The purpose of this book was to explore what each system of understanding can learn from its counterpart, and we have now considered many specific examples, but left many unmentioned. This final chapter considers some remaining areas where the Buddhist philosophy of mind and the Western science of the brain may be able to benefit from one another, emphasizing areas where one of the systems excels and the other may not have ventured in as much depth.

NEW IDEAS FOR WESTERN SCIENCE
Forming a link between subjective experience and empirical science

A continual conundrum of Western philosophy and science has been the boundary between introspective descriptions of subjective experience and empirical observations of physical form. This may prove to be the most useful area of contact between Asian thought in general and Western science. It is becoming more and more clear that if a scientific understanding of consciousness, even in its simplest aspects, is ever to arise, then new methods of observing internal mental phenomena are going to have to be developed, because these phenomena are such a fundamental part of consciousness itself. An understanding of the mind which does not include subjective experience will always be

incomplete. For this reason, circumstances now demand a reconcilia-
tion of subjective experience and empirical measurement, one which
has not yet been found.

The careful internal observations of formally trained meditators may
provide a middle ground between traditionally mistrusted Western
introspection-through-logic and empiricist observation. They may
yield an alternative to the philosophical systems which aim to be ex-
haustive and internally consistent but which are not based in verifiable observations, and the scientific treatments which are empirically
verified but do not fully address the issues of the mind. Perhaps a
useful step for science in restarting its approach to consciousness is to
look to some of the highly developed systems of internal analysis which
already exist, for example, the detailed catalogs of the mind which
have come from the Tibetan meditators. Using the Buddhist approach
as a starting point may encourage scientists to find new empirical
methods of measuring the mind from the inside—to find a psychophysics for studying internal experience.

Philosophical underpinnings and a definition of consciousness

Many neuroscientists are keenly aware of the fact that the scientific
approach to consciousness does not have a sufficient philosophical
underpinning. There is no generally accepted scientific definition of
what consciousness is, what awareness is, what a mind is, what a subject or an object is, what experience is, and so on. These issues have
been resolved to a self-consistent system within the context of Buddhist thought, and this system is now becoming available. Tibetan
Buddhism can be one of the many sources of a challenge to neuroscience to reach upwards from an emphasis on the biology of simple
behavior and to try to come to terms with the mind itself. Perhaps the
detailed philosophical explanations of consciousness found in Buddhism can serve as one model in this search.

The issue of the subject

Neuroscience almost entirely neglects the role of the subject in conscious awareness. For the most part the brain is studied as a passive
organ which merely processes information fed in from the outside.
Comparatively little neurobiological work has been dedicated to studying how the mind takes an active role in experience, as in shaping
perceptions through attention, creating images through recollection,
or generating behavior through choice. As the field begins to more

wholeheartedly address questions of consciousness, perhaps the Buddhist emphasis on understanding the concept of a subject and its role in experience will be helpful in providing examples. Moreover, perhaps the Buddhist perspective of putting consciousness itself as the primary factor in experience can serve as an example.

NEW IDEAS FOR BUDDHISM

There is also a tremendous amount for Buddhists to learn from neuroscience, both in methods and in facts. Having looked at some quite detailed examples, I would like to end by re-emphasizing the most basic point, which is that the experiential mind is intimately related to the physical brain, and that knowledge of either one can give insights into the other. This most fundamental fact has been itself largely absent from the traditional Buddhist presentation. For those who are unfamiliar with Western brain science a few examples taken from a huge body of literature will illustrate clearly this most fundamental finding.

Each conscious function is related to its own particular set of processes and areas of the brain. The general seats of many of the simpler mental functions, such as sensing, seeing, hearing, moving, and so on, have already been quite definitely localized within the brain in a number of ways. The simplest is merely that if a person has an injury to a part of the brain associated with a function, this function will often be lost, while the person is otherwise relatively unaffected. For example, there are patients who have lost only their hearing, or their sight, or even their ability to recognize a particular kind of object, because they have been injured in the corresponding brain areas. It is also now possible to measure the activity in different parts of the brain while people are engaged in different mental functions, and in this way to show that a given function uses particular parts of the system, even down to the level of single brain cells in some cases.

Taking the reverse approach, if scientists artificially activate particular parts of people's brains using electricity, it is possible to crudely *generate* mental operations. Patients are often awake during brain surgery, which is not painful, so they can report how their experiences are changed when the pathways in their brains are artificially activated. Depending on where the brain stimulation takes place their limbs may move, they may hear or see things, and they may even recollect complex memories from childhood as if from nowhere. Although it is not at present possible to control the mind in any systematic way by using this technique, it nonetheless shows that phenomena of experience can be directly "injected" into the brain.

Finally, much of the anatomy of the millions of pathways which make up the brain have been described in great detail and, for example, it is possible to trace the connecting pathways from the eyes to the various areas involved with sight. From volumes of data of this sort, it now seems an unquestionable fact that mental functions are very closely related to underlying brain hardware, and in one sense can be thought to be produced directly by it. This means that an understanding of the mind can be informed tremendously by an understanding of the functioning of the brain.

Here are two final examples of the many kinds of information about the mind that might come from brain science.

Subtle channels and physical anatomy

Tibetan Buddhism in general speaks of many subtle channels through which the *lung* (*rlung*), or winds of consciousness, flow in the body. Modern anatomy has also compiled an extremely detailed description of the neural pathways that run throughout the body and carry neural signals, and this body of knowledge remains virtually unexplored by Buddhist scholars. The advantage of the anatomical approach is that viewing physical pathways is comparatively easy, so it is possible to trace the individual fibers that make up bundles of millions of fibers which are the coarse anatomical tracts of the nervous system. In fact, any pathway can be explored in detail within a few years by a relative novice who receives the right training and has the right tools. It is not clear what the relationship between these two systems of anatomy might be, but it is clear that anatomy can provide a whole new source of information, and it has not yet been studied in detail by most Tibetan Buddhists.[169]

Mechanistic analysis

The explanatory power of mechanistic analysis has been made adequately clear by the revolution that it has wrought, but does it offer anything to Tibetan Buddhism? It offers a way of thinking about the mind that is almost entirely different from that provided by tradition. It brings a whole new set of challenges to old beliefs because it involves a different language of inquiry, a language that Tibetan scholars are as unfamiliar with as Western scientists are unfamiliar with

Buddhist dialectical reasoning. Whether this approach can help a meditator towards the elimination of confusion is an open question, but perhaps the recent interest in science among Tibetan Buddhists suggests the possibility.[170]

Tibetan Buddhism has only just begun to explore what can be learned from the outside about the complex physical system of the brain. Many Tibetans even deny that there is *any* relationship between particular types of conscious awareness and the brain.[171] This is simply no longer a tenable position, as was just discussed. It is now possible, within narrow limits, to make valid inferences about how the mind works based on the functioning of the brain. These sorts of inferences have been shown to be valid in diagnosing and treating numerous illnesses of the mind, such as manic-depressive disorder, schizophrenia, or impairments of the senses, such as deafness. It seems clear that this kind of objective understanding of the mind has some practical and theoretical import for the Buddhist view.

BRAIN PLASTICITY AND THE BUDDHIST IDEA OF
TRANSFORMATION

The purpose of Buddhism is human change, and the physical sciences are now coming to understand in detail how the brain changes and what effects this has. Many different studies have shown that the functional, physical properties of the brain can be dramatically changed by experience and through training. For example, using the fingers extensively increases the amount of brain area that processes information from the fingers, at the expense of other areas.[172] Similarly, extensive practice listening to particular sounds causes the auditory system to specialize for these sounds, devoting more of its resources to their processing in order to allow these sounds to be heard better.[173] The brain is constantly remodeling its own physical structure to reflect how it is being used. Moment by moment we choose how we will behave in the present and the future, and these choices are embossed on the physical material of our minds. This has the implication that the transformative processes described in Buddhism may have discoverable physiological underpinnings, and that an understanding of this physiology might someday lead to insights into how to change the mind more effectively. Findings of this sort have already made it possible to learn how to best guide the nervous system through changes in order to reach a desired goal, such as in learning, or in recovering mental function after an injury, or in people with learning disabilities.[174] Through further research it will become possible to understand how to best encourage the nervous system to change in more complex ways.

TIBETAN BUDDHISM AND WESTERN SCIENCE— COMPLEMENTARY VIEWS

In many ways the Tibetan approach is exactly complementary to the tradition of Western brain science, as has been alluded to throughout. Whereas the Buddhist scholars have an enormous *descriptive* understanding of consciousness, viewed from the *internal* perspective and addressing *complex* aspects of mind, complete with a framework for defining what questions are important and what classifications are most useful, neuroscience has none of these things. Indeed it has largely avoided the issues of consciousness, introspection, and complex mental phenomena altogether. Conversely, while science libraries in the West are filled with objective, *extrospective* data on the minute details of the *mechanisms* underlying different functions of the brain, as well as its microscopic anatomy, the Buddhists have almost completely ignored both the question of the mechanisms of mind and the understanding that can be gained by detailed external observations.

Knowledge of mind and its limits

Science and Buddhism both seek liberation from the bondage of ignorance, but the two disciplines pursue opposite ends of the continuum of the complexity of mind. While Buddhists are mainly concerned with the most complex aspects leading towards liberation, neuroscience considers no aspect of consciousness too mundane, and in fact favors thoroughgoing analyses of the simple over metaphorical descriptions of the complex. As a result, the areas covered by the two disciplines are largely complementary—the Buddhists have mostly explored sophisticated mental phenomena, starting with thoughts and emotions and working up through meditative states and ultimately toward the possibility of enlightenment, while the neuroscientists have mainly concerned themselves with reflexes, sensations, and are just beginning to approach simple cognitive processes. Although these two views augment each other beautifully, at present there is still a rather considerable void between them remaining to be explored.

Sense of self

The area of the most profound agreement between Buddhist philosophy and Western physiology may be the issue of the self. Buddhists have attempted through meditation and logical reasoning to demonstrate the lack of any substantial self. They are left with a simple question: "Well then, who am I?" Neuroscientists have attempted to demonstrate through mechanistic analysis and theoretical models that there is no need for any little homuncular pilot guiding the brain, no need for any ghost soul operating the machine. They too are faced by the criticism: "I see all of the mechanisms, but where am *I*?" The two systems seem to offer different sides to the same essential answer: "There is no need for a belief in a self, there is only a process taking place which is our individual experience."

Acknowledgments

I would like to express my deepest gratitude to Dr. Michael M. Merzenich whose encouragement and support made this project possible, and of course to the teachers who blessed me with their knowledge, and to the translators who made it available to me in my own language. This project was supported by a National Science Foundation Graduate Fellowship.

Notes

1. B. A. Wallace, *Choosing Reality: A Contemplative View of Physics and the Mind* (Berkeley: Shambhala, 1989). J. W. Hayward, *Perceiving Ordinary Magic: Science and Intuitive Wisdom* (Boulder: New Science Library, 1984). J. W. Hayward, *Shifting Worlds, Changing Minds: Where the Sciences and Buddhism Meet* (Boston: New Science Library, 1987). J. W. Hayward and F. J. Varela, *Gentle Bridges* (Boston: Shambhala, 1992). F. Capra, *The Tao of Physics: An Exploration of the Parallels Between Modern Physics and Eastern Mysticism* (Berkeley: Shambhala, 1975). W. F. Jayasuriya, *The Psychology and Philosophy of Buddhism: An Introduction to the Abhidhamma* (Kuala Lumpur, Malaysia: Buddhist Missionary Society, 1963). K. N. Jayatilleke, R. F. Spencer, W. U. Shu, and J. R. Oppenheimer, *Buddhism and Science: Collected Essays* (Kandy, Sri Lanka: Buddhist Publication Society, 1980). His Holiness the 14th Dalai Lama, H. Benson, R. A. F. Thurman, H. E. Gardner, and D. Goleman, *MindScience* (Boston: Wisdom, 1991). F. J. Varela, E. Thompson, and E. Rosch, *The Embodied Mind: Cognitive Science and Human Experience* (Boston: MIT Press, 1991).

2. The author wishes to make clear that the points in this book are distilled mainly from discussions with lamas or from secondary sources as cited, not from the original Sanskrit or Tibetan texts. For more complete, authoritative, and scholarly discussions of these issues please consult the sources noted. Particularly, on the treatment of mind and consciousness within Tibetan Buddhism, consult the following references (which will be abbreviated in the following text): J. Hopkins, *Meditation on Emptiness* (London: Wisdom, 1983); A. C. Klein, *Knowledge and Liberation* (Ithaca: Snow Lion, 1986); A. C. Klein, *Knowing, Naming and Negation: A Sourcebook on Tibetan Sautrantika* (Ithaca: Snow Lion, 1991); D. Perdue, *Debate in Tibetan Buddhism* (Ithaca: Snow Lion, 1992); Lati Rinpoche and E. Napper, *Mind in Tibetan Buddhism* (Ithaca: Snow Lion, 1986).

It is more difficult to suggest general introductions to cognitive neuroscience, but I would recommend sections of: H. Gardner, *The Mind's New Science—*

A History of the Cognitive Revolution (USA: Basic Books, 1985). E. R. Kandel, J. H. Schwartz, and T. Jessel, *Principles of Neural Science* (New York: Elsevier, 1991).

3. They included discussions with H. H. the Dalai Lama; Lati Rinpoche; Kamtrul Rinpoche; Ven. Geshe Lobsang Gyatso, Principal of the Institute of Buddhist Dialectics; Geshe Damcho, an authoritative instructor in Abhidharma at the Institute of Buddhist Dialectics; Gen Lamrimpa, a Tibetan meditator of the highest stature who has engaged in numerous long retreats in isolation; Dr. Yeshi Donden, former physician to the Dalai Lama and founder of the Tibetan Medical Institute in Dharamsala, and others.

4. The Buddhist presentation of mind is discussed in somewhat different terms in two different levels of teachings of the Buddha, which are included in two different divisions of the canon, the Sutras and the Tantras. The Sutra level texts are considered to constitute the fundamentals of the Buddhist teachings and the Tantric texts provide much more advanced and complex practices. In general, Tantric teachings are reserved for those who have already mastered an understanding of Sutra and who have had appropriate "empowerments" or "initiations" from a qualified teacher.

5. The Tibetan Buddhists posit four main schools of tenets, Vaibashika, Sautrantika, Chittamatra, and Madhyamika, each one complete in itself, but each one more subtle in its presentation than the last. The system which is considered highest of all, and espoused as the paramount teaching, is that of the Prasangika division of the Madhyamika school.

6. This presentation will be discussed in detail later. Briefly, the aspect is a reflection of the object which is cast to the mind and allows perception to take place.

7. Two examples, one from the West and one the East, are: F. Capra, *The Tao of Physics: An Exploration of the Parallels Between Modern Physics and Eastern Mysticism* (Berkeley: Shambhala, 1975). K. N. Jayatilleke, R. F. Spencer, W. U. Shu, and J. R. Oppenheimer, *Buddhism and Science: Collected Essays* (Kandy: Buddhist Publication Society, 1980). I have also heard many dharma teachers make comparisons between science and Buddhism during teachings to Westerners.

8. Terms like "subjective," "inside," and "outside" are the standard usage, so I use them here, but I find them very confusing and often a hindrance to understanding.

9. R. Descartes, *The Philosophical Works of Descartes*, trans. Elizabeth S. Haldane and G.R.T. Ross (Cambridge: Cambridge University Press, 1911).

10. I mean to connote a "standard" Western usage of the word dualism, not just within cognitive neuroscience, but within Western thought in general.

11. In fact, Nagarjuna teaches that it is additionally mistaken to suggest that it is both or that it is neither, but this can quickly become confusing. This material is most definitively presented from a Mahayana viewpoint by Nagarjuna; for examples see *Nagarjuna's Philosophy* (Delhi: Motilal Banarsidass, 1987), or J. Hopkins, *Meditation on Emptiness* (London: Wisdom, 1983).

12. J. Hopkins, *Meditation on Emptiness.*

13. Kamtrul Rinpoche, oral teachings.

14. This point was made to me by a number of Tibetan doctors and philosophers. Finding detailed mechanistic explanations is often described as "counting crows' teeth."

15. Gen Lamrimpa, oral teachings.

16. Audience with H.H. the Dalai Lama, October 1992.

17. A. C. Klein, *Knowledge and Liberation*, 29.

18. T. Stcherbatsky, *The Central Conception of Buddhism and the Meaning of the Word "Dharma"*" (Delhi: Motilal Banarsidass, 1922), 62.

19. E. R. Kandel and J. H. Schwartz, *Principles of Neural Science* (New York: Elsevier, 1985), 3.

20. Lati Rinbochay and E. Napper, *Mind in Tibetan Buddhism* (Ithaca: Snow Lion, 1986), 49.

21. A. C. Klein, *Knowledge and Liberation*, 63.

22. Ibid., 46-50.

23. Ibid., 15-17, 206-216.

24. T. Stcherbatsky, *The Central Concept of Buddhism and the Meaning of the Word "Dharma,"* 9; J. Hopkins, *Meditation on Emptiness*, 273.

25. Lati Rinbochay and E. Napper, *Mind in Tibetan Buddhism*, 17.

26. Ibid., 52.

27. Gen Damcho, oral teachings.

28. A. C. Klein, *Knowledge and Liberation*, 58.

29. Ibid., 34.

30. Gen Damcho, oral teachings.

31. A. C. Klein, *Knowledge and Liberation*, 49, 50-52; D. Perdue, *Debate in Tibetan Buddhism*, 300-304.

32. A. C Klein, *Knowledge and Liberation*, 35; D. Perdue, *Debate in Tibetan Buddhism*, 9, 283.

33. Ibid., 283.

34. J. Hopkins, *Meditation on Emptiness*, 419.

35. A. C. Klein, *Knowledge and Liberation*, 98-100; D. Perdue, *Debate in Tibetan Buddhism*, 292; A. C. Klein, *Knowing, Naming and Negation: A Sourcebook on Tibetan Sautrantika*, 31.

36. A. C. Klein, *Knowledge and Liberation*, 34.

37. Gen Damcho, oral teachings.

38. Ibid., 35. D. Perdue, *Debate in Tibetan Buddhism*, 9, 283.

39. A. C. Klein, *Knowing, Naming and Negation: A Sourcebook on Tibetan Sautrantika;* 32. D. Perdue, *Debate in Tibetan Buddhism*, 273.

40. Ibid., 92; Lati Rinpoche, oral teachings.

41. D. Perdue, *Debate in Tibetan Buddhism*, 292; A. C. Klein, *Knowledge and Liberation*, 63; Lati Rinbochay and E. Napper, *Mind in Tibetan Buddhism*, 99-106; A. C. Klein, *Knowing, Naming and Negation: A Sourcebook on Tibetan Sautrantika*, 53.

42. A. C. Klein, *Knowledge and Liberation*, 63-65, 91-100. Also Anne Klein, personal communication.

43. Ibid., 91.

44. Ibid., 39.

45. In some presentations a fourth factor is added, the ripening of a karmic seed or potential, which serves as the causal condition for perception. Lati Rinpoche, oral teachings.

46. Lati Rinbochay and E. Napper, *Mind in Tibetan Buddhism*, 17-18; D. Perdue, *Debate in Tibetan Buddhism*, 217, 360; Lati Rinpoche, oral teachings.

47. Ibid., 218-220. I am unaware of further explanation of these brief descriptive terms available in translation.

48. Lati Rinbochay and E. Napper, *Mind in Tibetan Buddhism*, 67.

49. A. C. Klein, *Knowledge and Liberation*, 104.

50. Ibid., 100-106.

51. Ibid., 102.

52. Ibid., 63-65, 91-100.

53. Lati Rinpoche, oral teachings.

54. Ibid.

55. A. C. Klein, *Knowing, Naming and Negation: A Sourcebook on Tibetan Sautrantika*, 158.

56. This point is refuted in the teachings of the higher schools within the Gelugpa presentation. Gen Damcho, oral teachings.

57. A. C. Klein, *Knowledge and Liberation*, 106.

58. Ibid., 33-88.

59. Ibid., 40-42.

60. T. Stcherbatsky, *Buddhist Logic*, cited in A. C. Klein, *Knowledge and Liberation*, 29.

61. Ibid., 44-52.

62. Ibid., 49.

63. E. R. Kandel and J. H. Schwartz, *Principles of Neural Science* (New York: Elsevier, 1985).

64. M. G. McGee and D. W. Wilson, *Psychology—Science and Application* (St. Paul, MN: West Publishing Company, 1984).

65. K. V. Ramanan, *Nagarjuna's Philosophy as Presented in the* Maha-Prajñaparamita-Shastra (New Delhi: Motilal Banarsidass, 1966), 127.

66. D. Perdue, *Debate in Tibetan Buddhism*, 200-205.

67. R. von der Heydt, E. Peterhans, and G. Baumgartner, "Illusory contours," *Science* 224 (1984): 1260-1262.

68. The Prasangika is considered a higher or more subtle Buddhist teaching than the Sautrantika. Gen Damcho, oral teachings, and A. C. Klein, *Knowledge and Liberation*, 49, 64.

69. In fact, in special circumstances where more information is available it is possible to see finer detail than any one receptor cell alone can see; but the point remains that there is an absolute limit to the smallest size object that the eye can sense, and that it is extremely large in atomic terms.

70. As an amusing coincidence, I have heard this question raised at a scientific meeting by Nobel Laureate Francis Crick, co-discoverer of the structure of DNA, and I was recently asked almost the exact same question by Lati Rinpoche, a highly distinguished scholar of Buddhism.

71. M. M. Merzenich, C. Schreiner, W. Jenkins, and X. Wang, "Neural mechanisms underlying temporal integration, segmentation and input sequence representation; some implications for the origin of learning disabilities," *Annals of the New York Academy of Sciences* 682 (1993).

72. R. von der Heydt, E. Peterhans and G. Baumgartner, "Illusory Contours," *Science* 224 (1984): 1260-1262; B. R. Sheth, et al., "Orientation maps of subjective contours in visual cortex," *Science* 274 (1996): 2110-2115.

73. A. C. Klein, *Knowledge and Liberation*, 106-108.

74. Ibid., 106.

75. A. C. Klein, *Knowing, Naming and Negation: A Sourcebook on Tibetan Sautrantika*, 160.

76. A. C. Klein, *Knowledge and Liberation*, 110.

77. A. C. Klein, *Knowledge and Liberation*, 29-32, 33-58, presents a thorough discussion of this debate, which I summarize here. See also D. Perdue, *Debate in Tibetan Buddhism*, 317.

78. A. C. Klein, *Knowledge and Liberation*, 69.

79. Ibid., 68-88.

80. Ibid., 77.

81. Ibid., 86.

82. I have heard several Buddhist teachers or scholars draw this comparison during teachings or discussions.

83. It is possible to argue for odor or taste that the "quantum unit" is a single molecule received in the nose or mouth; however, most tastes and odors arise from complex mixtures of molecules, and the odors and tastes produced by different kinds, sizes, and numbers of molecules do not follow simple rules that would support this approach.

84. This is only possible in very special experimental circumstances, and it is not possible to perceive a single photon.

85. Gen Damcho, oral teachings; A. C. Klein, *Knowledge and Liberation*, 64, 49.

86. In the Tibetan system the energy of the mind is called *lung* (Tib. *rlung*, pronounced "loong"). It is said to support the mind as a horse supports its rider. Some have drawn the analogy between *lung* and neural activity, but although the analogy may sometimes be useful, they are certainly not the same thing.

87. E. G. Jones and T. P. Powell, "An anatomical study of converging sensory pathways within the cerebral cortex of the monkey," *Brain* 93 (1970): 793-820.

88. A. R. Luria, "The functional organization of the brain," *Scientific American* 222 (1970): 66-79; O. Sacks, *The Man Who Mistook His Wife for a Hat and Other Clinical Tales* (New York: Summit Books, 1985).

89. Lati Rinbochay and E. Napper, *Mind in Tibetan Buddhism*.

90. Ibid., 111.

91. A. C. Klein, *Knowledge and Liberation*, 46-47.

92. Ibid., 123; J. Hopkins, *Meditation on Emptiness*, 347-349.

93. Lati Rinbochay and E. Napper, *Mind in Tibetan Buddhism*, 28.

94. A. C. Klein, *Knowledge and Liberation*, 14.

95. Ibid., 140.

96. Ibid., 130, 211-212.

97. Gen Damcho, oral teachings.

98. A. C. Klein, *Knowledge and Liberation*, 68-78.

99. Gen Damcho, oral teachings, and ibid., 38; Lati Rinbochay and E. Napper, *Mind in Tibetan Buddhism*, 28.

100. Ibid.; A. C. Klein, *Knowledge and Liberation*, 37-39.

101. Ibid.

102. Ibid.

103. Ibid.

104. Gen Damcho, oral teachings.

105. A. C. Klein, *Knowledge and Liberation*, 126-130; Lati Rinbochay and E. Napper, *Mind in Tibetan Buddhism*, 110-115; D. Perdue, *Debate in Tibetan Buddhism*, 289.

106. A. C. Klein, *Knowledge and Liberation*, 127-129.

107. J. Hopkins, *Meditation on Emptiness*, 349; A. C. Klein, *Knowledge and Liberation*, 103.

108. Ibid., 130, 211-212.

109. Lati Rinbochay and E. Napper, *Mind in Tibetan Buddhism*, 72.

110. Gen Damcho, oral teachings.

111. A. C. Klein, *Knowledge and Liberation*, 141-182; A. C. Klein, *Knowing, Naming, and Negation: A Sourcebook on Tibetan Sautrantika*; J. Hopkins, *Meditation on Emptiness*, 721-727.

112. J. Hopkins, *Meditation on Emptiness*, 722.

113. Ibid., 725.

114. A. C. Klein, *Knowledge and Liberation*, 153.

115. J. Hopkins, *Meditation on Emptiness*.

116. A. C. Klein, *Knowledge and Liberation*, 154; J. Hopkins, *Meditation on Emptiness*, 723.

117. Ibid., 175-182, 212-215.

118. Ibid., 169.

119. Ibid., 166.

120. A. C. Klein, *Knowledge and Liberation*, 166-169; A. C. Klein, *Knowing, Naming, and Negation: A Sourcebook on Tibetan Sautrantika*, 151.

121. A. C. Klein, *Knowledge and Liberation*, 169-172; A. C. Klein, *Knowing, Naming, and Negation: A Sourcebook on Tibetan Sautrantika*, 151.

122. Lati Rinbochay and E. Napper, *Mind in Tibetan Buddhism*, 35.

123. A. C. Klein, *Knowledge and Liberation*, 153-175.

124. Ibid, 154-157; A. C. Klein, *Knowing, Naming, and Negation: A Sourcebook on Tibetan Sautrantika*, 91-113.

125. Gen Damcho, oral teachings.

126. Lati Rinbochay and E. Napper, *Mind in Tibetan Buddhism*, 116-129.

127. Ibid., 84.

128. Gen Damcho, oral teachings; Lati Rinbochay and E. Napper, *Mind in Tibetan Buddhism*, 18-19, 54-59.

129. Lati Rinbochay, oral teachings.

130. Lati Rinbochay and E. Napper, *Mind in Tibetan Buddhism*, 85-86.

131. A. C. Klein, *Knowledge and Liberation*, 117, 127; J. Hopkins, *Meditation on Emptiness*, 348.

132. Gen Damcho and Kamtrul Rinpoche, oral teachings.

133. Lati Rinbochay and E. Napper, *Mind in Tibetan Buddhism*, 75.

134. A. C. Klein, *Knowledge and Liberation*, 129.

135. M. M. Merzenich and R. C. deCharms, "Experience, change and plasticity," in R. Llinas and P. Churchland, eds., *The Mind Brain Continuum* (Boston: MIT Press, 1996).

136. H. Gardner, *The Mind's New Science* (Boston: Basic Books, 1987).

137. J. J. Hopfield, "Neural networks and physical systems with emergent collective computational abilities," *Proceedings of the National Academy of Science USA* 79 (1982): 2554-2558; D. W. Tank and J. J. Hopfield, "Neural computation by concentrating information in time," *Proceedings of the National Academy of Science USA* 84 (1987): 1896-1900.

138. Ungerleider and Mishkin, *Two Cortical Visual Systems* (Cambridge, MA: MIT Press, 1982); E. R. Kandel, J. H. Schwartz and T. Jessel, *Principles of Neural Science*.

139. S. Zeki and S. Shipp, "The functional logic of cortical connections," *Nature* 335 (1988): 311-317.

140. M. J. Farah, "Mechanisms of imagery-perception interaction," *Journal of Experimental Psychology [Human Perception]* 15 (1989): 203-211. R. N. Shepard and J. Metzler, "Mental rotation of three-dimensional objects," *Science* 171 (1971): 701-703.

141. Another possibility, which was more commonly believed until recent years, was that most cognitive processing such as mental imagery and so on took place in the frontal lobes, rather that in areas associated with sensory processing.

142. M. J. Farah, F. Peronnet, M. A. Gonon and M. H. Giard, "Electrophysiological evidence for a shared representational medium for visual images and visual percepts," *Journal of Experimental Psychology [Gen]* 117 (1988): 248-257.

143. J. M. Fuster, "Unit activity in prefrontal cortex during delayed-response performance: Neuronal correlates of transient memory," *Journal of Neurophysiology* 36 (1973): 61-78; J. M. Fuster, "Inferotemporal units in selective visual attention and short-term memory," *Journal of Neurophysiology* 64 (1990): 681-697.

144. M. E. Raichle and M. I. Posner, *Images of Mind* (New York: Scientific American Library, 1994).

145. D. I. Perrett, E. T. Rolls and W. Caan, "Visual neurons responsive to faces in the monkey temporal cortex," *Experimental Brain Research* 47 (1982): 329-342.

146. Ibid.

147. A. C. Klein, *Knowledge and Liberation*, 198-203; A. C. Klein, *Knowing, Naming, and Negation: a Sourcebook on Tibetan Sautrantika*, 64-65, 78.

148. Ibid.

149. S. Ullman, "Sequence seeking and counter streams: a computational model for bidirectional information flow in the visual cortex," *Cerebral Cortex* 5/1 (1995): 1-11.

150. A. C. Klein, *Knowledge and Liberation*, 117-121; A. C. Klein, *Knowing, Naming, and Negation: A Sourcebook on Tibetan Sautrantika*, 126-140.

151. Lati Rinbochay and E. Napper, *Mind in Tibetan Buddhism*, 129-132; A. C. Klein, *Knowledge and Liberation*, 118.

152. Ibid., 130.

153. Lati Rinbochay and E. Napper, *Mind in Tibetan Buddhism*, 130.

154. Ibid.

155. A. C. Klein, *Knowing Naming, and Negation: A Sourcebook on Tibetan Sautrantika*, 129.

156. Ibid.

157. M. S. Gazzaniga and C. S. Smylie, "Dissociation of language and cognition. A psychological profile of two disconnected right hemispheres," *Brain* 107 (1984): 145-153; R. Sperry, "Some effects of disconnecting the cerebral hemispheres. Nobel Lecture, 8 December 1981," *Bioscientific Report* 2 (1982): 265-276; R. Sperry, "Some effects of disconnecting the cerebral hemispheres," *Science* 217 (1982): 1223-1226.

158. Ibid.

159. Lati Rinbochay and E. Napper, *Mind in Tibetan Buddhism*, 56-59.

160. Ibid., 57.

161. Ibid., 58.

162. Ibid., 59.

163. J. Hopkins, *Meditation on Emptiness*, 348.

164. Ibid; A. C. Klein, *Knowledge and Liberation*, 49.

165. M. S. Gazzaniga and C. S. Smylie, "Dissociation of language and cognition. A psychological profile of two disconnected right hemispheres," *Brain* 107 (1984): 145-153; R. Sperry, "Some effects of disconnecting the cerebral hemispheres. Nobel Lecture, 8 December 1981," *Bioscientific Report* 2 (1982): 265-276; R. Sperry, "Some effects of disconnecting the cerebral hemispheres,"*Science* 217 (1982): 1223-1226.

166. L. Ungerleider, "Functional brain imaging studies of cortical mechanisms for memory," *Science* 270 (Nov. 3, 1995): 769-775.

167. W. James, *Psychology-A Briefer Course* (New York: Holt1892).

168. J. Hopkins, *Meditation on Emptiness*, 368.

169. Almost no one that I spoke to was even familiar with it, although many were interested upon hearing of it.

170. His Holiness the Dalai Lama has been a leader in this regard.

171. I discussed this a number of times with Tibetan doctors, philosophers and meditators.

172. W. M. Jenkins, M. M. Merzenich, M. T. Ochs, T. Allard and R. E. Guic, "Functional reorganization of primary somatosensory cortex in adult owl monkeys after behaviorally controlled tactile stimulation," *Journal of Neurophysiology* 63/1 (1990): 82-104.

173. G. H. Recanzone, C. E. Schreiner and M. M. Merzenich, "Plasticity in the frequency representation of primary auditory cortex following discrimination training in adult owl monkeys," *Journal of Neuroscience* 13 (1993): 87-103.

174. W. M. Jenkins and M. M. Merzenich, "Reorganization of neocortical representations after brain injury: a neurophysiological model of the bases of recovery from stroke," *Progressive Brain Research* 71 (1987): 249-266; M. M. Merzenich and R. C. deCharms, "Experience, change and plasticity." In R. Llinas and P. Churchland (eds.), *The Mind-Brain Continuum* (Boston: MIT Press, 1996); M. M. Merzenich, W. M. Jenkins, P. Johnston, C. Schreiner, S. L. Miller and P. Tallal,"Temporal processing deficits of language-learning impaired children ameliorated by training," *Science* 271(1996): 77-81; P. Tallal, S. L. Miller, G. Bedi, G. Byma, X. Wang, S. S. Nagarajan, C. Schreiner, W. M. Jenkins and M. M. Merzenich,"Language comprehension in language-learning impaired children improved with acoustically modified speech," *Science* 271 (1996): 81-84.